Conflict Management Program
Field Trip to Ukraine

Participants

Mark Brass	Ross B. Hurwitz
Dorothea E. Cheek	Karina Panyan
Chloe Colbert	Ashley Patton
Christina Connelly-Kanmaz	Linan Peng
Anna Goodman	Christina Pushaw
Rebecca Grenham	Alex Simon
Qifan Huang	Kevin Toda
Gabriella Huddart	Angelica Valdez

P. Terrence Hopmann is the former director of the Conflict Management Program at the Johns Hopkins Paul H. Nitze School of Advanced International Studies

Jacket Design: Zindzi Thompson, SAIS, Washington, DC

<u>Front Cover Photos:</u>
Professors Leonid Kistersky and P. Terrence Hopmann with the SAIS Students in front of the Presidential Office, Kyiv

Saint Sophia Cathedral and Maidan Nezalezhnosti (Independence Square), Kyiv

<u>Back Cover Photos:</u>
SAIS students with students and faculty of Donetsk National University, Vinnytsia

"Tree of Friends," Donetsk National University, Vinnytsia

Table of Contents

List of Acronyms

AA	Association Agreement
CSIS	Center for Strategic and International Studies
CSO	Civil Society Organization
CFSP	Common Foreign and Security Policy
CFV	Ceasefire Violations
DCFTA	Deep and Comprehensive Free Trade Agreement
DDOS	distributed denial of service
DNU	Donetsk National University
DPR	Donetsk People's Republic
EaP	Eastern Partnership
EBRD	European Bank for Reconstruction and Development
EEAS	European External Action Services
EEU	Eurasian Economic Union
EIB	European Investment Bank
ENP	European Neighborhood Policy
EU	European Union
FBI	Federal Bureau of Investigation
FSB	Federal Security Service of the Russian Federation
FSU	Former Soviet Union
GCA	Government-Controlled Area
GCSP	Geneva Centre for Security Policy
GoU	Government of Ukraine
GDP	Gross Domestic Product
HRMMU	United Nations Human Rights Monitoring Mission Ukraine
ICG	International Crisis Group
ICJ	International Court of Justice
IDP	Internally Displaced Person
IMF	International Monetary Fund
INEKO	Institute for Economic and Social Reforms

KGB	USSR Committee for State Security
LPR	Lugansk People's Republic
MoSP	Ministry of Social Policy
MP	Member of Parliament
MTOTIDP	Ministry of Temporary Occupied Territories and Internally Displaced Persons
NABU	National Anti-Corruption Bureau of Ukraine
NATO	North Atlantic Treaty Organization
NGCA	Non-Government Controlled Area
NGO	Non-governmental organization
OCHA	Office for the Coordination of Humanitarian Affairs
ODIHR	Office for Democratic Institutions and Human Rights
OECD	Organization for Economic Cooperation and Development
OHCHR	Office of the High Commissioner for Human Rights
OOSC	Out-of-School Children
OSCE	Organization for Security and Cooperation in Europe
OSMM	Committee of Soldiers' Mothers in Moscow
OSMU	Organization of Soldiers' Mothers of Ukraine
PBC	Peacebuilding Commission
PPB	Petro Poroshenko Bloc
PTSD	post-traumatic stress disorder
RT	Russia Today
SAIS	School of Advanced International Studies
SBU	Security Service of Ukraine
SMM	Special Monitoring Mission
TCG	Trilateral Contact Group
UN	United Nations
UNEF	United Nations Emergency Force
UNGA	United Nations General Assembly
UNHCR	United Nations High Commissioner for Refugees
UNICEF	United Nations International Children's Emergency Fund
UNSC	United Nations Security Council

USD	United States Dollar
USIP	United States Institute for Peace
USSR	Union of Soviet Socialist Republics
UWF	Ukrainian Woman's Fund
WWII	World War II

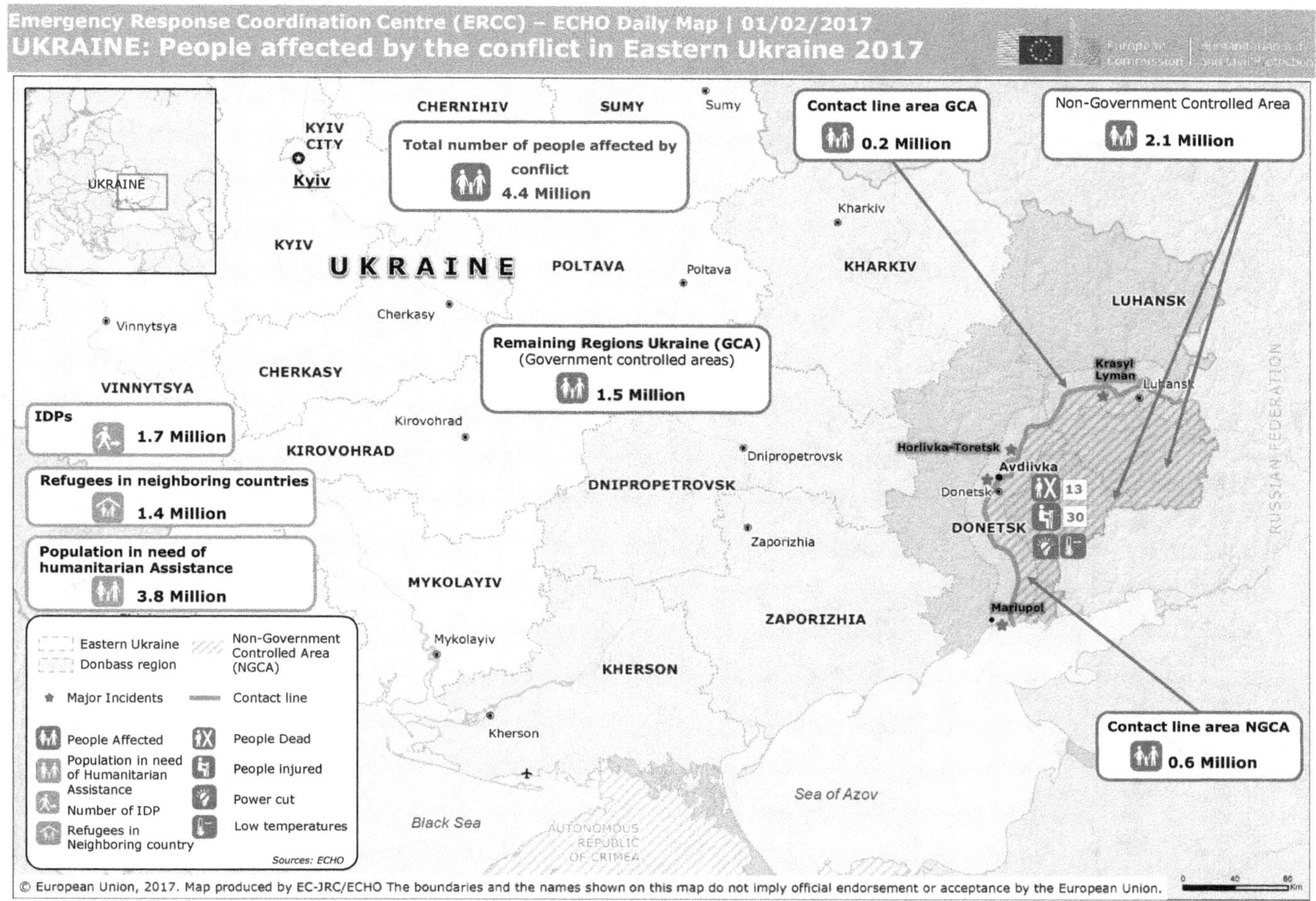

Source: European Union, 2017. Map produced by EC-JRC/ECHO. Used with permission.

Introduction

P. Terrence Hopmann

Violent conflict in Ukraine, both in Crimea and the Donbas region of eastern Ukraine, has presented a significant challenge for international security. Ukraine was the second largest, after Russia, of the 15 "union republics" of the Soviet Union that became independent and sovereign states in late 1991. That sovereignty seemed to have been guaranteed when Ukraine was admitted into the United Nations (UN) and the Organization for Security and Cooperation in Europe (OSCE) in 1992 within its post-Soviet borders. Ukraine's status was further assured in the Budapest Memorandum of 1994, when the United States, France, the United Kingdom and the Russian Federation acknowledged Ukraine's sovereignty within its 1994 borders in exchange for Ukraine's turning its nuclear warheads over to Russia and joining the Nuclear Non-Proliferation Treaty as a non-nuclear weapons state. These recognized borders of Ukraine included the peninsula of Crimea that had been transferred from the Russian Federation to Ukraine in 1954.

Throughout its first two decades as a sovereign state, Ukraine seemed to be constantly torn between its historic ties with Russia and closer relations with Central and Western Europe, a tension that was reflected in regional differences within Ukraine and in the competition for political power within the newly independent state. In November 2013, however, Ukrainian President Viktor Yanukovych cancelled an Association Agreement with the European Union and turned to Russia, which offered a large aid package without conditions. This decision provoked demonstrations in the Maidan Nezalezhnosti (Independence Square) in central Kyiv. Although these demonstrations were initially peaceful, they escalated as police and Ukrainian special forces attacked demonstrators, setting off several months of escalating violence. The situation culminated in President Yanukovych fleeing Ukraine in February 2014, after which an interim government was established to prepare for elections of a new president. However, the Russian government branded this an illegal *coup d'état*, and shortly thereafter soldiers without insignia seized major buildings and infrastructure in Crimea. On March 1, 2014, the Russian Duma (parliament) approved a request from President Vladimir Putin to deploy Russian troops openly in Ukraine. A hastily constructed referendum was held in Crimea on March 16, boycotted by most ethnic Ukrainians and Crimean Tatars, in which allegedly 97% of the population voted to secede from Ukraine, although no international monitors were allowed into Crimea to verify the election results. President Putin almost immediately signed a document annexing Crimea to the Russian Federation. Given overwhelming Russian military superiority in Crimea, Ukrainian forces had little alternative but to withdraw, and Ukraine essentially acquiesced in Russian occupation of the peninsula, while refusing to recognize the legality of its accession to the Russian Federation.

Shortly thereafter, rebel groups in the Donetsk and Luhansk oblasts in eastern Ukraine began fighting for autonomy or outright separation from Ukraine, supported by Russian military aid, soldiers, and mercenaries. This "hybrid" war thus combined a civil conflict focusing on regional secession in the eastern regions, economically disadvantaged and traditionally closer to Russia, and an international war pursued by the Russian military in eastern Ukraine against the government in Kyiv. In a meeting among heads of state in Normandy, France in 2014, celebrating the anniversary of D-Day in

World War II, leaders of France, Germany, Russia, and Ukraine created the "Normandy Format" to try to manage the conflict. In addition, the OSCE promoted the creation of a Trilateral Contact Group, including Russia, Ukraine, and the Special Representative of the OSCE Chair-in-Office as facilitator. The OSCE also deployed an unarmed Special Monitoring Mission (SMM) to Ukraine to observe the conflict and to try to prevent its escalation. The Trilateral Contact Group subsequently negotiated the Minsk Protocol in the capital of Belarus, calling for a cease-fire; a second Minsk Agreement was signed in February 2015 calling for a cease-fire along the line of contact and withdrawal of military hardware in a set of zones in order to separate forces at the line of contact and reduce civilian casualties. This agreement is monitored by the OSCE's SMM, consisting in March 2017 of over 700 personnel, mostly stationed in and around the conflict zones in eastern Ukraine. Although the line of contact has not moved since that time, extensive fighting continues throughout the cease-fire zone, and some 1.7 million persons have fled the region and have become internally displaced persons (IDPs) in other parts of Ukraine.

The Trilateral Contact Group has created four working groups to try to build confidence and reach agreement on concrete issues in the conflict. These groups focus on security, political issues, economic conditions, and humanitarian affairs. At the time of this writing, they have realized a few specific agreements but have been unable to resolve the fundamental issues underlying the conflict. Negotiations have been caught in a "chicken and egg" dilemma in which the Donbas regions demand substantial autonomy and elections for local governments, whereas the Government of Ukraine insists that these reforms cannot be enacted while extensive violence continues in the region.

This dilemma provided the focal point for a course and study trip by 16 students and 2 faculty members from the Johns Hopkins School of Advanced International Studies in spring term 2017, highlighted by a field trip to Ukraine, March 20-25, 2017. The chapters that follow represent the analysis by the 16 students of the situation in Ukraine at the time of our visit and their policy recommendations to relevant parties about how to manage this conflict situation more effectively. These chapters are organized along the lines of the four substantive working groups of the Minsk peace process, with a fifth section stepping outside the domain of the conflict to examine the role of international institutions in managing the conflict. I then present a conclusion in which I seek to integrate these 16 chapters into a broad overview of the conflict management challenges faced in Ukraine.

For a trip of this nature, there are many contributions that need to be acknowledged and thanked. At SAIS, first and foremost we recognize the incredible role played by Isabelle Talpain-Long, Program Coordinator for the Conflict Management Program, in helping to organize this trip, maintaining all financial and logistic details, and finally preparing this text for publication. We also thank Professor Daniel Serwer, Director of the Conflict Management Program, for his strong support in all stages of this project. In Washington, we also express our gratitude to Ambassador William Taylor and Steve Steiner of the US Institute of Peace for their assistance with identifying contacts in Ukraine; Ambassador Valeriy Chaly, representative of Ukraine to the United States, and his Deputy Chief of Mission Oksana Shulyar, for their assistance in preparing our trip and briefing us prior to our departure; to Ambassador John Herbst and Dr. Anders Aslund of the Atlantic Council for their informative briefings and assistance in developing contacts in Ukraine; and to Ambassador William Hill, Professor at the National Defense University, for his sage advice and excellent briefing on the historical background to the current Ukraine conflict.

In Kyiv we give special thanks to Prof. Leonid Kistersky, Director of the Institute for International Business Development, for his assistance in both logistics and identifying speakers in Ukraine; to George Kent (SAIS '92), Deputy Chief of Mission at the US Embassy in Ukraine, who hosted a dinner reception at his home in Kyiv for our group with SAIS alumni and friends in Ukraine and who provided invaluable assistance in arranging meetings with key officials of the Ukrainian Government, as well as Monica Sendor (SAIS '11) of US Embassy, Kyiv. Of course, we also express our appreciation to all of the many informative speakers with whom we met during our time in Ukraine, whose names and positions are all listed in the Appendix. Special thanks goes to Prof. Tatiana Orekhova, Vice-Rector for International Affairs at the Donetsk National University in Vinnytsia, for arranging a remarkable day in that city with students and IDPs from eastern Ukraine now living in Vinnytsia in exile; their courage, determination, and warmth of spirit in the face of many obstacles was heart-warming and very much appreciated by all of us.

Finally, this volume is dedicated to Serhy Kemskiy, and all the "heavenly hundreds" who died for the freedom and dignity of Ukrainians. We passed the memorial pictured above many times every day near our hotel in Kyiv, one of hundreds such memorials around the Maidan. Men and women like Serhy deserve to be remembered around the world for their struggle for justice and peace in Ukraine, and we dedicate our efforts to the cause for which they gave their lives.

Part I: Security Issues

Military Options and Outcomes

Mark Brass

The present war in Ukraine requires an innovative approach in conflict management. The nature of the conflict and fighting, the personalities of the parties, and the involvement of government and non-government players invite a perspective that considers the root causes of the conflict and contemplates the possible outcomes. At the outset in 2014, following the annexation of Crimea by Russia and the arrival of separatist forces in the Donbas region of eastern Ukraine, many Ukrainians and Russians anticipated a short-lived conflict. Now more than three years later, the annexation of the Crimean peninsula by the Russian Federation remains unchanged, the fighting along the conflict line in eastern Ukraine continues, and there is no immediate restoration to normalcy in sight. Meanwhile the people of Ukraine live in a world of great uncertainty and economic instability while Western nations look on and international institutions seek appropriate mediation measures.

This chapter will weigh the military options for Ukraine as an independent nation, as well as for the United States and nations of the North Atlantic Treaty Organization (NATO) that have indicated an interest in providing support to end the conflict and restore international security in the region. It will also examine the possible outcomes for the military engagement and fighting in eastern Ukraine. Briefly the chapter will provide a snapshot of the current situation in Crimea, where Russian naval forces and troops maintain a military presence following the annexation of the peninsula in 2014. Finally it will provide recommendations to the United States, NATO, the European Union (EU), and the Ukraine government.

Parties of the Conflict
Vital to understanding the possible outcomes to a conflict is understanding the strategies of the parties in conflict. In this case, the positions of Russia and Ukraine are relevant to plotting the potential outcomes, and a look at the asymmetry of power between the nations is prudent.

<u>Russia</u>

In the case of the conflict in Ukraine, the policy of Russian President Vladimir Putin remains erratic at best and mostly self-motivated. His decision to annex Crimea and send support to separatist forces in the Donbas region of eastern Ukraine in 2014 came soon after his return to the presidency in 2012 and immediately following the 2014 Winter Olympics hosted by Russia in the city of Sochi (Wood et al. 2016, 133). While Putin's agenda may be little more than headline dominance, Donbas does contain expansive facilities that once formed substantial steel, mining, and chemical industries in the region. Despite a dependence on Russia for fuel to facilitate operation and production, the region of the Donbas produced 16.6% of Ukraine's Gross Domestic Product (GDP) as recently as 2011, highlighting the area's richness and potential for economic growth (Wilson 2014, 122). While Putin's rationale behind sending armed forces to Donbas in 2014 could relate to a desire to reap the benefits of the region's Soviet-era facilities and their capability to contribute to Russia's economy, the more likely explanation is his propensity to disrupt international order and display the power of Russia. Putin also strives to harbor ethnic Russians and those who speak the Russian language; in fact he rationalized the annexation of Crimea in 2014 by articulating a need to protect their compatriots in the region (Yekelchyk 2015, 6). This ideology may very well represent the background to Putin's interests in Ukraine.

<u>Ukraine</u>

In the wake of the conflict outbreak in early 2014 and following the election of Ukrainian President Petro Poroshenko in June 2014, Ukrainian forces suffered major defeats in the region of Donbas (Yekelchyk 2015, 159). The subsequent collapse of the Minsk agreements and the internal struggles between Poroshenko's team and the new Ukrainian parliament at the time of publication contribute to Ukraine's ongoing struggle to reach a unified position and establish a foundation on which to effectively confront Putin and address Russia's objectives. Divided public opinion about Ukraine's identity and history further complicate Ukraine's position on its future in eastern Europe and its relationship with Russia and other post-Soviet nations. Families quarrel over origins and lineages, and this divisiveness breeds and compounds in the communities and regions of Ukraine.

<u>Power Asymmetry</u>

It is no secret that a power asymmetry exists between Russia and Ukraine. As conflict management expert Terry Hopmann states, power "refers to both resources that the parties to the negotiation may hold and their ability to exert influence on one another through the process of negotiation" (Hopmann 1996, 101). Ukraine's history as a part of the former Soviet Union gives it an inherent relationship with Russia that brings with it implications of power and influence, whether explicit or implicit. The policies and reign of Putin suggest that he has an interest in Ukraine, and that he understands that leveraging power to achieve his objectives in Ukraine is an option.

Fighting in Donbas

Separate from Russia's annexation of Crimea in February and March 2014, armed conflict began in the Donbas region of eastern Ukraine during the spring of 2014. The causal factors of this fighting have peculiar origins, as the majority of the population in this region did not support separating from Ukraine (Yekelchyk 2015, 141). The region became a base for armed conflict due to the political and identity divisions of Ukraine and Russia, namely nationalism, sovereignty, statehood, and empire (Wood et al. 2016, 69). The historically multinational makeup of the Donbas region of eastern Ukraine brings an added complexity to the conflict. Ruled by nomadic masters in medieval times, eastern Ukraine did not belong to the state of Kyivan Rus (Yekelchyk 2015, 134), a fact that translates to an identity struggle even in the present day.

The conflicting identity problem is exacerbated by a failure of Ukrainians and Russians to reach a consensus on the nature of the conflict. Russians submit that their presence in eastern Ukraine is strictly for humanitarian aid purposes, and this position is reflected even in the Minsk agreements, a tactic to get Russia to sign the document. Some parties internal and external to the conflict believe it to be a civil war, while others maintain the Russian forces in Donbas represent an invasion that started an international war. The population of eastern Ukraine is heavily pro-Russian, further complicating the identity question in the conflict region and likely hampering the incentive of policymakers in Kyiv to act hastily toward bridging the gap and ending the armed conflict.

The Organization for Security and Cooperation in Europe (OSCE) Special Monitoring Mission (SMM) deployed to Ukraine in March 2014 following the annexation of Crimea, and their mission still operates in eastern Ukraine. While serving in a strictly observe-and-report role, the OSCE SMM prides itself on not making conclusions based on the information gathered (Permanent Council Journal No. 991, 2014). Yet the data points coming from the SMM unit in eastern Ukraine paint a vivid picture of the status of the armed conflict in Donbas. Specifically, since the beginning of 2017, the SMM daily reports reveal that the number of ceasefire violations (CFVs) has increased along the line of conflict compared to previous years. Also, while the line of conflict has not moved in nearly a year, the mobilization of heavy artillery has shifted toward and away from the line multiple times, on both sides, in a bit of a game of cat and mouse. The number of CFVs combined with the movement of equipment and troops underscore the fact that ceasefire and peacekeeping efforts established by the Minsk agreements and other initiatives have not yielded a halt to the fighting in eastern Ukraine.

Furthermore, the mission and the consistent findings of the OSCE SMM clearly demonstrate that Russia and Ukraine have full knowledge of each other's presence in eastern Ukraine, despite claims of only being in the region for purposes of humanitarian aid and similar support. The reality is that the conflict in the Donbas region still thrives today and requires a fresh perspective and reformed accountability structure to establish control in the region and determine the way toward a stable peace between Ukraine and Russia.

Presence in Crimea

At the time of publication, Russian forces maintain total military control in Crimea. Following the withdrawal of Ukrainian forces in 2014 after Putin's annexation of the Crimean peninsula, Russia adopted a posture that remains mostly unchanged at the time of this publication. Satellite imagery collected following the annexation confirms that this posture contains a variety of ground and naval forces, centered mostly around the port city of Sevastopol. Specifically the presence of landing ships and armored personnel carriers confirm the presence of Russia's armed forces on the peninsula (American Association for the Advancement of Science). These forces, while not actively engaged in armed conflict, surely serve as Russia's deterrent, both throughout the peninsula and on the Black Sea, and could be mobilized at the outbreak of military engagement in Crimea.

Military Outcome

Through three years of fighting as of the time of publication, it is clear that the military conflict between Russia and Ukraine in the eastern Ukraine region of Donbas has three possible outcomes:

1. Military stalemate, where the Minsk agreements remain partially in effect, though with routine CFVs, and Russia and Ukraine enter a period of long-term frozen conflict.
2. Russian victory, where Putin's forces invade beyond the Donbas region and take over portions of eastern and possibly central or southern Ukraine.
3. Ukrainian victory, where separatist forces are defeated in eastern Ukraine, they reestablish control over territory lost in 2014, and they also reestablish control over their eastern border with Russia.

Of the possibilities, the most likely outcome is a stalemate. While a Russian invasion and victory is possible, this scenario presents huge global, political, and economic implications for Russia following the occupation that Putin and the Kremlin are not equipped to take on. Some believe that Russia might try to seize parts of southern Ukraine, moving westward through Mariupol, in order to establish a land corridor to Crimea. Such an occupation would avert sole dependence on a highly vulnerable bridge across the Kerch Strait currently under construction. Since a major part of Russia's military objective seems to be reestablishing itself as a naval power in the Black Sea, obtaining assured access to its naval base at Sevastopol could be extremely valuable.

A Ukrainian victory remains a possibility, and Ukrainian forces made several advances in the conflict during the summer months of 2014 (Menon 2015, 145-47). Ambassador John Herbst, in a meeting with SAIS, stated that he believed a Ukrainian victory could happen with military assistance (SAIS Group Meeting, Washington, DC, February 2017). However, this support would have to be unified and consistent to empower the Ukrainian forces to defeat the separatist forces. A Ukrainian victory also assumes that Russia does not launch any type of counter offensive that would reverse Ukraine's gains or even drive Russian forces further into Ukrainian territory.

Defense Options

Arming Ukraine with assistance from foreign countries and alliances remains a popular, well-discussed option, as doing so would provide Ukraine the military capability to match Russia's forces and eliminate or reduce the effect of the power asymmetry between the two nations. Especially in eastern Ukraine where the light Ukrainian military equipment barely provides an adequate defense posture, the bolstering of their artillery and an effective front-line force would give the impression that Ukraine could defend itself and reestablish its eastern border.

As confirmed during the SAIS meeting by Grigoriy Perepelytsia, Director of the Foreign Policy Research Institute, the concept of active defense also echoes among political and military leaders as an option for resolving the conflict in Ukraine. This posture takes many forms and therefore would have to be approached cautiously. In a successful active defense posture, Ukraine would receive a level of military support that would not ratchet up a counter response from Russia but would deter Putin and encourage Russia to withdraw forces. An appropriate balance of anti-tank and anti-aircraft weapons with a small reserve of offensive weapons such as tanks and heavy artillery would likely send a message of international backing to Russia without escalating the fighting underway at the time of this publication. Striking the right point along the continuum between no aid to a full military complement would provide the signal that Ukraine stands equipped to defend itself against a Russian offensive and engage fully at the outset of one.

Given the failure of Ukraine to establish a unified position and a clear identity for its people and nation, providing heavy artillery in a situation like the one in eastern Ukraine could be detrimental. With a lack of a clear national position, the likelihood of additional, heavier military equipment solving the issues facing Ukraine is unlikely. The most sustainable future rests in securing a common identity and foreign policy, the benefits of which will include a menu of options for border security and the prevention of the outbreak of future conflicts.

Conclusion

The anatomy of the conflict in Ukraine paints a unique picture in the world of conflict management. Ukraine's flimsy and shifting identity as a nation brings inherent dangers to the table of conflict resolution, as the solution one day could be void the next. Russia's quest for recognition as one of the great world powers often gives the impression that Ukraine to Putin is trivial and insignificant, yet the reality is that he uses the conflict with Ukraine as proof of his steadfastness in international relations and his drive for achieving his objectives for Russia. Most of the political and military leadership in Ukraine and the entirety of the speakers during the SAIS 2017 trip to Ukraine, including the most seemingly hawkish personalities, believe that Ukraine cannot achieve alone a military victory against Russia. The consensus suggests a frustration with the Minsk agreements and the diplomatic process in general, yet most do not see any alternative to holding the military status quo on the ground and hoping for an eventual political solution.

Recommendations

<u>To the United States</u>

- **Do not provide military assistance to Ukraine in the form of heavy artillery and weapons** to be used for a military offensive. The present inability of Ukraine to establish its identity as a people and its position as a nation foreshadow a real possibility for reckless destruction if provided with the means to exercise true military might. While support in the way of humanitarian aid remains popular and well received, its impact in country does little more than bandage human suffering and indirectly facilitate the conflict's continuation.

- **Encouraging the collective international embrace of the Minsk agreements** with capacity to update the negotiation measures and tailor them to the real circumstances of the fighting in Donbas will provide the best platform to end the fighting and work toward long-term stability and peace.

<u>To the North Atlantic Treaty Organization</u>

- **Discuss new alternatives to resolving the conflict in Ukraine.** The conflict has shifted from what many initially considered to be a short-lived offensive to a prolonged war. The change in timeframe and the nature of the fighting require a renewed approach by international players to break new ground in mediation and intervention measures. NATO's unique position in Europe provides unlimited potential to step up in conflicts such as the one in eastern Ukraine and inspire the collaboration required to end fighting.

- **Classifying the conflict on record as an international war with violated boundaries following an invasion by Russian troops, mercenaries, and "volunteers" in support of separatist forces will reinforce a motivation among NATO members to coordinate efforts and intervene where appropriate.** This would likely encourage Ukraine to seek NATO membership, and current NATO members to look more favorably on the possibility than in the past.

<u>To the European Union</u>

- **Restructure the strategy employed to manage the conflict in eastern Ukraine.** Since Ukraine faces pressure from both Russia and the international community at large (SAIS Group Meeting with the EU, Washington, DC, March 2017), the country and the government require assistance in formulating a unified position and capitalizing on its strong civil society to establish its character. By reinforcing the value of adhering to the ceasefire and withdrawing heavy weapons, the EU can build popularity and confidence in the Minsk agreements to overcome the lack of public support while emphasizing other provisions that can follow once the fighting ceases.

<u>To Ukraine</u>

- Above all, **Ukraine must reach a consensus on its character as a nation and its strategy for interacting with the neighbors of its region.** If Ukraine is an independent nation and desires to be a part of NATO and the EU, President

Poroshenko must make that objective clear to the Ukrainian people and then plot the course to realize these goals. The path to conflict resolution cannot be charted if there is no consensus on what the starting point is.

- **By strengthening trust in Ukraine and reinforcing the value that unity of state brings to the present situation as well as the future of Ukraine, the leadership of the state can influence the path that the nation takes in the coming years.**

Seeking Peaceful Resolution in Donbas
How Effective is the Minsk Agreement?

Linan Peng

Russia's annexation of Crimea and the conflict in Donbas occurred shortly after the 2014 Euromaidan Revolution when the former Ukrainian pro-Russian President Viktor Yanukovych ended up fleeing to Russia. A pro-Western government was welcomed by many Ukrainians after the revolution except for some areas in eastern Ukraine, particularly Crimea and territories bordering Russia. It was the divergence between pro-Russian separatists and the pro-Western Ukrainian government that triggered the ongoing conflict in eastern Ukraine. Since eastern Ukraine is the traditional base of support for the pro-Russian policy that Yanukovych held during his tenure, some activists in eastern Ukraine refused to succumb to the new government. Especially after the annexation of Crimea, separatists in the east attempted to retain close ties with Russia through a referendum on independence and through a full-scale conflict against the Ukrainian authority.

It is widely believed by Ukraine and western European countries that these pro-Russian militants had received direct military and financial supports from Russia, even though the Kremlin claimed that the conflict in eastern Ukraine that began in 2014 was only an internal war (Altshuller 2017). The message conveyed through Russia's propaganda suggests that these areas in eastern Ukraine with a significant proportion of ethnic Russians need to be kept under Russia's protection or should even be incorporated into Russia (Clem 2014). On the contrary, a survey conducted by Oxford University in eastern and southern Ukraine outside rebel-controlled areas indicates that this separatist movement lacks the public foundation, as only 5% of their 900 respondents support the breakup of Ukraine (Chaisty and Whitefield 2015).

By March 2017, the UN Office for the Coordination of Humanitarian Affairs (OCHA) has announced 9,940 conflict-affected deaths and more than 22,431 injuries among the Ukrainian army, Russian soldiers and "volunteers," civilians and separatists since the beginning of the War in Donbas in mid-2014 (OHCHR March 2017). The major casualties in the war have been innocent civilians and the Ukrainian soldiers.

There is ongoing conflict in the region even though Ukraine, Russia, France, and Germany (the "Normandy Quartet") have created the Minsk process to help facilitate the negotiation and peaceful resolution. While the Minsk Agreement is widely believed to be a guideline that should be followed by all parties, questions arise about its effectiveness. This chapter is designed to evaluate the measures currently implemented in eastern Ukraine and to make policy recommendations to different parties involved in the conflict.

Map 1: Conflict zones in the Eastern Border of Ukraine

The Minsk Agreement and its Breakdown

Given the background of the annexation of Crimea by the Russian Federation and unrest in eastern and southern Ukraine, representatives from Ukraine, Russia and the Organization of Security and Cooperation in Europe (OSCE) formed the Trilateral Contact Group (TCG) in 2014 to involve separatist groups in talks within the TCG's framework and to promote direct negotiation between conflicting parties in Donbas. As a

---

[1] Source: The New York Times; Ukrainian National Security and Defense Council; Organization of Security and Cooperation in Europe.

result, the first Minsk Protocol and Memorandum were signed by four parties: Ukraine, the Russian Federation, the Donetsk People's Republic (DPR), and the Luhansk People's Republic (LPR) on September 5, 2014. It aimed at ensuring an immediate ceasefire, promoting peacebuilding, and facilitating the process of decentralization of power in Donetsk and Luhansk. Under the OSCE's monitor as the Protocol required, eastern Ukraine enjoyed a successful reduction of violence after the September ceasefire. For example, the UN reported "331 deaths in the month after the start of ceasefire on September 5 2014, compared with 756 deaths in the 18 days before the ceasefire was signed" (Nicoll 2015).

However, the ceasefire implemented by the Minsk Protocol and Memorandum was short-lived, as all parties returned to the battlefield merely ten days after the introduction of the Minsk Protocol. In January 2015, Donetsk Airport was entirely destroyed. In addition, the parties failed to reach an agreement on the demarcation of the contact line, not to mention that a 30-kilometer buffer zone, as the Minsk agreement specified, was still only a hope (Nicoll 2015). Instead, activists and militants expanded the rebel-controlled territories by more than 300 square kilometers. They entered into Mariupol and Kramatorsk, which were under control of the Ukrainian government.

Since the problem of refugees was becoming severe and the conflict in the east escalated again in January 2015, Ukraine, Russia, Germany, and France who formed the "Normandy Quartet" in June 2014, signed the Minsk II Agreement on February 11 2015. The Minsk II Agreement was designed to mitigate the antagonism in Donetsk and Luhansk. Similar to the first Protocol issued in September 2014, the Minsk II Agreement called for an immediate and full ceasefire in particular districts of Donetsk and Luhansk. However, the improvement was that the Minsk II Agreement moved a step further by forcing both sides to withdraw all heavy weapons to equal distance with the purpose of creating a security zone (OSCE 2015). "The zone was to be at least 50km for artillery of 100mm caliber or more and 70km for most multiple-launch rocket systems, with a 140km pull-back specified for Tornado-S, Uragan and Smerch Multiple-launch rocket systems and Tochka and Tochka-U tactical missile systems" (Nicoll 2015).

Map 2: Situation in Eastern Ukraine in April 2015

Source: Ukrainian Security Defense Council

<u>Evaluation of the Minsk Process</u>

As Florian Poetter (SAIS Group Meeting, Kyiv, 20 March 2017) from the Office of the Special Representative of OSCE Chairman-in-Office stated, the Minsk process was successful in ending heavy violence, although it remains far from perfect. Two years after the Minsk Agreement was issued, the parties involved in the conflict tend to regard themselves as passively participating in the Minsk process. A report posted on Interfax, a privately-held independent news agency in Russia, commented that "the process got extremely protracted and stagnated......but neither of the parties has the intention of quitting the Minsk process" (Interfax 2017).

First, the Minsk Agreement lacks legally binding force to restrict the behavior of non-state actors such as DRP and LRP. For example, Grigoriy Perepelytsia, Director of the Foreign Policy Research Institute affiliated with the Ministry of Foreign Affairs of Ukraine, emphasizes the importance of working within the framework of the Minsk process, on one hand. However, on the other hand, he claims that relying on active defense along with the Minsk process would constitute a more effective strategy for Ukraine to resolve the conflict in the east. He believes that the Minsk process can be successful only if it is applied to manage interstate conflicts. In other words, restricted by internationally binding laws, a state is more likely to fulfill its obligation under international treaties. However, the war in Donbas is a dispute with local separatists who may break the agreement at any moment without consequences, even though it also shares the characteristic of an interstate conflict due to the direct intervention by the Russian Federation. As for DPR and LPR, militants and separatists continue to Perepelytsia is pessimistic about the Minsk process and advocates for a new strategy named "active defense," which is based on the Minsk process but puts more weight on military deterrence against escalation by Russia, DRP, and LRP (SAIS Group Meeting, Kyiv, 21 March 2017).

Second, the Minsk Agreement is also violated by state parties involved in the conflict. As for Russia, Russia's military, financial and other types of support for DPR and LPR are incompatible with the Minsk process. For instance, the United States has recently warned Russia after President Putin announced temporary recognition of passports and other documents issued by self-proclaimed DPR and LPR on February 19, 2017 (BBC 2017). Russia is blamed for having escalated the conflict and violated the Minsk process (Interfax 2017). As for Ukraine, it is also importing and requesting more weapons from the United States. Thus, the parties in the conflict have not strictly followed the peaceful path suggested by the Minsk Agreement.

Third, the Minsk Agreement has limitations on enforcing the ceasefire and peacebuilding provisions. The OSCE is the only actor that is responsible for monitoring the ceasefire. However, unlike the third parties in other similar conflict areas, OSCE is an international organization which is not designed for a formal peacekeeping mission. Moreover, the OSCE SMM is only empowered to monitor the ceasefire, to report the misbehaviors on both sides, and to promote mutual dialogue, but it lacks powers to implement and enforce the ceasefire and peacekeeping rules that "Normandy Quartet" promulgated (see chapter by Angelica Valdez).

Fundamental Difficulties in Conducting the Minsk Agreement

As noted in Map 1, Donbas is bordered with Russia, which is reluctant to see the western influence spreading along its border. It is Russia's traditional sensitivity to its geo-political security on its western borders since the Cold War that has raised the fundamental difficulty for Ukraine and Russia to make a compromise and agree on a peaceful and diplomatic resolution in the future. Even worse, the conflict between Ukraine and Russia will likely intensify if Ukraine continues its trajectory towards EU and NATO partnerships.

From the Russian perspective, the issue in Donbas and Crimea is a zero-sum game, where a pro-Western Ukrainian government is believed to threaten Russia's security situation, not to mention that Ukraine is seeking a closer relationship with the western European countries through frequent cooperation with EU and NATO. Even though a zero-sum game does not necessarily mean that it is impossible for both parties to negotiate, the war in Donbas reveals the fact that neither Russia nor Ukraine are willing to compromise, since their vital interests overlap along their borders. The war in Donbas is stuck in a stalemate, which is different from the other successful cases of territorial disputes, such as the Camp David negotiation between Egypt and Israel which was mediated by the United States. In this particular case, Israel was willing to return the control of the West Bank because Israel was satisfied with the demilitarization in the West Bank and did not ask for more. The other important reason leading to this successful negotiation was the role of the United States as a partial but conducive mediator in the middle that pushed Israel to compromise.

However, there is a lack of such influential power in the region that can balance Russia, and meanwhile, even though Russia has signed the Minsk accords and agreed to these provisions, it does little or even nothing to get their surrogates to implement them.

Therefore, as for the Ukrainian government, cooperating with EU or NATO and embracing a Western identity might provide a solution that could boost its national economy and legalize its policies. However, the other side of the story that is usually neglected by the public is that the process of seeking closer ties with the EU and NATO may further deteriorate Ukrainian security in the east, while the effectiveness of current measures to resolve the eastern conflict is still unclear.

Conclusion

The Minsk process is the main diplomatic measure to manage the conflict in eastern Ukraine. The Minsk process is believed to be the standard resolution process that has gained legitimacy from the UN Charter, the Geneva Convention and other international laws and treaties. However, two years after its implementation, the Minsk process has stagnated since the parties have made little contribution to facilitate the process so far, and the parties have even violated the Minsk process to different degrees. The Minsk Agreement is viewed as ineffective and unsuccessful even by the Ukrainian government, and the more fundamental factor that impedes the peaceful resolution is the difficulty for parties to compromise and agree with each other on this issue.

Effectiveness of Other Measures to End the Conflict in Donbas

The future of a peaceful resolution in Donbas is viewed as more pessimistic, even considering the other non-military measures that are available. Economic sanctions are one of the other measure used in Donbas issue apart from the Minsk process.

When Russia began its aggressive annexation of Crimea and disguised interference in eastern Ukraine in early 2014, the Western countries responded with packages of economic sanctions targeted at Russian enterprises, and some Russian high officials directly. "In July 2014, sanctions were enacted in a coordinated manner by the European Union, the United States, Canada, and other Allies and partners" (NATO 2016). These sanctions were further strengthened and extended by 2017 and the types of sanctions may be placed in three categories. The first type of sanctions restricts designated Russian state-owned enterprises in important sectors, such as banking, energy, and defense, from getting access to Western financial markets and services. The second type issues a ban on exports to Russia of designated high-technology oil exploration and production equipment. The third is an embargo on exports to Russia of designated military and dual-use goods (NATO 2016).

The impact of the Western economic sanctions on Russia is controversial. As NATO and EU claim, the sanctions they impose on Russia have helped worsen the macroeconomic difficulties that Russia was already encountering. For example, there was a pronounced oil price shock in 2014 when economic sanctions first came out. Furthermore, the combined effect of these sanctions and the fall of oil price increased downward pressure on the value of the Ruble and the exchange rate. As a result, data suggest that Russia entered into recession after January 2015 with a GDP growth of

-4.5% for the second quarter of 2015 and nearly zero growth for all of 2016, and the Russian economy started to recover from negative growth only after January 2017. Therefore, it is widely believed that Western sanctions have been a success in regard to the crucial goal of causing damage to the Russian economy.

Graph 1: Russia GDP Annual Growth Rate

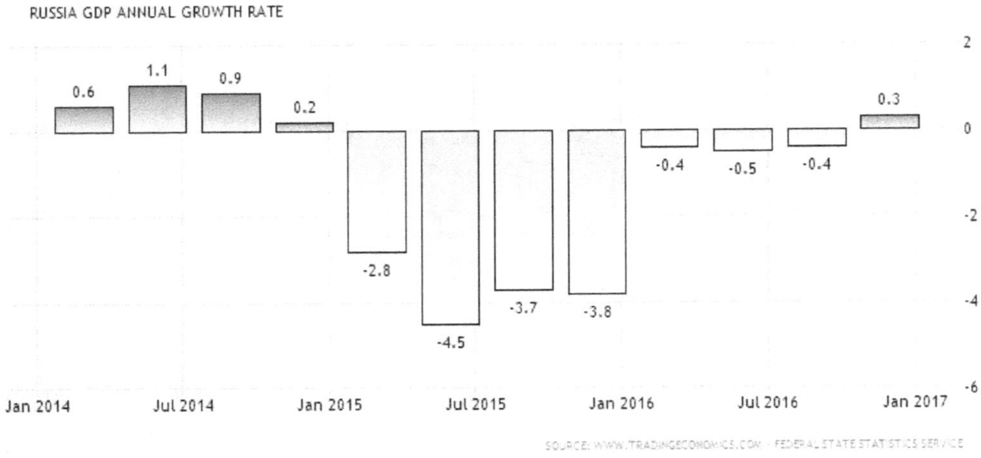

Source: Tradingeconomics.com: Federal Statistic Source

However, there are two noticeable flaws in the argument above.

First, the impact of the Western sanctions on Russian economy is stated ambiguously, since what matters when evaluating the sanctions is determining the magnitude by which Western sanctions could exacerbate the Russian economy, not whether they had any effect at all. According to Grigoriy Perepelytsia (SAIS Group Meeting, Kyiv, 21 March 2017), sanctions are not effective because the sanctions imposed on Russia concern only 6% of Russia's entire economy, based on their calculation, which is far less than what people thought previously. Additionally, as the data of global growth suggest, the economic growth of Russia fits in with the world growth. From 2011 to 2016, the global economic growth and Russia's economic growth both kept slowing down at the same pace. This broad background of current global economic situation can also be an explanation of the Russian recession.

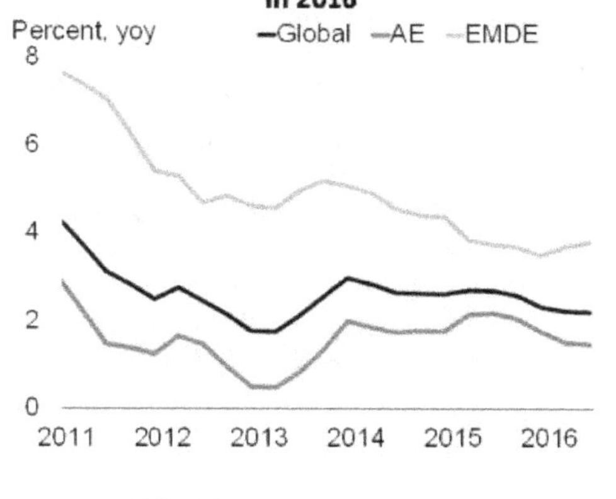

Figure 1: Global growth continued to slow down in 2016

Source: World Bank.

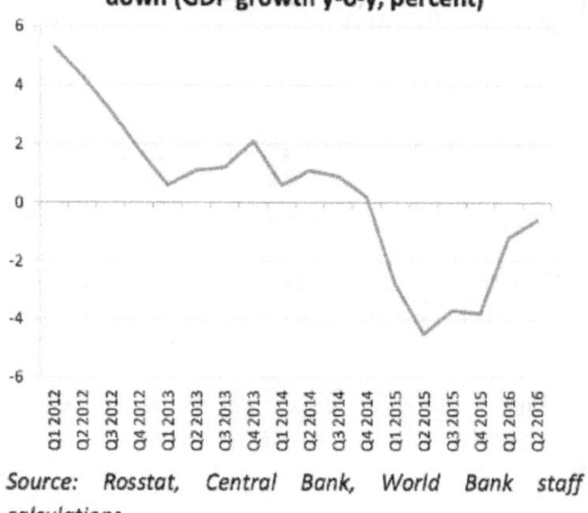

Figure 2: The pace of the Russian recession slowed down (GDP growth y-o-y, percent)

Source: Rosstat, Central Bank, World Bank staff calculations.

Second, it is more important to consider the impact of those sanctions on the implementer when evaluating sanctions. In other words, particularly noteworthy are the influence of sanctions on Ukraine and European countries themselves. Russia may have lost 6% of its economic growth due to sanctions, but Ukraine has lost most of its trade partnership with Russia and at least half of its trade volume after the breakout of Ukrainian crisis in 2014, according to the former Foreign Minister Leonid Kozhhara (SAIS Group Meeting, Kyiv, 22 March 2017). In comparison, the sanctions that Russia can impose on Ukraine and EU countries are much more robust, since Russia is the major gas provider for Europe. Therefore, the Western sanctions have not only exerted negligible impacts on Russia, but they also can have dangerous consequences for Ukraine and the West.

Conclusion and Prospects

It is generally agreed that the Minsk process provides a platform where all parties are encouraged to pursue peaceful resolution in Donbas under the protection of international law and supervised by OSCE, but the Minsk process is stagnant and ineffective after being implemented for two years. There are various reasons: The Ukrainian government started to doubt the effectiveness of the Minsk process after the continuous conflicts with DPR and LPR that have not been halted over the past three years. Russia refuses to compromise, such as withdrawing its military support from Donetsk and Luhansk. DPR and LPR keep violating the Minsk agreements, and EU countries are not strong enough to balance Russia in the region. As a result, the future of the Minsk process is widely viewed pessimistically.

Even though there are other measures available, such as the Western economic sanctions, the impacts of those measures are meager and not effective either. Ukraine is a country with weaker military force compared to its neighbor, Russia, so a military response is not a good option for Ukraine. That leaves Ukraine with no choice but to pursue diplomacy and either to find ways to strengthen the Minsk process or to replace it with a more effective one.

Recommendations

The following policy recommendations are addressed to different parties in Ukraine.

<u>To the Ukrainian Government</u>

- **Permit all sides in Ukraine to express their feelings and opinions of the eastern conflict.** For now, this process is mainly driven by civil society rather than the government. Civil society organizations such as the Ukrainian Women's Fund are working on reporting stories of IDPs, making the public feel an emotional outpouring around these issues. The support from the Ukrainian government on these issues is important, since the nationality and identity of Ukraine as a whole can be advanced if the government actively takes the lead.

- **Act as a unified voice to gain greater bargaining benefits in the negotiations.** The attitude on the Minsk process and other peaceful resolution measures within the Ukrainian government is diversified, which is conducive to making better policies, but hazardous to the negotiation process with other parties in the conflict.

- **Introduce peacekeepers who are from outside of Russia's and Western Europe's sphere of influence to the conflict in the east.** Even though the Normandy Quartet agreed that peacekeepers could provide a way to end the conflict, they disagreed over the composition of a peacekeeping force. Therefore, peacekeepers should neither come from European Union countries nor from the former Soviet states, but should come from nations with a neutral stance.

- **Strengthen the Minsk Agreement in terms of the enforcement of**

demilitarization. Demilitarization is available only if Ukraine and Russia agree to stop transporting weapons and armies to the front lines.

- **Continue reform on decentralization to cede some autonomy to the conflict zone in exchange for the opportunities of de-escalation and peaceful resolution.**

To the EU and NATO

- **Assist Ukraine's capability to defend itself rather than providing Ukraine with new weapons for offensive military operation.** The EU and NATO need to balance between guaranteeing protection for eastern Ukraine and initiating a security dilemma with Russia. Providing unambiguously defensive military support is regarded as a measure that could prevent the security dilemma from escalating.

Monitoring and Enforcing the Cease-Fire

Angelica Valdez

The contact line, between the Ukrainian armed forces on one side and armed separatists on the other, is 500 kilometers long. The conflict, that turned violent following the 2014 public demonstrations in Kyiv, has continued even after a 2015 cease-fire agreement. The Special Monitoring Mission (SMM) to Ukraine, having been established to manage the unrest after the 2014 Maiden revolution, was deployed to eastern Ukraine when the military conflict intensified. All OSCE participating states, on an annual basis, must renew the SMM's mandate and deployment, and this is not dictated by the Minsk agreements. In March 2017, OSCE participating states agreed to extend the SMM's mandate to monitor the security situation in eastern Ukraine to 31 March 2018. The SMM, composed of civilian monitors, is deployed to 14 locations throughout eastern Ukraine, on both sides of the contact line (SAIS Group Meeting, Kyiv, March 2017).

Unrest in the Donetsk and Luhansk regions, following the 2014 Ukrainian revolution and the Russian annexation of Crimea, resulted in a military conflict between the Ukrainian central government and eastern separatists. The Ukrainian military, relying on Western support, has deployed military forces to eastern Ukraine, while separatists have reportedly received extensive support, in the form of weapons, fighters, and propaganda, from Moscow. Armed conflicts are usually waged between two opposing entities which, after being unable to reach an agreement, decide to use military force to impose their will on the opposing side. The situation in eastern Ukraine, however, where opposing sides are not well defined or understood, is different. The Ukrainian government is fighting for territorial integrity and national unity on one side, but the other side is being defined as either Ukrainian separatist, rebelling against their central government, or Russian military forces invading Ukrainian territory to support local fighters and create instability in the country. Moscow insists its only role in the current situation is as a mediator between the Ukrainian central government and eastern Ukrainian separatists. Russian official claim the instability in Ukraine is between a weak and corrupt central government and eastern separatists, demanding the right to "self-determination." Weapons, fighters, and events on the ground would indicate otherwise.

Events on the ground, such as cease-fire violations and the mobilization of troops and weapons, indicate there are two militarily equipped sides engaging in an armed conflict. These sides are composed of Ukrainian armed forced and Russian-backed separatists, Russian soldiers and "volunteers." The cease-fire and withdrawal of weapons cannot be successfully enforced until all members of the conflict are clearly identified and their objectives are adequately addressed.

The Minsk agreements and subsequent arrangements have attempted to reach a diplomatic solution to the military conflict in eastern Ukraine. By 21 March 2014, the OSCE had deployed the SMM to observe and report on the security situation in the conflict zone (see chapter by Linan Peng). In Normandy, France in February 2015, Ukrainian, Russian, French, and German leaders reached a cease-fire agreement that also included the removal of all heavy weapons from the front line. The implementation of a monitoring and verification system was agreed upon to prevent ceasefire violations and to guide the conflict towards a peaceful resolution.

The SMM, charged with observing and recording cease-fire violations, consists in March 2017 of 716 unarmed civilian observers, from 44 OSCE participating states, and an additional staff of 427 personnel. There are currently more than 600 SMM unarmed civilian observers working in the Donetsk and Luhansk regions. The Chief Monitor of the mission is allowed to increase the number of monitors to up to 1000 (OSCE December 2016). All 57 OSCE participating states must approve the SMM's deployment and mandate annually. Currently, the SMM is mandated with observing and reporting the security situation on the ground, without any investigative or enforcement authorities and without drawing any conclusions as to who violates the cease-fire agreement or who moves prohibited weapon systems into unauthorized areas. They produce daily reports about observed violations without overtly identifying the violating parties; it is evident, however, that there are numerous violations from both sides on a daily basis.

The Agreement

Minsk II, or the "Package of Measures for the Implementation of the Minsk Agreements," agreed upon by the Trilateral Contact Group, outlines thirteen points to be considered for a peaceful resolution. The Trilateral Contact Group agreed on the following items on 12 February 2015.

1. Immediate and comprehensive ceasefire

2. Withdrawal of heavy weapons by both sides at equal distances in three sub-zones related to the weapon's range of fire: heavy artillery must be withdrawn beyond 25 kms. from the line of contact on each side, rocket launchers must be withdrawn 35 kms. on each side of the line, and tactical missiles must be pulled back 70 kms from the front line.

3. Effective monitoring and verification of the cease-fire and withdrawal of heavy weapons by the OSCE

4. Launch a dialogue on modalities of conducting local elections

5. Pardon and amnesty of persons connected with persons connected with events that took place in certain areas of Donetsk and Luhansk

6. Release and exchange of all hostages and prisoners of war

7. Ensure the safe access, delivery, storage, and distribution of humanitarian assistance

8. Define modalities of full resumption of socio-economic ties including pension payments

9. Reinstate full control of the state borders by the government of Ukraine

10. Withdraw all foreign armed formations, military equipment, and mercenaries

11. Adopt permanent legislation on the special status of certain areas of the Donetsk and Luhansk regions

12. Local elections will be discussed and agreed upon with representatives of certain areas of the Donetsk and Luhansk regions. Elections will be held in accordance with OSCE standards and monitored by OSCE's Office of Democratic Institutions and Human Rights (ODIHR) (United Nations Peacemaker December 2016).

13. Intensify the work of the Trilateral Contact Group through the establishment of working groups on the implementation of the Minsk agreement

The agreement provides a framework from which to plan a diplomatic resolution, but it is vague and does not provide details for implementation, verification of adherence from both sides, consequences for violations, or timeline in which each item should be achieved. The package of measures does not outline how each task will be accomplished or how to address violations that obstruct a peaceful solution. For instance, vague language such as the introduction of an "immediate and comprehensive ceasefire," does not articulate specific measures required to ensure they can be properly monitored or appropriately enforced. Likewise, the point on the "withdrawal of heavy weapons" does not specify exactly how these heavy weapons will be removed, how it can be verified, and most importantly, what the consequences will be for maintaining heavy weapons within range of the contact line. While this package of measures outlines optimistic actions that should lead to peace, it lacks details, steps required to achieve each objective, a pragmatic enforcement and verification system, and a specific consequence linked to each violation.

Although this agreement was signed in 2015, after more than two years it is yet to be fully implemented. Both sides continue to violate the cease-fire agreement and both continue to maintain heavy weapons well within range of the contact line. Examining the measures of the cease-fire and removal of heavy weapons might help in reaching a diplomatic solution in eastern Ukraine. Evaluating the role of the SMM, its major challenges in enforcing its mandate, and the implications it has on the negotiation process may reveal areas that could lead to an acceptable resolution.

The Role of the Special Monitoring Mission to Ukraine

The Minsk package of measures declares the OSCE's Special Monitoring Mission will conduct effective monitoring and verification of the cease-fire and withdrawal of heavy weapons. The SMM has over 700 unarmed civilian monitors altogether, with the vast majority are based in eastern Ukraine, although it also has small observer missions in many cities in western Ukraine. It receives its mandate from the OSCE Permanent Council, not the Minsk negotiations, which means all 57 participating states must agree on the SMM's purpose and objectives. The SMM's mandate allows them to report the facts as they observe them, without speculating on external factors, such as motive or intent, and without drawing any conclusions on which side caused a violation. These unarmed observers are responsible for gathering facts and information on the daily security situation in Donetsk and Luhansk, reporting on the humanitarian situation and needs, and helping to establish a dialogue between Ukrainian government officials and separatists. The OSCE has established over 14 SMM locations in eastern Ukraine, on both sides of the contact line, in order to monitor and record cease-fire violations. Forward bases are established on both sides of the line, with additional smaller posts spread throughout the area. These smaller posts have anywhere from six to twenty unarmed civilian observers. While SMM officials report on the security situation including cease-fire violations and the movement on heavy weapons, they do not conduct investigations or intelligence collections. In fact, an OSCE official stressed that the SMM is not collecting intelligence and is not drawing any conclusions, but is rather monitoring and reporting on the security situation on the ground as they see it unfold. These civilian monitors are simply recording each time they observe the firing of weapons or any explosions, without annotating who fired the weapon or who caused the explosion. Humanitarian requirements are also reported, but the SMM does not deliver humanitarian aid (SAIS Group Meeting, Kyiv, March 2017).

The SMM was deployed to the conflict zone precisely to monitor and verify adherence to the cease-fire and withdrawal of heavy weapons. However, the SMM is unable to either enforce the agreement, or provide enough details on violations so that an appropriate consequence can be authorized for any given violation. SMM officials publically release documents, reports, and data on the security situation to inform on the current situation and create some form of accountability. The SMM has written over 700 reports on the security situation, outlining cease-fire violations, explosions, and the location of such events. SMM publications also include weekly reports and "Thematic Reports" on topics such as human rights, gender dynamics, access to water, and civil society operating in the conflict regions. Observers have attempted to track the movement of heavy weapons by recording serial numbers and comparing them to specific equipment on the ground, but this has become a major challenge since neither side has been willing to provide a full inventory of military equipment that is located along the contact line. Observers also conduct "impact site assessments" and attempt to facilitate a dialogue and access between the two sides. An OSCE official also reiterated that it is up to the two sides to stop the fighting, especially since the SMM can only report on its observations and is not being deployed to enforce or punish either side (SAIS Group Meeting, Kyiv, March 2017). Additional work to facilitate a peaceful resolution is also being done by the Trilateral Contact Group (TCG).

The Trilateral Contact Group, formed by representative from Ukraine, the Russian Federation, and the OSCE, along with representatives from separatist regions of Donetsk and Luhansk, signed a "Framework Decision" on 21 September 2016. The agreement is an attempt to outline specific methods to implement and enforce the "package of measures." The framework was constructed with the guidance and recommendations of military advisers from the Normandy Quartet, which convened in June 2016. These military advisers relied on their background and principles on the development of force and military means to construct a framework to address the shortfalls found in the "package of measures" (OSCE September 2016).

The "Framework Decision" agrees to specific steps for the withdrawal of military troops and military equipment from the contact line to prevent the violation of the cease-fire. The goal is for both sides to remove forces and military equipment from their current fighting positions by an area of at least 2km wide by 2km deep, and thus creating specific demilitarized areas along the contact line. These zones are specified in the document's annex and are monitored by the unarmed SMM observes. The role of the SMM, as a verifying body, is once again emphasized, but remains restricted. The SMM is to verify adherence to the cease-fire within seven days of each demilitarized zone being established. SMM observers, recording geographic coordinates of each designated demilitarized zone, will track and document the movement and withdrawal of all military troops and equipment from each specific area. Additional demilitarized areas can be agreed upon and added to the framework in future meetings as members of the TCG agree on specific locations. The framework was first implemented in the Petrivske, Zoole, and Stanytsia Luhanska areas with the goal of creating areas of disengagement. Disengagement is defined in the agreement as the withdrawal of armed forces and military equipment from their current positions, starting in the three above mentioned areas. Once these areas are cleared and verified, moving forward into such disengaged areas is prohibited (OSCE October 2016).

Both sides are required to deliver baseline information including the current location of troop and equipment to facilitate monitoring by the SMM. Civilian observers are also to record and monitor information on anticipated troop and equipment destinations once they have departed their specific combat positions. Once both sides clear a designated 2km by 2km zone, they are to inform SMM observers within 24 hours of withdrawal. These cleared areas must be deemed safe and secure before SMM observers arrive to monitor and verify the disengagement process, which will be completed by unarmed observers patrolling and observing the area. The Ukrainian Armed Forces are to provide free and safe access for SMM observers to complete their verification mandate in disengaged zones. Unfortunately, unexploded ordinance and mines have prevented unarmed observers from reaching and monitoring all areas of the conflict zone. The Ukrainian military does provide limited de-mining support to enable the safe passage of civilians, but the task and process needed to address the large number of mines and unexploded ordnance littered across the conflict zone outweighs the military's capability (OSCE October 2016). Although the 19 September 2016 TCG Memorandum prohibits the laying of mines and declares existing mines must be removed, implementing and enforcing this policy has been difficult. On 23 April 2017, an SMM patrol vehicle, traveling on a road without any visible mine hazard signs, exploded after hitting a possible mine. An American paramedic was killed and two other patrol members were injured (OSCE April 2017). Not only does this type of event complicate the monitoring mission, but it also undermines the Minsk process since measures that have been agreed upon are clearly not being followed or enforced.

The Trilateral Contact Group and representatives from the separatist areas of Donetsk and Luhansk met on 1 February 2017 and once again called for the need to implement and enforce a cease-fire in the vicinity of the Donetsk Airport and along the contact line. The announcement states that weapons outlined in the Minsk agreement should be withdrawn to appropriate distances by 5 February 2017. It calls for a safe and secure passage and access to designated areas for SMM observers and the secure facilitation of humanitarian assistance, including water, electricity, and heating (OSCE February 2017). While the SMM continues to observe, monitor, and report on cease-fire violations and the presence of heavy weapons along the contact line, both sides continue to demonstrate they are neither willing nor able to remove their weapons from within range of the contact line, nor to adhere to the cease-fire agreement. The Ukrainian government insists it is acting in self-defense and cannot remove heavy weapons required to defend its territory and people while Russian-backed separatists continue their hostilities in Ukraine. Moscow, along with the DPR and LPR, on the other hand, claims security cannot be established in eastern Ukraine without elections and a productive central government.

Challenges to SMM

There are two significant challenges to the SMM carrying out its mandate: its inability to enforce the cease-fire and withdrawal of heavy weapons, and its inability to provide enough details so that external entities can hold either side accountable for violations. The Trilateral Contact Group, a bilateral agreement between Russia and Ukraine, has not established terms of reference for how cease-fire and disarmament operations should be conducted in eastern Ukraine. There are no established disciplinary proceedings at the military level or political price to pay at the policy level for cease-fire violations or for refusing to remove heavy weapons from the conflict zone. Obtaining safe and secure access to specific areas has been an obstacle preventing SMM observers from documenting precise information on the location of heavy weapons, explosions, or cease-fire violations. Additionally, SMM equipment such as drones and vehicles have frequently come under fire while attempting to access areas with cease-fire violations. This has unfortunately prevented the proper documentation of violations to the Minsk agreement.

Disagreements between TCG members on defining underlying concepts of a military conflict prevent either a full-scale military campaign that would inevitably either leave a losing side having to accept the other's terms, or the complete enforcement of a cease-fire and removal of weapons. Instead, the SMM has been deployed and tasked with observing and reporting on violations to the agreement without having any authority to enforce a cease-fire or implement a set of consequences for violations. SMM observers and their public reports may, however, be able to provoke an international reaction to the failed implementation of the Minsk agreements and the continuous violations of the cease-fire agreement.

Recommendations

Stakeholders should address all significant obstacles to reaching a non-military resolution in eastern Ukraine. Reconsidering the disengagement framework might provide an opportunity to develop an enforceable way of removing weapons from the conflict zone while also implementing an enforceable cease-fire.

<u>To the OSCE</u>

- **Provide SMM with appropriate equipment to observe, monitor, and track the location of heavy weapons, explosions, and cease-fire violations**. These might include underground seismic detection devices, observations balloons, and motion detection cameras.
- **Work with the Ukrainian military to increase safe and secure areas for SMM observers.**
- Clarify the role of all involved **parties**: the Ukrainian and Russian governments.
- **Establish a process to enforce a cease-fire agreement and the removal of heavy weapons.**

<u>To the SMM</u>

- **Work with military advisers** to establish appropriate procedures in combat zones.
- **Establish training programs on ammunition and weapons recognition.**
- **Clarify the role of the Joint Centre for Control and Coordination (JCCC)** and rely on it to help implement and enforce the cease-fire agreement.

<u>To the Ukrainian Government</u>

- **Publically commit to enforcing the cease-fire.**
- **Establish consequences for violations**.

- **Decide whether or not a military option should be pursued in order to achieve Ukraine's military objectives** (see chapter by Mark Brass) **in the Donbas;** if it does not, then Ukraine should remove heavy weapons from the current conflict zone.

To the Russian Government

- **Acknowledge the level of support that is being provided to Ukrainian separatists fighters.**
- **Stop the movement of heavy weapons and fighters into eastern Ukraine.**
- **Work with the SMM to facilitate observation, monitoring, tracking, and enforcement.**
- **Return control of the legally recognized Russian-Ukrainian border to Ukrainian control.**

To Representatives from the Donetsk and Luhansk Regions:

- **Clearly define political and military objectives.**
- **Work with Ukrainian government and SMM to end hostilities.**
- **Permit local election in the two regions with international monitors.**

Part II: Political Issues

42

The *Other* Conflict: Ukrainian Politics at a Crossroads

Ross B. Hurwitz

The conflict in eastern Ukraine and the Crimean Peninsula receives significant attention from world leaders, policy makers, and academics. However, there is a second conflict currently underway in Ukraine with far-reaching implications for the future of the state, the crisis in the east, and the international community. Ukraine's domestic politics suffer from deep roots in a post-Soviet oligarchic structure, unfeasibly high ambitions for future European alignment, and a hybrid war redefining the very idea of what it means to be Ukrainian. Between entrenched corruption, fierce political opposition, mounting social pressure, and an increasingly intractable conflict, Ukraine's domestic politics might pose the greatest threat to its future stability and prosperity.

Background

A retired, high-ranking American diplomat described Ukrainian politics as a collection of hustlers learning to survive (SAIS Group meeting, Washington, DC, February 2017). In the aftermath of the dissolution of the Soviet Union, survival was essential. Economic uncertainty and political turmoil threatened the stability of the newly independent state. Unlike numerous Central European countries, Ukraine did not declare independence in the aftermath of a popular uprising that removed the Soviet era elites from power. Instead, for the first decade after independence, the state was run by the same bureaucrats who had been in power throughout the Soviet era (Yekelchyk 2015). Consequently, high levels of corruption have led to an inefficient, kleptocratic government controlled by an oligarchic class of ultra-wealthy entrepreneurs. These individuals took advantage of the post-Soviet transition to gain wealth and power. As a result, some consider Ukraine to be one of the world's defective democracies; more specifically, an illiberal democracy. This term refers to a state in which "the principle of the rule of law is damaged, affecting the actual core of liberal self-understanding, namely the equal freedom of all individuals" (Merkel 2004). While a notoriously corrupt judicial system certainly weakens Ukraine's rule of law and the oligarchs hinder necessary economic and political reforms, Ukraine's democracy is quite strong in other areas, in particular, freedom of the press. So, while "defective" might be too strong a term for the state of Ukrainian governance, a history of corruption and cronyism, coupled with current internal and external obstacles, have placed significant pressure on the Ukrainian government's ability to govern the state and achieve success in the current conflict.

In order to analyze the extent of Ukraine's political problems and the impact it is having on the conflict in the Donbas and Crimea, it is first necessary to understand how Ukraine's government is organized. Over the last two decades, political unrest and social transformations have forced significant changes in the government's structure, often oscillating back and forth between parliamentary and presidential authority depending on the party in power. These changes have not been merely statutory; in many cases, they have been constitutional (Way 2004; Pleines 2016). In both the 2004-05 Orange Revolution and the 2013-14 Euromaidan, or Revolution of Dignity, a key element of popular unrest was the rise in presidential power at the expense of parliament (the Rada). Understanding the constitutional authority of each branch will help frame further discussion of Ukraine's political landscape. Additionally, understanding the role of political parties and societal stakeholders can contribute to our understanding of Ukraine's political climate.

<u>The Presidency</u>

The role of the president, as discussed above, has changed numerous times since independence was declared in 1991. As of the last elections in 2014, Ukraine operates under a semi-presidential system of government, meaning that the president acts as the head of state, while the prime minister is the head of government. Under this system, the president appoints governors of Ukraine's 24 oblasts (regions) and nominates both the prime minister and the cabinet, but both are only answerable to the Rada. He or she is elected by popular vote in national elections for no more than two terms of five years each. The president's duties include serving as commander-in-chief of the armed forces as well as representing Ukraine in all matters of international affairs, foreign policy, national security, and the negotiation of treaties and agreements (The Constitution of Ukraine 2016).

The history of the Ukrainian Presidency since independence is defined by oscillation between pro-Russian and pro-Western points of view, highlighting a significant divide between the western and eastern parts of the country. The east-west dynamic is certainly not universally applicable; however, the strong ethnic and linguistic connections of populations in the eastern oblasts with Russia and in the western oblasts with Europe have impacted the domestic political ideologies of the regions and of the state as a whole. The fact that this division resulted in the presidency shifting between the two orientations with considerable frequency explains the ambivalence that many presidents took toward policies regarding Russia and Europe. As soon as a president took decisive action in terms of defining Ukraine's geo-political position, protests or even revolution often ensued. As a result, presidents often played a delicate balancing game to ensure that neither point of view gained too much ground.

The Rada

The Verkhovna Rada is the unicameral parliament of Ukraine. It consists of 450 deputies (though as of March 2017 only 422 seats are occupied due to the conflict in Donbas). Elections are based on a mixed voting system where fifty percent of the seats are filled through proportional representation from political parties and the other half is based on first-past-the-post in single-member voting districts. All political parties must reach a 5% threshold to be eligible (Election Law of Ukraine No. 4061-VI 2011, Whitmore 2014). Deputies are elected for five-year terms and while in office are granted immunity. The constitution assigns numerous authorities to the Rada, including adopting all laws, adopting state budgets, approval over principles of foreign policy, approval of the president's nominees for prime minister and cabinet positions, as well as introduction of amendments to the constitution (The Constitution of Ukraine 2016).

Political Parties

Ukraine is a multi-party system where parties rarely receive enough support to govern without forming a coalition. In the last national election in 2014, there were 52 separate political parties that put forward candidates for parliament (Central Election Commission 2014). Total membership in political parties in Ukraine is low, estimated around 3.5

percent of the population. Financing comes from a mix of private and public sources, with parties needing to clear two percent support to receive state funding (Meleshevych 2016).

Political parties in Ukraine tend to exercise significant control over national political discourse, even while 80 percent of Ukrainians say they don't trust any political party (Meleshevych 2016). This dynamic is a consequence of Ukraine's historic political culture, where political personas usually outweigh policy or ideology. As a result, political parties in Ukraine are often cults of personality that focus far more attention on pursuing the interests of its leaders and donors, rather than achieving significant political reforms necessary for Ukrainian development. The fact that many political parties take on the names of their leaders (e.g. the Poroshenko Bloc, the Tymoshenko Bloc) highlights this phenomenon. Parties merge and split so often in Ukraine that referencing the party by the name of its leader is sometimes the only way to achieve public recognition. The actual party names remain so vague and change so frequently that voters rarely know what positions each party stands for; being able to associate parties with political personalities makes this process easier, though it often fails to delineate political philosophies.

<u>Oligarchy</u>

No conversation about politics in Ukraine can be conducted without understanding the role of the oligarchs. In the classical Greek definition, oligarchy refers to "the rule of a few self-interested elites" (Pleines 2016). In the context of Ukraine, these elites, totaling 29 by some estimates (Pleines 2016), are the entrepreneurs and politically well-connected individuals who made millions, and in some cases billions, of dollars during the privatization of state-owned enterprises in the 1990s. These individuals control Ukraine's major industries, including energy, natural resources, metallurgy, communications, transportation, and manufacturing (Yekelchyk 2015). These considerable fortunes were obtained through the close partnership of politicians and savvy businessmen in the early post-Soviet era. As oligarchs consolidated power and built wealth, they used their wealth and resources to support political parties that would continue to support their monopolistic enterprises. Eventually, the line between government, political party infrastructure, and the oligarchy began to fade (Abrams and Fish 2016). For a Western audience, it is difficult to comprehend how deeply rooted the oligarchic culture is in former Soviet countries, particularly in Ukraine. As mentioned earlier, Ukrainian independence did not come as a result of a violent overthrow. The existing Soviet authorities had opportunity and motive to ensure that they could enrich themselves and their allies in the transition toward democracy and a market economy. Unfortunately, this came at the expense of the Ukrainian people.

Government Composition in 2017

The head of state in 2017 is President Petro Poroshenko, the "chocolate king," an oligarch estimated to be worth $1.3 billion US (Forbes 2017). He is also the head of the Petro Poroshenko Bloc (PPB), a political party which achieved a majority in the Rada following the post-Euromaidan elections. While it failed to win an absolute majority of seats, it formed a governing coalition with People's Front. Together, these two parties hold 221 of the 450 seats. As of March 2017, the opposition consisted of a coalition of six political parties holding 154 seats as well as 47 seats occupied by deputies with no party affiliation. Within this opposition there are a few notable parties, including the Opposition Bloc, the Yulia Tymoshenko Bloc (Fatherland), and Self Reliance.

As stated earlier, the particular ideologies of each party are relatively unimportant in the broader scheme of Ukrainian politics. The PPB is composed of members representing almost every end of the ideological spectrum and this can be said about many of the parties. Timofey Milovanov, an associate professor of economics at the University of Pittsburgh, recently described the Self Reliance party by saying: "They have no ideology. Some of their laws are conservative, some are populist, and some are liberal" (Gorchinskaya 2015). Politicians join parties based on the opportunities for their personal gain and not necessarily because they agree with the leader politically. As a result, party membership and leadership is focused more on obtaining and retaining power, regardless of what must be said or done to achieve it.

<u>The Ukrainian People</u>

The final element of Ukraine's political landscape is the people themselves. For much of the last 25 years, the Ukrainian people have taken a sideline in politics to the interests of the political elite and their oligarchic benefactors. This was primarily a result of the lack of a cohesive understanding of what it meant to be Ukrainian. There was no national identity that solidified strong political or social forces to enact positive change on behalf of the people. However, beginning after the Orange Revolution and growing even stronger after the Euromaidan and the subsequent conflict in the East, a tangible sense of Ukrainian national identity began to emerge. It is predicated primarily on opposition to Russian influence, but also on a pro-European alignment and anti-corruption and rule of law reforms. This political identity has developed in conjunction with the rise of a powerful civil society, which has been successful at putting pressure on key politicians to move reforms through the Rada. Despite clear regional and ethnic differences as well as variations in support for specific policy positions, the Ukrainian people are more unified than in any period in recent history. It is unclear, however, how the protraction of the conflict in the east, coupled with increasing political discord and growth of civil society, will affect the nascent national identity.

What This Means for Ukraine

Between a government built on the unstable foundations of post-Soviet plutocracy and kleptocracy and the hybrid conflict with Russia and the insurgents in Donbas, the Ukrainian political system has never been so close to a catastrophic collapse. At the same time, however, it has never been so close to a political and social, democratic breakthrough. The question remains, will the budding sense of Ukrainian nationhood coalesce into an effective voice for profound political transformation or will the entrenched political mechanisms derail reform efforts, condemning Ukraine to political and economic instability?

To answer this question, it is vital to evaluate the current state of the Poroshenko government and their efforts to deal with pressing internal and external dynamics. In short, the government is under extreme pressure. The opposition is attacking from the left and the right and the only way to maintain power is to either win a victory in Donbas, to succeed in significant anti-corruption reforms, or to resort to the methods of past governments and consolidate power to silence their opposition. Unfortunately, none of these options currently seem feasible.

The government's strategy for handling the conflict is difficult to delineate. This is primarily due to the growing number of politicians seeking to increase their political capital by exploiting the public's mounting dissatisfaction with Poroshenko's conduct of the war as well as his failure to quickly implement needed domestic reforms. These politicians represent a growing voice of opposition to the PPB from both the left and the right. The nascent national identity has resulted in an emerging opposition seeking a political rhetoric that will find traction and support from the people. In an effort to guard both his left and right flanks, Poroshenko has found himself in a strategic headlock in which he is unable to avoid the international community's cries for a negotiated peace out of fear of losing their needed financial assistance, while simultaneously needing to satisfy a growing nationalist sentiment through a commitment to use any means necessary to repel Russian aggression.

The government's actions have demonstrated a lack of any clear strategy for achieving success on either of these fronts. Therefore, they have been unable to achieve domestic buy-in from the Ukrainian people which will be necessary to conduct a successful, unified response to the conflict. It is becoming clear that the Minsk II Agreement, signed in 2015, is dead in the water. After two years, neither side has successfully implemented even the most basic provisions of the deal, particularly the ceasefire and the drawback of heavy weapons. Opposition to Minsk is growing in intensity in the Rada, led by Self Reliance member and the Rada's Deputy Speaker, Oksana Syroyid. Ms. Syroyid's rising political influence in Ukraine is based mainly on her vocal and unyielding opposition to Minsk or any deal that threatens Ukrainian sovereignty (an emerging element of Ukrainian national identity). The Deputy Speaker does not mince words when discussing the conflict. She describes the occupation of Donbas, and the subsequent failure of the international community to respond appropriately, as having been "raped in the view of the whole world" (SAIS Group meeting, Kiev, March 2017). This provocative language has made Syroyid the center of the anti-Minsk movement and propelled her to national prominence, but it has also failed to make her many friends in the international community. This rhetoric is tapping into the growing frustration amongst the population that too much is being asked of Ukraine, while Russia is getting what it wants without even having to admit that they are a party to the conflict.

While simultaneously seeking peace through the Minsk process, Poroshenko is also executing a brutal war against the self-proclaimed People's Republics of Donetsk and Luhansk. Predicated on the failure of Russia or the separatists to implement the security protocols of Minsk and attempting to force the rebels into submission, the Ukrainian government imposed an economic blockade of the region beginning in March 2017. The blockade enjoys widespread popular support, particularly from the opposition parties and the growing nationalist elements in the population. While authorizing the blockade, Poroshenko and other centrist politicians remained opposed to the measure due in large part to the heavy toll it takes on the Ukrainian economy—and by extension the oligarchs, including the richest of them all, Rinat Akhmetov. Prime Minister Groysman referred to the protesters, who started a makeshift blockade of the region in January 2017, as "populist PR" (Jacobsen 2017). However, after separatists seized Ukrainian businesses in the non-governmental controlled areas (NGCA), especially those belonging to Akhmetov, Poroshenko ordered the official blockade to continue until all property had been returned.

While this blockade is certainly scoring political points for Poroshenko and other politicians thought to be too willing to compromise on the war effort, it is unclear what benefit it will bring in the medium- or long-term. The economic cost to Ukraine is likely to be high, and the pressure on the separatists to surrender is likely to be small. As the economic consequences begin to be felt, left-leaning opposition parties, such as the Socialist Party of Ukraine, which has taken the helm from the mostly defunct Party of Regions, will capitalize on the growing burden. The Socialist's message, articulated by party spokesman and former Foreign Minister Leonid Kozhara, posits that Ukraine cannot survive without strong economic ties to Russia (SAIS Group Meeting, Kiev, March 2017), While perhaps unpopular today, it is difficult to say whether this line of reasoning will become more palatable as Ukrainians begin to feel the pinch.

The West's, particularly the EU's, failure to engage economically with Ukraine in a more robust way could increase the potential for an easing of social and economic animosity toward Russia. In 2015, for example, the EU was Ukraine's top trading partner, accounting for 40 percent of its total trade, while Ukraine only accounted for 0.8 percent of the EU's total trade (European Commission Statistics 2017). The Association Agreement signed in 2014 does not prevent disillusionment among the Ukrainian people. The reluctance of the EU to engage more fully with Ukraine leaves the door open for more pro-Russian parties to make the case for Russian alignment. Regardless of the emergence and strength of the new Ukrainian identity, the power of the purse might force many Ukrainians to reconsider where their interests truly lie. While hardline nationalists might be more resistant to easing relations with Russia, many Ukrainians, who are mainly looking to work hard and support themselves and their families, could be convinced of a more promising economic future in the East.

Between the technically (though not openly) pro-Russian political parties and the more hawkish nationalists, exists a fairly popular sentiment among realists. From their point of view, the only way for Ukraine to win in this conflict is to become the more attractive option. This involves anti-corruption reforms, economic liberalization, and a greater Western alignment. The aim is to beat Russia through soft power inducements of a high quality of life and better economic and social opportunities.

One long-standing voice for this push toward radical domestic reform is former Prime Minister Yulia Tymoshenko, leader of the Fatherland Party (more commonly referred to as the Tymoshenko Bloc). In a meeting with the SAIS delegation, Fatherland's Deputy Chairman Sergei Sobolev stressed the necessity of overhauling Ukraine's judicial system, particularly the courts. This is part of a broader effort to fight corruption in the government and loosen control by the reigning oligarchs and to return power to the people. This reform movement has recently seen a significant victory in the successful implementation of the e-declaration process. This law, passed by the Rada in March of 2016, has forced around 100,000 Rada deputies and other political leaders to declare all financial holdings, including the cash that many members keep in their homes (Hiemstra 2016). The e-declaration is the first step in providing greater transparency and accountability within the Ukrainian government. It is unclear what political ramifications these declarations will have in future elections, but the fact that deputies and officials complied with the new law is a promising sign in an environment that has seen few successes in the push for anti-corruption reforms.

This growing populist movement is being echoed by former Georgian President and subsequently Governor of Ukraine's Odesa oblast, Mikheil Saakashvili and his new Movement of New Forces Party. As a political outsider with no party members currently in the Rada, Saakashvili is able to reiterate many of the anti-corruption and judicial reform goals of the Tymoshenko Bloc while differentiating himself (and aiding his own political rise) by denouncing all current politicians as political elites and insiders who are incapable of enacting the necessary reforms due to entrenched ties to the oligarchs (SAIS Group Meeting, Kiev, March 2017).

Saakashvili's new political movement perfectly encapsulates the problems within Ukrainian politics. While his Movement to New Forces Party and the Tymoshenko Bloc share political objectives, their leaders' personal ambitions prevent the formation of a unifying force to achieve substantial reforms. Saakashvili is not shy about his personal aspirations. He has referred to a meeting where he informed President Poroshenko that his ambitions in Ukraine went beyond prime minister and even president; in his words, "I'm just like Simón Bolívar" (SAIS Group Meeting, Kiev, March 2017). Saakashvili might want to liberate Ukraine from the clutches of the political elites, but his efforts could potentially fall prey to his own ego and ambition. Personality politics and self-promotion, rather than policy driven principles, make effective opposition impossible. As a result, existing oligarchic powers retain control over a government defined by political posturing and infighting, preventing necessary reforms.

Unfortunately, at the end of the day, the current state of Ukrainian politics is nothing less than a rhetorical circus. No party honestly intends to solve the conflict because every side gains too much from using the crisis as a political lever. Just as American politicians are accused of failing to pass necessary immigration and infrastructure reform for political purposes, so too does the Ukrainian political elite use the conflict for campaign purposes. Admittedly, it would be a fallacy to say that every single politician behaves this way, but the problem certainly runs deep, crossing party lines. If corruption, kleptocracy, gridlock, and political opportunism are the symptoms of

Ukraine's flawed democracy, the primary cause is a political structure designed to serve, not the masses, but the fortunate few who have the money, connections, and desire to rig the system for personal gain.

Recommendations

It might seem odd for an outsider to be giving Ukrainians advice on how to run their country, but I do not think it's particularly revolutionary to propose that what Ukraine needs more than anything else is to end the economic and political control of the oligarchy and the political party structure that sustains it. The plutocrats who have been running the country for nearly three decades have plundered their nation of its wealth and resources, preventing one of the most resource rich nations in Europe from achieving a true and prosperous economic and political life.

There are numerous steps that can be taken by the Ukrainian government, civil society, and the international community to assist Ukraine to achieve its ultimate goal. It will not be easy. A state is like an organism. Like any organism, it will try to protect itself at any cost. The entrenched interests within the country will not easily loosen their hold. It is up to others to make sure they must.

<u>To the Civil Society</u>
- **Continue to foster and support emerging candidates and political parties who have no financial or political ties to the oligarchs.**
- **Continue to pressure MPs and other government officials to abide by campaign promises to enact needed judicial, economic, and fiscal reforms.**
- **Develop an action plan to determine how best to communicate needed reforms to constituencies** throughout the country.
  - **Empower local communities through training** about how to become active in the political process and to hold their deputies accountable.
  - **Develop and launch an information campaign** to create buy-in among the electorate to persuade them that their engagement is the only way to truly reform the corrupt system.

- o **Incorporate new technologies**, geared toward younger generations that can galvanize existing political momentum across the country.
- **Use social media to publically hold politicians responsible for their actions**. Whether through publicizing MPs' newly disclosed financial records or keeping score cards on votes, this public dissemination of information is the best tool the public possesses to ensure deputies remain accountable.

<u>To the Government</u>

- **A unified national identity is necessary** for any democracy to succeed. National identities create buy-in among the population and foster greater civic engagement and pride in the form and process of government. The Ukrainian government must encourage the continued development of the nascent national identity through **educational and community programs that build greater social cohesion.**
  - o These programs must foster multicultural national identity to mitigate the negative influences of radical ethnic and ideological animosities. **Education and social programs should celebrate Ukraine's history** as a crossroads of civilizations and as a center of Eurasian history and culture. These developments can act as a bulwark against destabilizing influences from both within Ukraine and from abroad.
- **The government must continue its efforts to institute desperately needed reforms.**
  - o If party members and MPs want to maintain their positions, there must be recognition that the political tide is moving against oligarchs and that civil society, with the assistance of the international community, will eventually succeed in liberalizing Ukraine's democracy. **MPs with the education and government experience necessary should be leaders in this movement** and not just for the sake of political posturing. The recent e-declarations are a great first step, but more is needed.
- **Greater transparency is necessary for effective government**. Making government positions easier to understand and follow is vital to ensure a healthy

democracy. While it might be too difficult to achieve in the short-term, moving political parties away from personality driven and toward easily definable political platforms will simplify the campaign and election process while also creating more unified and efficient political parties.

To the International Community

- **International organizations**, such as the OSCE whose mission in the country has provided necessary support for economic and democratic liberalization, **must continue to support the reformation of Ukrainian democracy**. The country is on the verge of a significant breakthrough and, properly handled, the right incentives could spur the government toward reforms that have stalled.

- **Anti-corruption efforts are the most important reform necessary** to the future growth of Ukraine. Foreign governments, particularly the US and UK, could assist in the efforts to dismantle the oligarchy's control by making it easier for Ukrainian prosecutors and the new Anti-Corruption Ministry to access financial information of oligarch's international accounts. In this way, the Ukrainian people can finally know just how much money these individuals have stolen from the state and can hold them to account.

- To the European Union: **It is vital that the EU develop a clear message regarding its intentions for its future relations with Ukraine**. While the Association Agreement has laid out terms for further integration, the reality is far more ambiguous, allowing political entities in Ukraine to capitalize on misinformation and pipe dreams to win political power and influence. By clearly articulating what the Ukrainian people can reasonably expect from their relationship with the EU and communicating that message directly to the population, the political manipulators will lose a powerful tool in their efforts to sway voters.

The Role of Media and Propaganda in the Ukrainian Conflict

Gabriella Huddart

As relayed to us by an employee of OSCE (Organization for Security and Cooperation in Europe) in Kyiv, journalism has the power to cause conflict or build peace (SAIS Group Meeting. OSCE, Kyiv, 20 March 2017). In the case of the Ukrainian conflict, the media has been used by Ukraine, the international community (especially the West), and by Russia to promote competing narratives on what is "really" going on in the region. The term "hybrid war" was used in many of our meetings to describe the combination of military force and propaganda through media that Russia has employed throughout the conflict to attempt to bring credence to its aims. While both Western and Ukrainian media are, for the most part, free of government control, Russian media is controlled by the Kremlin and therefore only portrays its own, obviously biased (and oftentimes, false) side of the story in regards to the Ukrainian conflict.

Furthermore, journalists reporting on the conflict frequently fear for their safety. According to OSCE Representative on Freedom of the Media, Dunja Mijatovic, "We have reports of more than 300 journalists being attacked in the past year, 10 journalists killed, seven in Eastern Ukraine, and there are cases of journalists being kidnapped and detained" (Bell 2015). Physical violence against the journalists trying to preserve freedom of speech is the most direct method of attack on the media, whereas propaganda is a much more subtle, though arguably even more dangerous tool of war used throughout the crisis.

It is no secret that Russia has made ample use of propaganda throughout its modern history. However, the motives behind the employment of propaganda by the state have evolved from ideological during Soviet times, more open during the 1990s through the early 2000s, to opportunistic and nationalistic under Putin today: "Unlike the Socialists of the 1930s, the Kremlin and its friends today are driven not so much by ideology as by opportunism (and, in Russia's case, corruption). Mr. Putin's primary goal is not to present an alternative political model but to undermine Western democracies whose models present an existential threat to his rule at home" (*Economist* December 2016). This motive for propaganda development was corroborated by many of our interviewees who stated in no uncertain terms that Ukraine's desire to be a part of the "West," both politically and culturally, is a direct threat to Putin and the Russia he has built. Almost all of the people with whom we met, both in the government and NGOs, spoke of the incredible strength of Ukrainian civil society, especially when compared to that of other post-Soviet countries. According to Ambassador Oleksandr Motsyk, the lead Ukrainian representative on the Minsk Political Working Group, the conflict between Ukraine and Russia is a war against European values, democracy and freedom of speech (SAIS Group Meeting, Minsk Political Working Group, Kyiv, March 2017). Freedom of the press is one of the liberties that most democracies in the world consider paramount to the functioning of an open and just society, and when that liberty is allowed to prosper, it becomes a threat to all those nations that oppose it.

This chapter examines the media and propaganda tools employed by Russia that heavily contribute to its influence in the occupied territories of Ukraine. It also discusses both Ukraine's and the Western press's attempts to counter such propaganda, both successfully and unsuccessfully. It concludes with recommendations about how Russia, Ukraine and the Western press can use the media as a force for peace as opposed to a means of conflict escalation.

The "Information War" Explained

While the term "hybrid warfare" is used to explain the combination of military and soft tools that have been used thus far in the Ukrainian conflict, "information warfare" describes the sophisticated and pervasive methods employed by Russia's media and cyber communities to wage war against "western" values. Salome Samadashvili from the Wilfried Martens Centre for European Studies further explains the goals and methods of Russia's information war in Ukraine:

> The Russian government's information warfare strategy pursues two main and interrelated objectives. On the defence capabilities front it aims to curtail the freedom of information at home in order to avoid a 'colour revolution' scenario, using information as the tool to indoctrinate Russian voters and preferably Russian-speaking populations beyond Russia too. Offensively, it seeks to build and sustain a powerful infrastructure in the West in order to advance Russian interests by influencing public perception. (Samadashvili 2015 25)

Thus, the defensive and offensive aspects of the Russian government's propaganda campaign allow it to curb the growth of democratic ideals domestically while simultaneously spreading anti-western propaganda abroad. A concrete example of the start of informational warfare in Ukraine can be found in the arrival of Russian forces to Crimea. Armed Russian security forces entered Crimea in 2014, dressed in military uniforms and driving with Russian military license plates. As a result of the arrival of the Russian forces, Russian, Ukrainian and Western media began to clash: "In the blogosphere the sparring reached epic proportions. Western reporters Tweeted photographs of Russian license plates. Pro-Ukrainian bloggers sarcastically referred to the uniformed forces as "little green men." Pro-Russian bloggers and journalists used the catchword "polite men" and released pictures of them in camouflage, cradling automatic weapons, chatting amiably with little children" (Dougherty 2014, 3-4).

In this media environment described by Dougherty, it is easy to mix up fact and fiction, truth and lies, and therein lies the effectiveness of the Russian propaganda machine.

The Role of the Media in Russia's Propaganda Machine

According to Karlsen, there are four elements that make up Russia's "propaganda apparatus"—media, social media, political communication and diplomacy, and covert active measures (Karlsen 2016, 182). In order to stay true to the theme of this chapter, media and social media will hold the focus.

<u>Examples of the Influence of Russian Media in Ukraine</u>

There are three Russian news sources that are instrumental in spreading the Kremlin's messages: RT (formerly known as *Russia Today*), Sputnik, and *Pervii Kanal* (First Channel). Karlsen reveals that a NATO study of the three Russian news sources "…identified the use of 22 manipulative techniques used to influence Euro-Atlantic values. The analysis covered political rhetoric, content, and narrative related to the crisis in Ukraine, and concluded that Russian media were used to redefine the meaning of democracy, media freedom, freedom of speech, and human rights. Furthermore, they aimed to divide Western society and have people question their foreign and security policies and the credibility of their political leaders" (Karlsen 2016, 188-189).

The most interesting aspect of Russian propaganda in Ukraine is that it comes in multiple forms—blatant disinformation and manipulative indoctrination. For example, when Alexei Volin, Deputy Minister of Communication in Russia, was questioned about a fabricated story about an alleged crucifixion of a child in the eastern Ukrainian city of Sloviansk, his response was to imply that TV channel ratings were more important than the truth (Samadashvili 2015, 28). In this case, it appears that there was no attempt by the Kremlin to even hide the fact that the news was falsified.

Another example of the dissemination of blatant misinformation by the Russian government relates to its handling of the shooting down of Malaysian Airlines Flight MH17 in July of 2014. Not only did Russia's Ministry of Defense hold a press conference providing explanations for the tragedy that absolved Russia of any complicity, four months after the crash Russia released poorly doctored satellite images implying that the airplane had been shot down by Ukrainian forces. Although these outright lies and falsified documents might initially appear to discredit the efficacy of Russia's manipulative propaganda regime, the government's blatant disregard for the truth actually strengthens its indoctrination efforts. According to Keir Giles of Chatham House, "A primary objective of Russian disinformation campaigns is to cause confusion and doubt. The provision of multiple, contradictory alternatives to the truth serves the purpose of undermining trust in objective reporting, and especially in official statements by Russia's adversaries and victims" (Giles 2016, 37). Thus, mixing occasional truths with outright lies creates subconscious confusion and as time goes by, it is difficult for viewers/readers/listeners to discern the true facts.

In addition to the unapologetic dissemination of false news, Russian TV channels pursue more subtle, manipulative tactics in their propaganda techniques through entertainment programming. Themes include military victories and many new soap operas have been produced focusing on the "Great Patriotic War" (i.e. WWII) that praise the bravery of the Soviet people. In Ukraine specifically, Russian television has promoted the narrative that Ukrainian "fascists," prompted by orders from the West, have initiated a war against Russia and its values (Samadashvili 2015, 28-29).

Purposeful distribution of misinformation through biased news, along with subliminal political messages through entertainment are clearly important factors in Russia's information warfare tactics. In addition to news media, social media and cyberwarfare have proven to be valuable vessels for propaganda dissemination.

<u>Social Media and Cyberwarfare</u>

The use of social media for propaganda purposes by Russia has been targeted at both Ukraine and the West. For example, after the conflict arose in Ukraine and Russia was targeted with sanctions, there appeared to be a large, funded increase in international trolling. Karlsen states that *The Guardian* has actually noticed trolling for several years and has assessed that there have been planned attempts by pro-Kremlin campaigns to hinder or destroy debate on its comment boards on any topic related to Russia or the Ukrainian conflict (Karlsen 2016, 191). Furthermore, Pavel Durov, Founder and CEO of Russia's most popular social networking site Vkontakte, has informed the media that the FSB (formerly the KGB), demanded that he provide them with personal information of the activists who took part in the uprising in Kyiv. When he refused, he was purportedly fired (Dougherty 2014, 10).

According to Senate testimony on March 28, 2017 by Dr. Olga Oliker, Senior Advisor and Director, Russia and Eurasia Program at Center for Strategic and International Studies (CSIS), and in reference to the protests on the Maidan:

> Social media disseminated both intercepted and apparently doctored recordings of Western officials discussing the situation in Ukraine, with the intent to both embarrass and to suggest a Western hand behind Kyiv's emerging government. The narrative emphasized unrest in Kyiv and elsewhere and reported that fascist gangs were roaming the capital city's Streets. (Oliker 28 March 2017)

This narrative that the Maidan protests were orchestrated by so-called "fascists" has been an integral aspect of Russian propaganda in and about Ukraine. Furthermore, it has been stated that Russia actually "…deploys equipment in eastern Ukraine and elsewhere which not only filters the information available to internet users, blocking access to a range of websites and replacing them with Russian sources, but also harvests data from personal electronic devices. Combined with the demonstrated capability of trolling on an industrial scale, this poses a potential challenge if at a moment of crisis large numbers of servicemen and civilian officers are simultaneously targeted" (Giles 2016, 63).

In her testimony to the Senate, Oliker also pointed out that escalatory trajectory of cyber attacks on Ukraine at first remained relatively petty, consisting of distributed denial of service (DDOS) and defacement attacks targeted at Ukrainian government and NATO websites. However, she claims that, "[M]ore debilitating was a December 2015 attack on Ukraine's power grid, which shut down electricity to hundreds of thousands of people for several hours. Both Ukrainian and U.S. officials blamed Moscow. If this was, indeed, an orchestrated attack by Russia, it is an example of precisely the type of cyber operation that could be seen as warfare, in that it approximates effects similar to those that might be attained through the use of armed force" (Oliker 28 March 2017).

The combined TV news, social media, and cyber components of Russia's propaganda machine in Ukraine are indeed troubling and appear to be sophisticated enough to have garnered the Russian government significant influence in the country. Ukraine as a country that prides itself on the freedom of its press has indeed made efforts to combat Russia's information war on its Eastern territories, but unfortunately has missed the mark in several incidents.

Ukraine's Reactions to Russian Propaganda in the East

Russia is not the only party involved in the conflict that has used media to influence opinion. While Ukrainian media has not blatantly used methods of indoctrination for its own aims, unabashed criticism of Russia is paramount. In August of 2014, BBC Monitoring declared that Ukrainian news channels were beginning to take a very critical stance on Russia's actions in the eastern provinces, escalating to the point where, if the Russian stance on any issue was mentioned, it would immediately be dismissed as "Kremlin propaganda." Supplementing news broadcasts were documentaries and live discussion programs that promoted anti-Moscow views. These included the "Freedom of Speech" program on ICTV and "Shuster Live" on Kyiv's state-run UT1, which feature multiple Ukrainian officials and politicians delivering harsh criticism of Russia. The BBC points out, however, that despite the smear campaign of Russia by Ukrainian media, "alternative opinions are also aired, and presenters make no attempt to block dissent" (*BBC* 2014).

It is important to note that, in the early stages of the conflict in 2014, Ukrainian media, despite being openly critical of Russian actions, did not block dissent and still considered a variety of opinions on the matter. After all, it is never advisable to fight fire with fire. However, President Poroshenko's creation of the Ministry of Information Policy in 2014 drove Ukraine and its free media back in history a few decades, with a mission to spread propaganda of its own, thus making the press decidedly less free. The Ministry has been wildly unpopular among Ukrainian journalists and civil society and has been compared to a nonfiction version of George Orwell's Ministry of Truth. According to Samuel Ramani in a *Huffington Post* article:

> The ministry's lack of traction can be explained by two factors. First, media market saturation and the Russian state media's massive financial resource advantage have restricted Poroshenko's ability to spread the Ministry's line. Second, the ministry's use of propaganda to fight propaganda has severely eroded its credibility among moderate Ukrainians. Russian media stations have also exploited the ministry's stated mission and rhetoric as proof that Ukraine's leaders are authoritarian extremists. (Ramani 2015)

Thus, not only does the Ministry of Information Policy suffer from financial issues, it was formed to combat the same type of propaganda that it supposedly disburses. This is both counterproductive and hypocritical, and gives the Russian government even more fodder to vilify the Ukrainian government and praise its own.

According to Gaetan Vannay from the Geneva Centre for Security Policy (GCSP), most main Ukrainian media sources demonstrate a patriotic bias. Furthermore, various NGOs and the OSCE have reported many cases of journalists and the media being threatened by the Ukrainian government for not being patriotic enough. For example, Savik Shuter, one of Ukraine's most famous televisions hosts, came under fire from Ukraine's National Council for Television and Radio Broadcasting for inviting on air a Russian journalist who criticized the Ukrainian government's killing of civilians in a "fratricidal war." As a result of Shuter's attempts to bring balanced opinions to the

Ukrainian media regarding the conflict, the Council issued him with a warning for violating a law against war propaganda and the incitement of hatred (Vannay 2016, 3-4).

There has, to Ukraine's credit, been some progress made by the Poroshenko government to make Ukrainian media more free. In April of 2015, for example, Poroshenko signed a bill that defines the legal status and basis for the creation of a potentially independent public broadcasting organization. He also signed a law a few months later that is designed to ensure the transparency of media ownership in Ukraine (Vannay 2016, 4). Although some promising steps have been taken, the government and patriotically charged journalists in Ukraine must not continue to fall into Russia's trap. Not only does the restriction of a free press by the government provide Russia with more ammunition for its own propaganda, it threatens Ukraine's progress in becoming the truly democratic and "Western" society that it desires to be.

Western Media: Countering or Exacerbating the Russian Propaganda Problem?

It is no secret that freedom of the press in the West is a huge threat to Putin and his propaganda machine. According to Karlsen, "Russia has competed with the West in the media sphere since Radio Moscow's first broadcast in German in 1929. However, the perceived media monopoly attained by the West became a growing source of concern for Russia. The first major step to field a competitive international media outlet was the launch of *Russia Today* (now *RT*) in 2005. Its mandate was, according to President Putin, to "break the monopoly of the Anglo-Saxon mass media"" (Karlsen 2016, 186). *RT* is well on the way to achieving Putin's goal, as, despite efforts by the UK to sanction the news channel for being "unfree," there is no coordinated Western response to combat it. Giles suggests, however, that "[H]esitancy in appearing to target free media should be offset by recognition that RT and similar outlets are not free media, nor does their programming constitute journalism" (Giles 2016, 53).

Furthermore, Western media has become quick to a vulture-like degree in picking up news stories as soon as they occur, whether they are true or not. For example, despite the false "explanations" or scenarios provided by Russia for the shooting down of MH17 (described earlier), "…the scenarios' instant rejection by foreign and Russian experts did not prevent them from being reported in the West as well as receiving broad coverage within Russia" (Giles 2016, 37). Additionally, the doctored satellite images of the airliner that were instantly seen to be fake were initially still reported without qualification by Western media (Giles 2016, 27). Samadashvili echoes this opinion that Western media essentially, and often subconsciously, actually aids the dissemination of Russian propaganda, and suggests that, "[U]nfortunately, unlike Ebola or other epidemics, the epidemic of misinformation has no easily identifiable symptoms. It is the job of the independent Western media and public-opinion-forming outlets, such as think tanks and NGOs, to explain to the European public the danger they are facing" (Samadashvili 2015, 44).

Overall, Western media is unconsciously legitimizing the propaganda of Russia, (especially that disseminated through *RT*) by either citing it or unconsciously reporting its stories as true. In this sense, it is exacerbating the Russian propaganda problem, and steps need to be taken to stop this (described in recommendations below).

Conclusion

Despite small efforts by Ukraine and the West, to curb the effects and spread of Russia's information war in Ukraine, the war continues and does not show signs of stopping any time soon. Russia uses TV news sources and social media in a savvy and cunning manner, and the Ukrainian government has misguidedly tried to combat this propaganda with its own. While Poroshenko has signed some promising media reforms and there is clearly a great amount of will and desire among Ukrainian civil society for a free press and objective journalists, until the government and its people work together to combat propaganda, it will continue to permeate the country.

Recommendations

<u>To the Ukrainian Government</u>

- **Either abolish the Ministry of Information Policy, or alter its purpose.** Fighting propaganda with propaganda justifies Russia's methods and diminishes the progress the government has made in creating an open and free society.
- **Do not influence or intervene in Ukrainian news broadcasting.** Opposing viewpoints about the conflict should be neither quelled nor punished. Debate is

the key to a vibrant and open society and hindering it only gives Russia more fodder for its propaganda.

- **Ensure swift implementation of laws signed to promote free press.** Creating and signing such laws is a good first step, but unless they are implemented in a timely manner, they will not incite any change in the Ukrainian media environment.

To Ukrainian Civil Society

- **Empower the Youth!** The youth is the future of Ukraine and a powerful force for change. In our meeting with the Donetsk University students, we saw how impassioned and motivated they were to continue Ukraine's development as a free and open society. One student told us about her grandparents who continue to live in Donetsk and have been victims of the information war. She makes every effort to call her grandparents and visit them and to constantly explain to them that they are victims of a propaganda campaign and that they should resist (SAIS Group Meeting, Donetsk University, Vinnitsiya, 23 March 2017). Perhaps with enough of Ukrainian's young working to combat disinformation among the elderly, the propaganda will not have as pervasive an effect in the occupied territories.
- **Both domestic and international NGOs must work together to teach the victims of propaganda how to both recognize and resist it.** Since the Ukrainian government is, as of now, circulating its own propaganda, it is the duty of NGOs to do the community-level work to make sure vulnerable populations in the eastern territories do not continue to be indoctrinated.

To the Western Press

- **Do not legitimize Russian propaganda by citing it or reporting it as fact.** The United States is facing its own crisis of "fake news," and we should not be supporting this movement in the East, whether consciously or unconsciously.
- **Create a universal framework of guidelines to regulate behavior and activity of the press,** so if any media sources violate said guidelines, there can be consequences. Russian media should not be the sole target of media "sanctions,"

but all news sources that report fake news should be legally required to account for their actions.

- **Support Ukraine in continuing to build up an independent media**, and discourage the government from intervening in its operations.

The Women's Narrative in the Ukrainian Conflict

Chloe Colbert

The Beginning: Maidan and The Revolution of Dignity

"Every Ukrainian has to take responsibility for Ukraine" (Onyshko 2014). Those were the words of a woman in the Maidan Square in Kyiv, Ukraine as she publicly protested the Yanukovych government in December 2013. She demonstrated her resolve to fight for Ukrainian association with Europe and against government corruption. Beginning in November 2013, when Ukrainian President Victor Yanukovych refused to sign an Association Agreement between Ukraine and the European Union (EU), protests broke out in Kyiv (Yekelchyk 2015). From November 2013 to March 2014, protestors (who identified as Ukrainian) came to the Maidan Nezalezhnosti (Independence Square, Maidan for short) in Kyiv. The numbers swelled from hundreds of protestors in November 2013 to hundreds of thousands by December of that year. They were protesting Yanukovych's broken promise to sign the EU association agreement and the police brutality his government implemented against the protestors.

The women who helped organize the anti-Yanukovych, anti-corruption protests were crucial to the Revolution of Dignity's (the Maidan Revolution) success. It was the mothers who first criticized the Berkut (Ukrainian special police) for beating the youth and who then mobilized their husbands, sons, and daughters to join the protests in the Maidan (Onyshko 2014). Without women in the movement, there would have been less food preparation, clinics to care for the injured, or spokespeople for the Revolution. Women were involved in each aspect of the Revolution, sometimes bringing their children with them. Yet, the presence of women on the Maidan did not bring peace or mediation to the Revolution between the government-backed police and the protestors; instead, women were also targeted and arrested by the Ukrainian police (Onyshko 2014).

When given the chance, Ukrainian women will fight back against oppression and aggression. In this chapter, I will consider the following question: why has Ukrainian women's involvement in the Revolution of Dignity and the war in the Donbas escalated the conflict rather than defuse it? This question defies preconceived notions that women's involvement in conflict leads to peace (Strasser 2017). In opposition to pacifistic,

Western feminist narratives, Ukrainian women have demonstrated that women in leadership do not necessarily create more peace but often encourage men and women to pursue conflict for a means to an end. Thus, this chapter will analyze the role of Ukrainian women in politics, in the security forces (e.g. the police and military), in civil society, and in the media. Lastly, I will present a set of policy recommendations to civil society organizations, Ukrainian government agencies, and the international community to include women in mediation roles so they can resolve the conflict, not continue it.

Ukrainian Women Leaders

Yulia Tymoshenko: Ukraine's Populist Politician

Ukrainian women in politics demonstrate that women in leadership do not necessarily advocate for women's rights agendas, but use their position to manipulate power for themselves and their political party's interests. This was the case for Yulia Volodymyrivna Tymoshenko, Deputy Prime Minister under Prime Minister Yushchenko in the 2000s (Skard 2014). Known as the Eastern "Joan of Arc" in the West or "dominating" and "power-seeking" in Ukraine, Tymoshenko was active in politics as well as managed private companies in the energy sector during the Soviet period prior to Ukraine's independence. When Tymoshenko ran for prime minister after Ukraine's Orange Revolution in 2005 and then in 2007, only five percent and eight percent respectively of Parliament were women, several of whom did not support Tymoshenko's Fatherland Party (Skard 2014). Thus, one cannot conclude that Tymoshenko depended on fellow female politicians for support in her bid for power. In fact, Tymoshenko distanced herself from women's movements and relied on her public support to build popularity and support for her party's agenda. Tymoshenko utilized her popularity to fight the real threat: government corruption and Russian aggression against Ukraine. Overall, it is more important to Ukrainian female politicians to mobilize themselves for causes than for women's agendas to achieve their purposes and to be in sync with the state's priorities (e.g. anti-corruption campaigns, anti-Russian aggression battles, etc.).

<u>Women in Parliament</u>

In 2015, the Ukrainian female members of Parliament (MPs) established a gender caucus, which was "effective in lobbying and bringing issues of gender rights to the table" (SAIS Group Meeting, Kyiv, March 2017). The female MPs also established a formal advisory council in partnership with the Ukrainian Women's Fund to research and create actions for civil society organizations (CSOs) in tackling women's issues. However, the War in the Donbas has overshadowed this caucus, thus marginalizing the women's rights agenda and prioritizing the Ukrainian efforts in the war in the Donbas.

Like Tymoshenko, Oksana Syrorid, the Deputy Speaker of the Verkhovna Rada (the Ukrainian Self-Reliance party), is a female politician who has not espoused greater gender balance in politics, but rather pushed for her "center-right" Self-Reliance Party— an opposition party of Ukrainian President Petro Poroshenko's party (SAIS Group Meeting, Kyiv, 22 March 2017). Syrorid acknowledged that Ukraine was one of the first European countries where women had civil rights dating back to the 17th century. She also mentioned that only 11% to 12% of the Rada (Ukrainian Parliament) were female MPs. On the contrary, Syrorid emphasized that her own party had 38% female membership. Even though Syrorid presented her party as more gender-balance, she did not encourage more female participation in the Rada. Rather, her party and her role as Deputy Speaker was to prioritize the party's interests, which primarily responded to Russian aggression in Crimea and the Donbas (SAIS Group Meeting, Kyiv, 22 March 2017). Thus, Syrorid illustrated that the role of women in Parliament did not necessarily lead to conflict resolution, as she prioritized stronger Ukrainian military efforts in the war in the Donbas over advancing the role of women in society.

<u>Women in the Police</u>

Ukrainian women in the police legitimize the role of Ukrainian women in larger security aspects (e.g. the military) because it changes the perspective of gender within the country. In the beginning of 2017, approximately 25% of the patrol officers in Ukraine were women, and thus, women police officers "[were] more approachable" (Solovey 2016). Thus, women in leadership in the security sector have represented a significant change in how women are viewed in Ukraine, from 'homemaker' to active public servant. They are changing the gender perspective of Ukrainian women as community builders to protectors and fighters, even in the military.

Women in the Military

Ukrainian women in the military upend the idea of women as peacemakers in conflict. To many Ukrainian women, Russian aggression in the war in the Donbas validates the use of violence in lieu of peacemaking efforts. Women in the Ukrainian military began on the battlefield of the Maidan during the Revolution of Dignity. By February 2014, several Ukrainian women formed the first women's "hundred"[2] on the Maidan—an all-female battalion that conducted offensive missions against the Berkut and that defended the Maidan protestors from attacks (Onyshko 2014). One of the founders of that hundred, Anna Kovalenko, has since mobilized women to join the military to fight on the front lines of the war in the Donbas. Yet, even in the military, Ukrainian women face sexism and inequality. Not too long after women started joining the Ukrainian military, the Ukrainian Ministry of Defense created a policy where only men could occupy the top leadership positions within the military, effectively banning women from any leadership roles or major combat roles (SAIS Group Meeting, Kyiv, March 2017). Instead of having the responsibilities of a sniper or soldier (as some women were previously trained), this edict demoted women to secretaries and cooks. It is imperative for the Ukrainian Ministry of Defense to fully integrate women into the military because women's deaths in combat could create more international outcry against the war in the Donbas. Ukrainian women are the backbone and protectors of Ukrainian society, and without them, Ukrainian society would collapse.

Women in Civil Society

Female participation in Ukrainian civil society is essential to creating a stable state within Ukraine. Ukrainian women were always involved in creating civil society and providing for their communities' needs because, throughout history, the state was sometimes unable to provide for many types of social welfare services (Phillips 2008). Ukrainian women

---

[2] The Maidan protesters borrowed a name and tactic from their Cossack ancestors and organized in small battle groups, each called a "hundred." Facing larger forces, the "hundreds" could attack their enemy from different sides and keep them off-balance to compensate for their smaller numbers.

viewed participation in civil society and community development as an extension of their motherly duties to take care of their children, spouses, extended family members and the elderly; thus, Ukrainian women were more likely to be organizers of CSOs.

In respect to civil society in wartime, Ukrainian women organized the Organization of Soldiers' Mothers of Ukraine (OSMU) as an affiliate of the Committee of Soldiers' Mothers in Moscow (OSMM) in response to Russian casualties in the Russian-Afghanistan War and the Russian-Chechnya War in the 1980s and 1990s (Phillips 2008). The OSMU and the OSMM existed to raise awareness of the maltreatment of new conscripts in the Soviet military and "the untimely deaths of soldiers" in war. Eventually, the OSMU transformed from a wartime organization to a peacetime organization by continuing to advocate for veterans of Soviet-era wars as the newly-created Mothers and Sisters for Soldiers of Ukraine. For a limited period, the Russian women and Ukrainian women collaborated when it came to the treatment of their sons in wars fought by Soviet Russia.

Wartime civil society mobilization continues today in Ukraine, as women have organized and helped internally displaced persons (IDPs) who are fleeing the war in the Donbas region (see the chapter by Ashley Patton). The Ukrainian Women's Fund supports research about IDPs from the Donbas coming to Kyiv and Vinnytsia (SAIS Group Meeting, Kyiv, 20 March 2017). The Fund's Director, Natalia Karbowski, and her colleagues established the Fund in the early 2000s to support civil society at a time when the Ukrainian government was cutting civil society programs. In addition, the Fund supports women in local elections and trains women leaders. Karbowski has also advocated for recognition of women in the military in combat roles after the Ukrainian government closed 63 careers positions (e.g. photographer, journalist, sniper, etc.) to women in 2014 (SAIS Group Meeting, Kyiv, 20 March 2017). Hence, some Ukrainian women organizers prioritize their agendas and interests more than peacemaking; in Karbowski's case, she prioritized equal opportunity for women in career positions in the military more than a cessation of hostilities. Thus, female leaders of CSOs are not necessarily supporters of peacebuilding as other women leaders have been in conflicts.[3]

---

[3] See Fred Strasser, *Women and Peace: A Special Role in Violent Conflict.* USIP. 2016, for more information about women in peacebuilding roles with examples in Liberia and Colombia.

<u>Women and Social Media</u>

Social media is a fundamental part of political revolutions in the twenty-first century. Specifically, Ukrainian female participation in social media was the game-changer in the 2013 "Revolution of Dignity." Ukrainian students were the first participants in the Maidan who protested the Yanukovych government, and they used social media to raise awareness and invite peers to protest with them in the Maidan (Piechota and Rajczyk 2015, 86-97). A survey of students conducted after the revolution found that more female than male students had blogs linking Kyiv and Lviv in the West. Thus, female participation in social media was a fundamental grassroots component to the organization and communication between peers.

<u>Women in the Media</u>

Women in media roles in Ukraine are essential to shaping the conflict's narrative, from the Maidan Revolution to the war in the Donbas. In 2014, there was a temporary government ban on female journalists and photographers in Ukraine after the Maidan Revolution (SAIS Group Meeting, Kyiv, March 2017). Before that, women were present documenting the conflict. Olha Onyshko directed an independent documentary on the women's involvement in the Revolution of Dignity on the Maidan titled *Women of Maidan* (2014). As a Ukrainian woman, Onyshko highlighted the work of Ukrainian women in the Maidan Revolution, from female students to food preparers, from nurses to volunteers, and finally to soldiers in the women's hundred. Onyshko captured the experiences that she encountered in the Revolution to share with Westerners and Ukrainians not only to raise awareness of the conflict but to encourage a means of healing for those directly affected by the conflict (Onyshko 2017). Ukrainian women with a mission and narrative have the means of communicating their interests, which is to garner more international support for the Ukrainian government in the war in the Donbas.

International Approach to Ukraine's Women

<u>International Support of Women in Civil Society</u>

International organizations like the Organization for Security and Cooperation in Europe (OSCE) help determine the legitimacy of Ukrainian women's participation in the war in the Donbas. The OSCE Special Monitoring Mission (SMM) to Ukraine indicated that too few CSOs in Ukraine have a component on "conflict resolution, reconciliation and dialogue activities" (OSCE SMM 2015, 3-11). The reason for the lack of dialogue and conflict resolution programs within the CSOs is because of the following: higher priority to IDPs' needs, delegation of mediation to the national government in Kyiv, and the negative perspective of communicating with "terrorists" (e.g. the separatists in Donetsk and Luhansk) (OSCE SMM 2015, 3-11). The OSCE SMM is one of the few international attempts to bridge dialogue between CSOs on either side of the conflict.

International Support of Ukrainian Women in the Media

The OSCE instrumentally assists the mediation process of the conflict by connecting journalists from both sides of the conflict (e.g. Russian aggressive forces and Ukrainian nationalist forces). In 2014, the OSCE began hosting meetings between Ukrainian journalists and Russian journalists to bridge dialogue and "discuss ways to improve professional standards and safety of journalists in the context of the crisis in and around Ukraine" (OSCE 2016). The Office of the OSCE Representative on the Freedom of the Media, Dunja Mijatovic, and the OSCE Senior Advisor on Gender Issues, Amarsanaa Darisuren, also addressed media issues with a focus on women journalists and how the media portrays men and women (OSCE 2016; OSCE 2017). Thus, women in journalism and the media in Ukraine help to shed light on the conflict in the Donbas and hopefully will help solve the conflict by creating a dialogue between both sides.

Conclusion

Ukrainian women have involved themselves in all parts of the conflict in the Donbas—from civil society to documenting the conflict to fighting in the military. As natural organizers, women in Ukraine have the necessary skills to create movements, influence policies, and create change in their society for generations to come. With the dawn of multi-platform media, Ukrainian women's voices will not be marginalized. Going forward, women in Ukraine must hold positions within the government not for Western feminism's sake (Phillips 2008), but as a means of advancing Ukrainian society and ensuring stability and state security. When the conflict eventually ceases, Ukrainian women must play a role in the peacemaking process as emphasized by the international community (UNSC 2012).

Recommendations

<u>To the Ukrainian Ministry of Defense</u>

- **Include female military members in combat roles on the frontlines of the war** in the Donbas region. More female participation could translate into more military aid and support for the Ukrainian army.
- **Grant leadership titles to Ukrainian women in the military**. Essentially, the military should not label each woman as a secretary or cook when she performs other duties beyond that label's scope.

<u>To the Ukrainian Ministry of Social Policy</u>

- **Create a mothers' dialogue for women from the GCAs and the non-government controlled areas (NGCAs)**. A renewed mothers' dialogue on soldiers' untimely deaths could pressure governments for a diplomatic solution to the war.
- **Include CSO female leaders as special representatives to the Ukrainian parliament to act as liaisons** between Parliament, the Ministry of IDPs and Occupied Territories, and field operations teams on IDP issues, especially those concerning women and their children.
- **Task these delegates with the responsibility of creating an inter-agency working group**. The working group will include monthly updates on the plight of IDPs in the country and steps on the mobilization of women in CSOs as mediators.
- **Include the following parties within the working group: female representatives of CSOs that work with IDPs, members of political parties, and members of the media**, with equal representation given to female journalists, photographers, and filmmakers.

<u>To the Ukrainian Women's Fund</u>

- **Conduct conflict resolution training for women volunteers in NGOs that currently work on the frontlines of the war.**
- **Partner with the United Nations High Commissioner for Refugees (UNHCR) cluster group to conduct training for women volunteers throughout the GCAs.**

Part III: Economic Issues

Economies at War: Digging in, Cutting Ties

Alex Simon

January 2017 brought with it two very different forms of escalation in eastern Ukraine. One was military, with Russian-backed separatists ramping up heavy artillery attacks in violation of the tenuous ceasefire stipulated by the Minsk agreements. The other was quieter, and almost certainly more dangerous: as ceasefire violations piled up, Ukrainian volunteers along the frontline were pushing a non-military offensive of their own, erecting a makeshift blockade to prevent certain goods from entering non-government controlled areas (NGCAs). In the months since, multiple actors on both sides of the contact line have ratcheted up their own forms of economic warfare, threatening to inflict both short- and long-term damage, while eroding the links that had previously connected communities on both sides of the conflict.

This latest escalation underscores the centrality of economic factors in Ukraine's three-year old conflict. With the political and military tracks thoroughly stalemated, some parties appear to view economic measures as the most promising path forward: while Kyiv and its Western allies hold out hope that targeted sanctions might someday force Moscow to negotiate in good faith, Ukrainian hardliners now seem to believe they can strangle the separatist enclaves into submission—or at least score political points by trying. Russian and separatist objectives remain opaque, but these actors have in any case been probing new forms of economic provocation in ways that invite one-upmanship.

Despite this flurry of activity, anyone hoping that economic attrition will force Ukraine's conflict toward a denouement will likely be disappointed—at least in the near-term. The war's protagonists are all suffering, but not enough to compromise on the conflict's thorniest issues. On the contrary, present dynamics are likely to push in the opposite direction, fraying ties between separatist areas and the rest of Ukraine, while deepening the political and social schisms that have long hampered efforts at diplomacy. This represents a pivotal challenge for those committed to an eventual settlement that would see the NGCAs reincorporated into the Ukrainian state; these actors must now work quickly to de-escalate the current crisis and to safeguard against further deterioration.

Ukraine's Not-Quite-Hurting Stalemate

Undeniably, Ukraine's conflict has imposed major costs on Ukraine, Russia and the separatists. After sharp initial shocks, all have settled into a status quo in which the war consumes precious resources, disrupts trade and undermines production. Some stakeholders hope that the cumulative costs of warfare will soften the demands of one or the other side, paving the way for a breakthrough in the stalemated Minsk process; this is particularly true in Western capitals, where decision makers have for three years maintained sanctions against Russia with the goal of pushing Moscow toward implementing Minsk in good faith. For now, no such concessions appear forthcoming from Moscow or any other party; all have adapted to bear the costs of protracted warfare, which they view as justified by the conflict's political rationale. In a word, the conflict is economically painful and effectively stalemated, but not so "mutually hurting" as to lay the groundwork for compromise (Zartman and Berman 1982).

Moscow: Making Ends Meet

In analyzing the economic dimension of the conflict and its implications for eventual settlement, Russia is the obvious place to start for two reasons. First, Western states have made economic punishment for Russian aggression a cornerstone of their approach to the conflict, with a package of sanctions woven into the fabric of the Minsk framework. Second, the Kremlin is arguably the only party that *could*, if it deemed the costs of violence too high, pull back and strike a compromise; the government in Kyiv has no plausible alternative to continued warfare, and the separatists are—in various ways— beholden to the Kremlin's will.

It is clear that Moscow's intervention and its knock-on effects have caused Russia considerable economic hardship. The sanctions imposed by the US, the EU and other Western states have dealt the most significant blow; the IMF in 2015 estimated that sanctions would initially cut Russian GDP by 1 to 1.5 percent in real terms, with the potential to reach a cumulative output loss of 9 percent of GDP over the medium-term (IMF 2015, 5). These costs are augmented by further expenditures on the war effort, and on civilian expenditures in support of the populations and local administrations in annexed or occupied territory. The International Crisis Group estimated in early 2016 that

Russia was spending over $1 billion per year on subsidies, government salaries and pensions in the Donbas (ICG February 2016, 5). Ultimately, sanctions—and, to a lesser extent, the direct costs of intervention in Ukraine—combined with low oil prices to fuel a recession that in 2015 saw Russia's economy contract by 3.7 percent in real terms (Christie 2016, 57).

What is less clear, however, is whether this pain might at some stage suffice to force a shift in Russia's posture in Ukraine. Indeed, such a rethink appears unlikely in the near-term, for three primary reasons. First, a variety of Western and Ukrainian observers from varying fields agree that Russian President Vladimir Putin has judged his country's involvement in Ukraine a matter of core national interest—above all as a way to impede Kyiv's path toward greater integration with the EU, but also as a way of reasserting Russian status as a global power. Russia's macroeconomic wellbeing has thus far taken a backseat to these calculations, and there is no clear reason why this would change in the near-term. Second, and relatedly, the Russian economy has begun to climb back from the nadir of its recession, performing better than anticipated in 2016 as the impact of sanctions leveled off and industry ramped up (Tanas 2017).

Third, Moscow has some reason to doubt that sanctions will stick for the long- or even medium-term, with Mr. Putin evidently hopeful that sympathetic figures in Washington or Europe will pave the way for an economic reopening. While several American and Ukrainian observers voiced skepticism that an embattled Trump administration could pursue such an opening anytime soon, an increasingly fractious EU may hold more promise. The EU's sanctioning mechanism requires that sanctions be reconfirmed semiannually and by consensus; this poses growing challenges as sanctions eat into EU states' own economies (Sharkov 2015), and as some more Putin-friendly figures such as Marine Le Pen gain currency. At the very least, it appears clear that a more aggressive package of sanctions is not in the offing—a fact that will assure the Kremlin of what it has deemed a tolerable status quo.

These dynamics, taken together, led a range of interlocutors—from current and former Western officials to Ukrainian politicians and independent analysts—to the same conclusion: while the costs of involvement in Ukraine could eventually force Moscow to reconsider its approach to the conflict, there's no telling when such a reassessment might take place. Moscow is prepared to bear the costs of low-intensity warfare for the foreseeable future, and there is little reason to expect a shift anytime soon.

Ukraine: Hunkering Down

Kyiv, too, is poised to fight on, despite massive costs incurred by violence that has undermined Ukraine's productivity, territorial integrity and trade links. Russia's intervention hit Ukraine's economy hard and fast. Economist Anders Aslund has argued that the loss of Crimea immediately carved 4 percent from Ukrainian GDP, which was then compounded by the partial loss of Ukraine's industrial heartland in the Donbas; a sharp drop in trade with Russia, Ukraine's biggest trading partner, which slashed the country's exports by 18 percent; and the virtual disappearance of foreign direct investment, which cost another 3 percent in GDP (Aslund 2015). In total, Ukraine's GDP fell by roughly 15 percent between 2013 and 2015, while a two-thirds reduction in the value of the hyrvnia eviscerated Ukrainians' purchasing power (*Economist* 2017). These woes were exacerbated by a sovereign debt crisis, including $3 billion in loans to Russia, that has incurred further costs while forcing considerable wrangling over write-offs and restructuring (Moore, Olearchyk and Buckley 2015).

But Ukraine's economy, like Russia's, appears to have weathered the most turbulent period of the storm. The IMF agreed in April 2014 to step in with a $17.5 billion loan package to prevent Kyiv from defaulting on its debts, conditioning the assistance on political and economic reforms (Moore, Olearchyk and Buckley 2015); Kyiv has made significant progress on this front, notably in the banking sector and system of energy subsidies, although the pace has slowed and a host of problems remain unaddressed—above all in the areas of judicial reform and rooting out high level corruption (*Economist* 2017). Meanwhile, the country's agricultural sector has been picking up, drawing investment from Western firms looking to capitalize on the country's rich soil and underexploited land (Bjerga and Verbyany 2016). Various indicators stabilized in 2016, including reduced inflation and the deficit-GDP ratio (Olearchyk 2016), such that the IMF predicted a growth rate of 2.5 percent for 2017 (*Economist* 2017).

In short, Ukraine's economy is by no means thriving, but it is not in a state of free-fall that prevailed between 2014 and 2015. Meanwhile, the prevailing mood in Kyiv and elsewhere in the country is one of outrage at Russia's "aggression" in Crimea and the Donbas. What this means is that, barring a genuine economic collapse or a major change in political climate, Ukraine is poised to forge ahead with a war effort that has brought defense spending up to 5 percent of Ukrainian GDP (Schofield 2015). Indeed, some more optimistic stakeholders on the Ukrainian side ventured to suggest that the country's economic fortunes could—far from undermining the war effort—in fact help Kyiv to prevail over the separatists by rendering reintegration into a united Ukraine such an appealing prospect. While this smacks of wishful thinking, political and economic progress could indeed help render Ukraine both more appealing to fence-sitters in the East and better equipped, in the long-run, to reincorporate swathes of alienated, war-ravaged territory.

The Separatists: Between Isolation and Interdependence

In between Kyiv and Moscow sit the separatist-controlled regions of Donetsk and Lugansk, which over the course of the conflict have developed a war economy reliant on a mixture of trade—both with Russia and across the contact line with government-held Ukrainian territory—and financial assistance from Moscow. While the precise dynamics of this war economy remain opaque, we may draw three broad conclusions of relevance to this discussion.

First, economic conditions and overall quality of life in the separatist areas are harsh, with many subsisting on savings or pensions. Prices have risen dramatically due to scarcity, by some accounts climbing to double or triple the levels in government controlled areas across the line (ICG February 2016, 5). Conditions are worst in the areas closest to the line, where mining, artillery fire and the expropriation of abandoned homes by military forces have wrought havoc on civilian infrastructures—a fact that holds true on the government-held side as well (ICG July 2016). Meanwhile, separatist authorities have increasingly restricted access for humanitarian actors, worsening an already dire situation.

Second, the occupied areas are profoundly reliant on Russia for economic, political and military survival. As noted above, ICG estimated in early 2016 that Moscow extended more than $1 billion in civilian assistance to the NGCAs, some $700 million of which was for pensions for the regions' largely elderly population (ICG February 2016, 5); this is in addition to considerable military expenditures, for which Moscow forms the separatists' sole lifeline. As a result, the ruble has become the *de facto*—and, as of February 2017, the official—currency in NGCAs.

Third, despite the depth of separatist reliance on Russia, the occupied territories remain intimately bound up with dynamics west of the contact line. One manifestation of this lies in the Donbas's continuing centrality to Ukrainian industry, which crisscrosses the front line in a convoluted war economy. The Associated Press sketched these dynamics in a 2015 investigation, focusing on the empire of billionaire oligarch Rinat Akhmetov: "Coal produced in Krasnodon mines, on rebel territory, travels to the Avdiivka coking plant on the government side. Coke is then shipped back to rebel lands, to a metals smelter in Yenakieve, and the metals produced there are transported to government territory on the Azov Sea—for shipping to the West." Add to this the widely-held view that Mr. Akhmetov's empire has been paying taxes to Kyiv and the separatists alike, and a picture begins to emerge of the complex economic linkages between government- and rebel-held areas (Vasilyeva 2015).

The connections, however, run deeper than industrial production. Basic services including water, electricity and heating rely on infrastructure that runs back and fourth across the line; many such services are administered by utilities controlled, again, by Mr. Akhmetov (Vasilyeva 2015). Maps provided by Ukraine's Ministry for Temporarily Occupied Territories and IDPs show the depth of this interconnection, with the electrical grid and waterlines crossing frequently over the frontline. Meanwhile, in an illustration of the highly personal linkages and blurred lines in the conflict zone, some elderly residents are said to engage in "pension tourism"—crossing back and forth across the contact line to double up on retirement benefits, some paid by Kyiv, others by Moscow via the separatists.

Three conclusions flow from the above dynamics. First, despite the separatists' reliance on Moscow and increasing willingness to close themselves off from the outside world, the NGCAs have remained closely interlinked—and as such tightly interdependent—with territory west of the contact line. Second, trade across the contact line creates considerable potential for profiteering and corruption, particularly given Mr. Akhmetov's influence in this area. Third, the interdependence between GCAs and NGCAs has all the makings of a double-edged sword, with the potential to either attenuate or exacerbate conflict dynamics. On the one hand, shared economic and infrastructural interests might in principle incentivize restraint, shoring up cross-line ties and providing fertile ground for dialogue; one EU official noted, for example, the potential for "peacebuilding" initiatives centering on the issue of water. On the other hand, however, this interdependence introduces a set of pressure points through which each side may—deliberately or otherwise—inflict pain on the other, inviting in the process escalation from across the line. Recent events, unfortunately, have moved rapidly toward this latter dynamic of economic warfare.

Spiraling Self-Inflicted Wounds

The first three months of 2017 brought with them what one European official called "a galloping reaction and counterreaction" in the realm of economic warfare. In late January, Ukrainian volunteer battalions launched a blockade of bulk goods entering NGCAs by train. These groups charged that trade with the NGCAs amounted to "doing business on blood," and had the effect of enriching corrupt officials while breathing life into the separatist war effort (Makarenko 2017). In the month that followed, Moscow announced that it would recognize documents issued by the separatist authorities while opening its borders to citizens from the NGCAs. A further escalation came on March 1, when separatists seized control of a set of industrial and telecoms firms owned by Mr. Akhmetov, while also shutting down the latter's charitable operation—the largest in the NGCAs. Kyiv retaliated, opting in mid-March to throw its weight behind the blockade, and affirming that trade could resume only once separatists had relinquished control over the expropriated properties (Isachenkov 2017).

The precise rationale behind each of these measures is open to debate, as is the question of who bears primary responsibility. The nationalist volunteers who initially launched the blockade appear to have been motivated, at least in part, by a mixture of frustration with the status quo and an expectation that the move would hamper the separatist military campaign. Petro Poroshenko's government seems to have been effectively dragged into supporting the move, which it initially opposed and which holds the potential to cost Ukraine's economy dearly. The motivations of the separatist and Russian escalations are harder to discern, and could be attributable to a range of factors (one Ukrainian observer cited, for example, rumors that Moscow chose this moment to lash out at Akhmetov for political reasons totally unrelated to the conflict).

What is clear, however, is that the latest back-and-forth has ominous implications not just for the immediate economic wellbeing of communities and industries on both sides of the contact line, but also for any long-term resolution to the conflict. In the near-term, the combined impact of the blockade and expropriations could be devastating. Mr. Akhmetov's enterprises are said to employ some 300,000 individuals in the NGCAs, whose output—above all in coal mining—is inextricably linked to other aspects of industry and service provision on both sides of the contact line. These enterprises today stand to suffer both from their expropriation by forces that may or may not prove administratively competent, and from the blockade's impact on the links between coal, coke, metal and electricity production across the front line. One Ukrainian NGO worker suggested that producers would inevitably find their way through the blockade through bribes to security officials, but that doing so would push prices still higher than their current levels—say, from 300 to 1,000 percent of market value. In short, the possible effects of this recent escalation include massive price hikes, disruption of basic services including electricity and water, rising unemployment on both sides of the line, and a further contraction of the already narrow humanitarian space in NGCAs.

The medium- and long-term effects could be equally pernicious. A European official noted concern that coal mines and metal plants, if sufficiently disrupted, could require shuttering and even dismantling, lending a measure of irreversibility to what is presently being billed as a temporary arrangement. He also suggested that, with coal from the NGCAs increasingly restricted, Ukrainian producers had begun seeking out alternative suppliers as far afield as Africa. Meanwhile, both the Ukrainian central bank and the IMF have warned of major economic consequences: while the former revised its 2017 growth forecast from 2.8 down to 1.9 percent, the latter announced it would delay the next $1 billion tranche of its loan to Ukraine in order to review the impact of the blockade (*Agence France-Presse* 2017).

In addition to these economic effects, Kyiv's decision to seal off the NGCAs formally from the rest of the country will serve to further alienate Ukrainians east of the contact line. Indeed, the blockade is likely to be particularly infuriating for communities who have, since long before the current conflict, harbored feelings of economic neglect. Moscow was swift to add fuel to this fire, incorporating the blockade into a running narrative whereby ultra-nationalists in the capital are said to victimize those on the country's periphery; in Putin's words, Kyiv has been "resolutely and consistently repudiating its own regions, condemning millions to living without social security, banking, medical and legal services" (Isachenkov 2017). As times get tougher, this narrative is likely to resonate; one Ukrainian student who in 2014 relocated from Donetsk to central Ukraine suggested that the blockade had already led friends back home to harden their views of the central government.

The precise impact of these dynamics will only crystallize in the months ahead. Broadly speaking, however, it seems clear that a continuation of current policies will corrode both the Ukrainian and separatist economies, with a particularly dramatic—and potentially irreversible—impact on the commercial and infrastructural ties that have until recently bound communities on both sides of the line. As these ties fray, the prospect of reintegrating the NGCAs into Ukraine will loom ever more complex and costly; separatist regions will deepen their reliance upon and integration into the Russian economy, while Ukrainians look elsewhere to make up for lost industrial output. This weakening of economic linkages will only deepen entrenched political fissures, adding fresh layers of intractability to the conflict's already stagnant diplomatic process.

Conclusion and Recommendations

Recent events underscore the fluidity of economic dynamics surrounding the crisis in eastern Ukraine. Even with the conflict's political and military tracks deadlocked, the various protagonists retain considerable maneuverability in the economic sphere. This has been on full display through early 2017, with Kyiv, Moscow and the separatists all ramping up their own distinct forms of economic pressure. Those invested in a settlement that preserves, to the greatest extent possible, Ukraine's territorial integrity must now work to tamp down this escalation while simultaneously working toward medium- and long-term objectives that will maximize the space for an eventual resolution to the conflict. To this end, the following recommendations may serve as a guide.

To the Trilateral Contact Group (Ukraine, Russia, OSCE)

- **Prioritize de-escalation of the recent crisis, with the goal of lifting the blockade and returning expropriated enterprises.** This should rise to the top of the agenda for the political, economic and humanitarian working groups, with OSCE stressing the costs to all sides and offering to monitor a de-escalation.

- **Absent successful reopening of the NGCAs, ensure that the blockade on economic goods does not spill over to humanitarian supplies.** In the event that Kyiv maintains its blockade on NGCAs, it is imperative that all parties negotiate an exception for humanitarian goods; while a hardline posture may yield short-term political dividends in Kyiv, it will come back to haunt Ukraine's political class in the form of an ever more embittered and impoverished Donbas.

To the Poroshenko Government

- **Mobilize public support for an end to the blockade.** President Poroshenko's government signed onto the blockade only reluctantly, and must now work to convince the Ukrainian public that changing course is the only way forward. The dire forecast from Ukraine's central bank and the specter of delayed IMF funding provide ample talking points, but Kyiv and its backers must work hard to overcome the government's weak track record of engaging with the public.

- **Push forward reforms to restructure the Ukrainian judicial system and rein in high level corruption.** Such reforms are essential to economic growth, and they may indeed create a more conducive environment for eventual reintegration of the NGCAs; and may help ease popular frustrations that contributed to the initial imposition of the blockade by volunteer battalions.

<u>To the US and EU</u>

- **Invest greater political and financial capital in the maintenance and rehabilitation of infrastructural links across the contact line,** in coordination with the OSCE and Ukraine's Ministry for Temporarily Occupied Territories and IDPs. While this is already a focal point of the Trilateral Contact Group's economic working group, it will benefit from greater attention and resourcing from international players.

- **Maintain targeted sanctions against Russia**. While these do not appear likely to force a compromise in the near-term, they nonetheless form a much-needed source of leverage at a stage when Mr. Putin appears to hold the initiative in most of his dealings with the West. An end to sanctions would, moreover, be widely perceived in both Russia and the NGCAs as a victory for Mr. Putin, with the likely effect of encouraging Russian maximalism in Ukraine and beyond.

Blockade of Peace: Corruption and Crime

Karina Panyan

Ukraine is not a unique example of corruption and crime at all levels. However, its ongoing conflict stresses the need for immediate and comprehensive reform, particularly in the judicial and legal systems, to address weakening trust in the state.

Manifestation of Corruption

In Ukraine, as in all other nations, illicit activity comes in many shapes and sizes. Corruption can be broken down into local, regional, and federal levels. It exists in nearly all aspects of the state: politics, administration, higher education, business, and many more.

Roots and Examples of Corruption in Ukraine

The history of corruption in Ukraine is intrinsically related to its past entrenchment in the Soviet Union system. During Soviet times, experts argued that corruption was embodied for one of two reasons, for private gain or for bureaucratic gain (Kramer 1977, 214). This trend appears to continue into the modern era, with corruption utilized for monetary benefit and to stay in positions of power for as long as possible. Corruption occurs at two levels; at the high level, encompassing the oligarchs and top government officials, and lower level, including daily and commonplace corruption such as bribes. Some predominant areas of corruption included the housing, education, and agricultural markets, with officials taking advantage of severe housing shortages by accepting bribes, admitting unqualified students into higher institutions for payment, and creating a black market for produce (Kramer 1977, 216)

After independence, Ukraine and many other former Soviet republics understandably struggled to implement reform, and most are still combating corruption over a quarter of a century later. A senior government official stated that Ukraine has a strong society, but weak institutions, as the years of corruption create a hard habit to break (SAIS Group Meeting, Kyiv, 22 March 2017). One reason for this is that Ukraine is still operating as part of "Soviet machinery" and does not have separated powers with checks and balances (SAIS Group Meeting, Kyiv, 24 March 2017)

<u>Public Perception</u>

The striking difference between the actuality of corruption and public perception is difficult to capture, but surveys attempt to do so. From polling conducted in 2014 and 2015, Ernst & Young described a significant increase in the number of individuals who believe that "bribery or corrupt practices happen widely in business in Ukraine," jumping from 60% of those polled in 2014 to 80% in 2015 (*UNIAN* News 2015).

Perceptions of the government itself matter greatly. A former high-level government official expressed frustration that the majority of the current administration is basically a "remix" of the 2005 government and that the current system practically grants you immunity from corruption if you are in the political elite. The people know that the government is corrupt, but the ways and manners in which it is corrupt have changed. This same official states that the corruption of former president Yanukovich were "direct and primitive," whereas the corruption of Poroshenko's government is smarter, less direct, and utilizes informal control (SAIS Group Meeting, Kyiv, 24 March 2017).

Perceptions of corruption differ based on what exactly one defines as corrupt behavior. For instance, a citizen stealing merchandise from his or her employer to provide for their family under economic hardship may not be seen as corrupt by some. However, if an official is in coordination with a citizen to steal merchandise and then sells it on a black market for personal gain, then it may be considered corruption. Ukrainian society, operating with the shared Soviet history, has different standards for what can and cannot be labeled as corruption. Bribes for simple government services, such as obtaining a drivers' license, might be seen as negligible, daily corruption. Embezzlement and backchannel business dealings may be seen as significantly more corrupt behavior, as it occurs on a larger scale. The lack of standards is detrimental to progress.

Furthermore, perceptions of corruption vary often by individual characteristics, such as whether citizens are urban or rural, young or old, and male or female, among others. When our delegation had the privilege to meet with students of Donetsk National

University, relocated to Vinnytsia, our conversations were frank and telling. Some of the students felt that their identity had always been one of a united Ukraine, as opposed to the perception of divide between East and West presented as a result of the conflict. Some students said that they have no illusions that their government is using the narratives of citizens in the conflict zone to push their own agenda, but reiterated that this was a conflict that had serious ramifications on thousands of people's lives (SAIS Group Meeting, Vinnytsia, 23 March 2017).

At a meeting with representatives in Vinnytsia, one of the SAIS students asked whether the panelists felt that the central government misused the plight of IDPs to accomplish their own goals. A female representative adamantly replied that her government does not mistreat its citizens. Upon speaking with a woman who studied in the US and assisted our delegation in Vinnytsia, she divulged that people in the region believe that their city is the best in Ukraine. They have such pride in their supposed advancement that they completely disregard reports of Vinnytsia's economic hardship and slowing development. Therefore, it may be possible that individuals in more rural locations do not experience daily levels of corruption like those in Kyiv and may have a skewed perception of reality in terms of corrupt officials.

That is not to say that those in rural areas do not feel corruption at all. While in Vinnytsia, our delegation met with individuals assisting IDPs in their integration and economic development. Some of the IDPs had multiple-child families and had significant issues registering their family in order to receive subsidies and discounts for child care. Residents may not as readily feel the ramifications of high level, macro corruption but certainly do feel the effects of bureaucratic corruption.

Corruption and the Conflict

The conflict in the East creates a gray zone that is conducive to many forms of corrupt and illicit activity. The conflict itself and the Revolution of Dignity in 2014 is a reflection of great corruption within the state and between individuals and Russian leadership. However, the environment of the armed conflict creates a plethora of new opportunities for corrupt behavior and criminal activity. Several such opportunities include:

1. <u>Payments across the border line</u>: Ukrainian legislation condemns payments across the border and the criminal code would consider paying businesses and individuals in occupied territories akin to funding terrorism (SAIS Group Meeting, Kyiv, 20 March 2017). This creates incredible problems for the thousands of people living in the region who depend on water, gas, electricity, and payments that cross the border. As official payment methods are not possible, the room for corruption is evident when people begin transporting suitcases of money across the border to pay their debts. Businesses in the occupied territories have begun to circumvent this policy by creating unofficially affiliated corporations in Ukraine proper to receive payment (SAIS Group Meeting, Kyiv, 20 March 2017).

2. <u>Arms sales</u>: Continuing from its Soviet history, Ukraine focuses heavily on manufacturing and industry, particular in arms and military equipment. Corruption is escalated with the growing need for more arms on both sides as a result of the conflict. Even though there are official sanctions against Russia, there is evidence that arms sales to Russia are "bigger than under the "pro-Russian" Yanukovich in 2013 ($230 million then, $310 million now)" (Marjanovic 2017). Another issue is that the conflict has taken government-controlled weapons and placed them into the hands of "irregular units unable to properly control them." Some of these weapons are lost due to pure negligence or theft, but countless others are "leaking out of the battlefield" and being sold to "buyers well beyond the conflict zone," creating a problem of global proportions (Prentice and Zverev 2016).

3. <u>Shadow Economy</u>: The border is used as a mechanism for smuggling and illicit transport of goods, particularly since the vast majority of it, about 400 km, remains uncontrolled. Even in the parts that are monitored, officers can receive calls ahead of time instructing them which individuals and vehicles should remain uninspected (SAIS Group Meeting, Kyiv, 24 March 2017). This border in particular is unique because it is the most trafficked in the world. Thousands of people cross it each month, many to receive their pensions on the Ukrainian side. Those in control of areas around the border

smuggle spirits, money, drugs, coal, medicine and much more because there is demand for the goods that people cannot readily access as a result of the conflict (SAIS Group Meeting, Kyiv, 21 March 2017). Just as with other crimes, much of this does not occur in a vacuum. The drug smuggling in particular then extends to Europe and the West.

4. <u>Human Trafficking</u>: For years, Ukraine has experienced significant trouble with the use of its territory as a "source, transit, and destination country" of human trafficking for sex and labor. The conflict further exacerbates this perpetual effort to combat the slave trade. According the US Department of State, there are reports of "kidnapping of women and girls from conflict-affected areas for the purposes of sex and labor trafficking." The most vulnerable victims include women, children (especially those in orphanages), and internally displaced persons. The OSCE mission reports that children as young as 12 years old are "recruited to participate in militarized youth groups that teach children to carry and use weapons" (US Department of State 2016). OSCE currently maintains a project to combat human trafficking, which provides significant expertise in legal reform to aid prosecution of perpetrators and conducts awareness campaigns (OSCE 2017). Representatives of Vinnytsia NGO Djerelo nady/"Spring of Hope" stated that they were continuing their battle against human trafficking by conducting information campaigns. They aim to teach people how to identify victims of trafficking and how potential victims can avoid being lured into trafficking, with the intent to reach a broad audience because anybody can be affected by this crime (SAIS Group Meeting, Vinnytisa, 23 March 2017). However, it seems as though the overall focus is on IDPs and local integration, so these crimes may be on the backburner until other issues are resolved first.

These are only some of the consequences of the gray zone environment that has resulted from the conflict and militarized border. The cessation of the conflict will not address all of these issues, as some are inherent to the country regardless of the conflict. That being said, peaceful resolution to the conflict can allow for other reforms, such as a reliable and safe banking mechanism in the occupied territories, whatever their status may be upon the resolution of the conflict.

Why Fight Corruption?

Corruption is detrimental to all nations to some extent. However, the effects are particularly brutal for Ukraine as it aims to peacefully settle the current conflict.

One of the most frequently repeated ideas from our meetings is the concept that Ukraine must become the ideal role model, so that the non-government controlled areas would see the immense benefit of reuniting with the nation and ending the conflict. That is, Ukraine must become non-corrupt, must embrace European standards, must improve its economic growth, and must take care of its people. While this idea does have merits for the future of Ukraine, it is neither the only path that Ukrainians should embrace, nor is it the end-all to the conflict.

Even though this idea will not singlehandedly solve the conflict, Ukraine must embrace it nonetheless. Combating corruption is essential to promote sustainable political, economic, and social development and is particularly important for a nation engaging in armed conflict. Ukraine needs all the resources it can dedicated to the conflict and its peaceful settlement, as well as its own strengthening and economic development. Those funds unfortunately are wasted through embezzlement, bribery, and misallocation. According to OECD, corruption increases the costs of doing business, perpetuates poverty by excluding the most vulnerable from needed resources, and reduces overall efficiency (OECD 2014). Possibly, most importantly of all, Ukraine needs to re-energize its people and regain much of the trust that continues to dwindle.

Ukraine needs international assistance, for humanitarian and development purposes. Therefore, it absolutely needs to prove that the funding is not going to waste. The World Bank estimated that 20-40% of its official development assistance is lost globally due to high-level corruption (OECD 2014, 3). Under the current circumstances of armed conflict and economic downturn, Ukraine simply cannot afford to be part of that statistic.

Current Endeavors to Combat Corruption

Ukraine began much of its current anti-corruption campaign in 2014, after the beginning of the conflict. The National Anti-corruption Bureau of Ukraine, or NABU, was established on October 14, 2014, as "one of the requirements set by the IMF and the European Commission for relaxation of visa restrictions between Ukraine and the European Union" (NABU 2017).

Two standout issues very much impede the mission and purpose.

First, the organization does not define what constitutes corruption. Its slogan is "Eradicate and Prevent" but does not provide a definitive list of corrupt activities and illicit behavior.

Second, the organization does not have the power to indict suspects and can only investigate and compile information for prosecutors (Kramer, McIntire and Meier 2016). While it does have an information sharing agreement with the FBI, this does not ensure that its investigations will come to fruition and make impactful change. When the investigations have concluded, it is still the decision of the prosecutor to bring about a criminal case, which means that NABU is limited severely in its operations. If the judicial and legal system is corrupt, possibly providing incentives and opportunities for prosecutors to pick and choose which cases to bring to trial, then the mission of NABU is moot.

As another measure, the government further mandated electronic disclosures by public servants. This is a large step forward, but is not completely foolproof. Even though some people may be honestly reporting their holdings, the current government will always have an atmosphere of doubt surrounding it. The implementation of the laws mandating these e-declarations was delayed. Furthermore, the revelations themselves were contradictory. For example, the minister of the Ukrainian central bank disclosed that he has millions in USD cash, but the sole purpose of his job function is to radiate confidence in the banking system.

Many officials reportedly have so much money that they don't know what to do with it, and it is especially the case post-9/11, as it is now much harder to move money into the West and even harder to access it (SAIS Group Meeting, Kyiv, 24 March 2017).

Therefore, public servants may declare more money than they have in reality, so as to justify future purchases.

Judicial and Legal Reform

Judicial and legal reform should be at the forefront of the government agenda, as it impacts many other sectors. Prosecution, property rights, international investment, and many other sectors stand to gain from a well-functioning and honorable judicial and legal system.

One of the most debated topics in our discussions on anti-corruption was the creation of an anti-corruption court. One must acknowledge the push and pull between two strong forces: the rule of law and anti-corruption. There is an apparent discord between which should come first. Actions that are taken to curb corruption and bribery may also be seen as an infringement on privacy and certain human rights (SAIS Group Meeting, Kyiv, 20 March 2017).

A potential hurdle to the implementation of these courts is Ukraine's constitution, which does not allow for special courts (SAIS Group Meeting, Kyiv, 20 March 2017). Another topic of debate is the utility of the courts themselves. Perhaps they could be useful in the immediate future, but may be abused in the long-run as a mechanism through which to attack political opponents.

Some national reforms have already begun, but the efforts must continue. Police reforms have already begun, with OSCE reporting a jump from 20% to 40% in public confidence (SAIS Group Meeting, Kyiv, 20 March 2017). Having a modernized police force does not ensure that investigations will be impartial and that investigations will continue to effective prosecution (SAIS Group Meeting with OSCE, Kyiv, 20 March 2017).

The OSCE recommends significant capacity building. Training Ukrainian judges in international programs is one option. The judges will obtain experience in international judicial systems and bring back European standards of practice. Furthermore, OSCE recommends reinventing the legal training system. Ukraine currently lacks a standardized examination system for graduates of its law schools. Perhaps the implementation of a Bar similar to the United States system would be beneficial to standardization and licensing practices (SAIS Group Meeting with OSCE, Kyiv, 20 March 2017).

In an opposing argument, Mr. Mikheil Saakashvili argued that reforming the system is not enough. He insisted that there must be an entirely new system that does not employ the same individuals from the old system. He recommends the employment of foreign judges and possibly utilizing foreign judicial systems as a template for a new Ukrainian one. This option is difficult to envision, however, as some officials and citizens believe that Americans and Europeans should stop meddling in Ukraine's internal affairs and politics. The reasoning is that outsiders do not understand the environment and may end up supporting corrupt candidates for positions of power (SAIS Group Meeting with Saakashvili, Kyiv, 21 March 2017).

The conflict poses great challenges to the execution of legal reform, particularly in election law. It is well known that bribery and corrupt practices are employed by people in power to maintain their government positions. Elections proceedings are not free and must be drawn to European standards. This involves monitoring and evaluation, particularly from the OSCE Office for Democratic Institutions and Human Rights (ODIHR). The overarching need to ensure these ODIHR missions are implemented properly is the guarantee of safety in the occupied territories. Many argue that the ceasefire and safety provisions must be absolutely and completely abided by in order to ensure free and fair elections, as well as the safety of the monitoring missions themselves. Furthermore, the election law of the country has remained unchanged since its introduction by Yanukovich (SAIS Group Meeting, Kyiv, 24 March 2017). The current laws allow for money to be the best campaign mechanism. By nature, this intertwines with corruption of the broadcasting and media environment of the country (SAIS Group Meeting, Kyiv, 24 March 2017).

Ukraine must address judicial and legal reform before it can successfully and wholeheartedly embrace other reforms. Anti-corruption endeavors are only feasible once there is a functioning and reliable judiciary to prosecute those who have engaged in criminal acts. Mr. Saakashvili referred to the Ukrainian elite as the twin of the Russian elite, and this is true for many of the oligarchs who maintain business and personal relationships with their counterparts in Russia (SAIS Group Meeting with Mr.

Saakashvili, Kyiv, 21 March 2017) One way to address the problem is to implement constitutional reform that emphasizes checks and balances and that places public monies under independent control, rather than in the hands of corrupt leaders. This should particularly concern the international communities and organizations that provide development assistance funding that can be stolen for personal gain. One official referred to this problem as "pouring financial water into a barrel of corruption holes" (SAIS Group Meeting, Kyiv, 24 March 2017).

Conclusion

The corruption in Ukraine is a long-standing habit, one which will take many years of painstaking reform to overcome. The conflict only serves to aggravate existing corruption and provides opportunity for new avenues of crime. The Ukrainian government must alter its own image if it hopes to find approval from its citizens and the international community.

If the people and the government of Ukraine aim to truly tackle corruption and increase trust in the administration, they must implement local, regional, and federal reforms. Once again, there will be the chicken-or-the-egg problem, as a result of which the nation must decide the order and plan of attack. I argue that reforms to the judicial and legal systems must outweigh all other goals, at least in the immediate term.

Recommendations

To the Ukrainian Government

- **Define corruption.** Who should be prosecuted? What should be considered so corrupt as to prosecute for damaging state interests? Establishing a clear definition and amending the legal code to reflect that is absolutely essential to initiating proper reform.

- **Implement judicial reform**. Judicial and legal reform will increase public trust, establish more reliable property rights, and promote an atmosphere for foreign direct investment. This endeavor begins with reforming the people who partake in the legal system.

- **Engage parties in the Minsk Agreement.** The people and the armed factions need to understand the importance of the Minsk Agreement and its calls for ceasefire. Without a ceasefire, there can be no elections or progress in engaging the occupied territories. This recommendation is also applicable to the international community.

- **Address kleptocracy and oligarchy.** This is a large endeavor that will not conclude quickly, easily, or without great resistance and must be addressed by both the international community and the Ukrainian government. If the government works to seal these holes of corruption, by addressing corruption both within the government and within its network of wealthy citizens, it can gain trust from both the international community and its own citizens. This may involve overseeing tax reform and implementation and restructuring state-run enterprises, among other reforms.

To the International Community

- **Continue monitoring and oversight missions.** Programs such as those implemented by the IMF and OSCE enable progress tracking and may provide additional confidence in the economy.

- **Ensure standards are attained for bailout funding.** The IMF has consistently urged faster and more efficient progress of anti-corruption programs, and should continue to monitor these standards to ensure that money is properly allocated and used.

- **Create avenues of dialogue for judicial and legal reform.** Connecting Ukrainian policymakers and participants in the legal and judicial systems with their European and American counterparts may allow for more comprehensive discourse on possible reforms and implementation.

Economic Impact of Internally Displaced Persons in Ukraine

Dorothea E. Cheek

The purpose of this chapter is to analyze the economic impact of Ukrainian internally displaced persons (IDPs) on the communities to which they move. Subsequent questions include where did the Ukrainian IDPs come from geographically, academically, and with regard to their socioeconomic background? To which regions did they migrate? What was the economic situation of these regions prior to the emigration of IDPs from the conflict-affected regions?

The issue of Internally Displaced Persons is covered in detail by the United Nations High Commissioner for Refugees (UNHCR). Internal displacement is characterized as "affecting some 25 million people worldwide, [and it] has become increasingly recognized as one of the most tragic phenomena of the contemporary world" (UNHCR 1998). The UNHCR defines IDPs in particular as "persons or groups of persons who have been forced or obliged to flee or to leave their homes or places of habitual residence, in particular as a result of or in order to avoid the effects of armed conflict, situations of generalized violence, violations of human rights or natural or human-made disasters, and who have not crossed an internationally recognized State border" (UNHCR 1998).

The case of Ukrainian IDPs is an oddity as noted in a report published by Brenzel, Betliy and Kirchner for the German Advisory Group Institute for Economic Research and Policy Consulting as "it can be summarized that [Ukrainian] IDPs moved to relatively prosperous regions with comparatively good working labor markets and not to already less well-off oblasts with already weakened labor market situations" (Brenzel, Betliy, and Kirchner 2015). I will show below that, not only have Ukrainian IDPs moved to economically well-off regions of the country, but that they also maintain some of the highest education levels of the entire Ukrainian population whether within the employed or unemployed citizenry. Unfortunately, despite this fact, Ukrainian IDPs continue to struggle to obtain the same level of rights and freedoms that non-displaced citizens enjoy, partially due to discrimination from within the host community and partially due to government failure to deliver.

This chapter endeavors to answer the questions listed above, define the economic parameters for stability as outlined by the *American Economic Review*, review the general impact and crisis situation of IDPs as recorded by the UNHCR, and examine the particular key variables involved in the type of economic impact (if any) IDPs have upon the region they move to—prior education, socioeconomic background, ability to relate i.e. cultural similarities or differences regarding language, religion, familial values etc. This chapter will conclude that, while Ukrainian IDPs have had an easier time of integrating into host communities than in other nations, due to the protracted nature of the conflict in the Donbas region, the Ukrainian government is obliged to take their IDP situation seriously and create a single policy towards the management of this worrisome humanitarian situation. Not only is it crucial for Ukraine to produce this policy so as to continue to adhere to international standards for human rights, but also for the purpose of sustaining national economic stability and decreasing tensions between displaced and non-displaced citizens.

Background Information Regarding IDPs and Ukrainian IDPs

While it is mandated by international bodies such as the United Nations that internally displaced persons should receive the same universal rights as non-displaced citizens, this experience of equal human rights is generally not a privilege that IDPs share once they have been displaced.

Based on international human rights and humanitarian law, the UNHCR developed a set of guidelines for governing and international bodies. This set of guidelines identifies the rights and needs of the internally displaced. There are 30 principles in total and they mandate the same rights for all citizens—displaced or not—without discrimination. They require all legal authorities to observe the principles and make every attempt to avoid "conditions that might lead to displacement of persons" (UNHCR 1998) inclusive of avoiding policies of apartheid, armed conflict, and/or collective punishment. They assert that, if individuals must be internally displaced, they have the right to proper accommodation so that they still have access to "safety, nutrition, health and hygiene, and that members of the same family are not separated" (UNHCR 1998), as well as full information about the procedures affecting their displacement.

Moreover the consent of the relevant individuals is required. Internally displaced people must be protected against all forms of violence from murder, genocide, rape, torture, and slavery. Children and all IDPs must be protected from being recruited into taking part in hostilities. All IDPs have the right to "liberty of movement and freedom to choose his or her residence,… the right to seek safety in another part of the country, the right to leave their country,… the right to be protected against forcible return to or resettlement in any place where their life, safety, liberty and/or health would be at risk" (UNHCR 1998). IDP families have the right to stay together. As noted above all IDPs should have the same exact rights as non-displaced citizens e.g. access to healthcare, education, legal representation, freedom of thought, religion, movement, freedom from violence and discrimination and so on.

There are current and ongoing issues regarding the access to full equal rights for IDPs within Ukraine that could be influencing the economic impact these internally displaced individuals are having upon the communities to which they have moved. The numbers recorded by various governing bodies vary greatly depending on registered individuals. There is a greater percentage of women registered as internally displaced than men, but this is in part due to the fact that men fear being registered and then drafted into the army. According to the Ministry of Social Policy, as of June 6, 2016 close to 1,800,000 Ukrainian citizens were registered as internally displaced, 1,100,000 women and 700,000 men. This total number differs from the Interagency Coordinating Headquarters for Social Security of Persons Displaced from Anti-Terror Operation Area and Temporarily Occupied Territories, which takes note of closer 1,000,000 IDPs in Ukraine as of June 7, 2016. This is because the Ministry "registers people who applied for pension or social welfare payments at a new place of residence… [their] data include not only internally displaced persons but also those who have declined temporary accommodation services and live in the occupied areas" (Smal 2016). Some of the rights that these people struggle to obtain are freedom from discrimination, access to education, and the right to vote.

According to the Minister of Temporarily Occupied Territories and IDPs one of the biggest issues in the conflict zones of Lugansk and Donetsk is access to potable water. The pipelines cross directly from government controlled regions to the non-government controlled regions, and this issue continues to go unaddressed (although this Ministry has written a proposal to be submitted to the Ukrainian Rada) (SAIS Group Meeting, Kyiv, 24 March 2017). Moreover, officials from the Organization for Security and Cooperation in Europe (OSCE) noted that there is a crucial need for the government to increase provisions of electricity, gas, and infrastructure upkeep within the Donbas in particular referencing the coal mines, funding, and abandoned equipment within the region (SAIS Group Meeting, Kyiv, 20 March 2017).

The government has made attempts at aiding IDPs where education is concerned by cutting costs for IDP families as well as allowing them to skip the 1-2 year period of a waitlist that most families have to endure. However, in so doing, there has been considerable backlash from the communities, when schools either refuse to accept IDP students unless their families pay full price, or host families object to the fact that IDP students can be immediately enrolled in classes. Moreover, according to the Ukrainian NGO Dzerolo Nadyy (Spring of Hope) the quality of education has decreased due to the increased ratio of students to teachers within the classroom (SAIS Group Meeting, Vinnytsia, 23 March 2017).

Furthermore it has been noted by multiple NGOs, Dzerelo Nadyy, Vis, and the Ukrainian Women's Fund that IDPs lack access to psychological aid. While early on in the conflict there was a need for material and monetary support, as the conflict endures IDPs have developed and continue to struggle with Post Traumatic Stress Disorder. The Ukrainian Women's Fund found through a series of information sessions that men in particular would shut down, stop communicating with their friends and family, and in many domestic situations resort to violence to relieve stress (SAIS Group Meeting, Kyiv, 20 March 2017).

Although bluntly worded, after examining the above analysis of Ukrainian management of their IDP situation, representatives of the Socialist Party of Ukraine noted that "at times it seems as if the government does not care about the IDPs resulting in the deepening of political and philosophical divergences" (SAIS Group Meeting, Kyiv, 22 March 2017). There continues to be a lack in a singular policy towards IDPs as well as coordination between agencies within the government which needs to be rectified as soon as possible (SAIS Group Meeting, Kyiv, 24 March 2017).

Policy Objectives

<u>Economic Stability</u>

During this period of conflict and as reference for the future reconstruction period of Ukraine, this chapter suggests that regional and national economic stability should take precedence as a policy objective within Ukrainian government agencies. In cases of conflict there is no guaranteed economic stability, yet by making it a policy priority, the Ukrainian government can take care of its both displaced and non-displaced people by ensuring their economic needs and decrease national and communal tensions.

While there is no singular standardized model for assessing financial system stability, for the purpose of gauging regional economic stability and potential variations therein over time due to IDP migration to and from various communities, this paper will rely on examining and measuring regional Gross Domestic Product (GDP) over time. Thus the economic stability variable will be defined off of the parameters of GDP.

GDP is considered by economists to be inclusive of three different approaches to the same answer i.e. GDP is a measure of value added with regards to national production, it is a measure of national income insofar as by producing goods and services individuals are receiving said income, and finally it is also a measure of national expenditure (Hoddenbagh 2016). GDP being defined as such, Hoddenbagh states that there are obvious signs that "GDP per person reflects income and standard of living," (Hoddenbagh 2016). As noted above, it demonstrates not only the value of the goods and services produced within a country but also an individual's income and therein his/her capability to purchase goods and services. Therefore, by using basic intuition it can be assumed here that as the indicator of economic stability, i.e. as GDP rises so too does an individual's capacity to buy goods and services. By regarding up and down swings in GDP one can infer a positive correlation in the up and down swings of regional economic stability as well.

Jones and Klenow (2016) provide a convincing analysis of a strong correlation between GDP and quality of life. They defined economic welfare by combining measures of consumption, leisure, mortality, and inequality. When compared to GDP per person within a nation, these two variables demonstrated a 95% positive correlation (Jones and Klenow 2016). As depicted in Figure 1, one can see the strong correlation between GDP and the independent variables of consumption, leisure, mortality, and inequality. Therefore, for the purposes of this paper, I will utilize measurements of past and current GDP to represent the economic stability of the regions within my case study. In so doing I will compare the influx of IDP populations into these regions with the peaks or crevasses in GDP accumulation to determine the impact of IDPs on a region's economic stability.

Figure 1

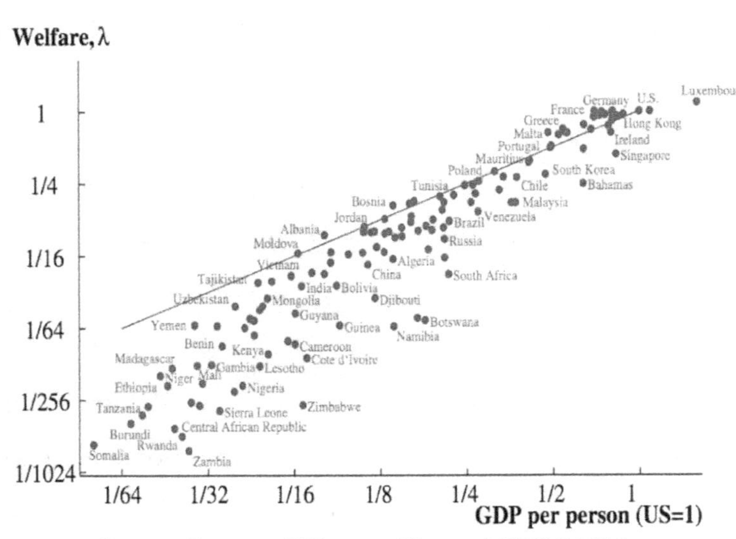

Source: Jones and Klenow, "Beyond GDP," 2010.

To review the status of Ukraine's GDP during this period of conflict, as of 2014 and 2015 Ukraine was already experiencing an economic downturn. This decline in GDP was due to "twin deficits in the current account and the fiscal balance [as well as] fixing the exchange rate to the US dollar" (Brenzel, Betliy, and Kirchner 2015) prior to 2014. Thus as IDPs were in movement, the Ukrainian economy was already in flux.

While the government had made an agreement with the IMF to take part in an adjustment program to stabilize the economy and while there was an expected 5% decline in real GDP, "due to the annexation of Crimea in 2014, 3.8-5% of Ukraine's GDP was lost" (Brenzel, Betliy, and Kirchner 2015) immediately as Ukraine engaged in conflict with Russia. The drastic drop in Ukraine's GDP continued as the military conflict raged on in the Donbas, reaching an overall loss of 15.8% by mid-2015. All of the above, as well as a 60% depreciation of the Ukrainian Hryvnia to the US Dollar, was a much larger loss than expected. Furthermore, consumer inflation reached 61% and banks "experienced liquidity (deposit flight) as well as solvency issues" (Brenzel, Betliy, and Kirchner 2015). The Ukrainian economy has recovered to a certain extent since 2015, however, due to the ongoing conflict in the Donbas there is no guarantee that Ukraine will be able to maintain economic stability in the near future. If economic competition increases between host and IDP communities the government might not only have to manage the conflict in the East but within its own population as well. Therefore the Ukrainian government must focus its policies on stabilizing regional and national GDP.

<u>Caring for Internally Displaced Persons in Ukraine</u>
The term IDP has already been defined above as persons or a group of persons forced to move from their homes due to imminent threat of violence in their area, yet the issue of IDPs goes hand-in-hand with economic concerns and therefore must be the second policy objective for the Ukrainian government. Due to ongoing military conflict in the Donbas, the population of internally displaced persons within Ukraine has grown to a level that placed Ukraine within the top ten nations managing such a population. Furthermore, the internally displaced persons of Ukraine are still lacking in access to crucial rights guaranteed in principle by UNHCR. Due to their lack of full access to universal human rights and due to community misunderstandings about the current and future situation of IDPs pertaining to access to housing, education, healthcare, and job markets there has been a notable increase in economic and social tension within the Ukrainian populace (see chapters by Ashley Patton and Christina Connelly-Kanmaz).

As of September 2016, the UN reported that its human rights expert [Mr. Chaloka Beyani], "called on the government of Ukraine to step up its response to prevent and address internal displacement and to provide durable solutions to the persons already displaced" (*UN Daily News* 2016). In particular, while he lauded the government's "continued efforts to address the IDPs' situation, including the adoption of a new law on internal displacement and the establishment of a ministry to deal directly with the issue," (*UN Daily News* 2016), he insisted that there is still much to be done. He recommended that the government detach registration from social security and pensions. Because the payment of these benefits depends on verifying the place of residence of IDPs, this has resulted in the suspension of payment of benefits affecting hundreds of thousands of IDPs in the Eastern regions of Ukraine. Mr. Beyani urged that IDPs should be able to receive these benefits no matter where they reside in the country, and if they do not it has caused secondary displacement as well as "unsafe spontaneous returns" (*UN Daily News* 2016). Moreover, he states that "the authorities must ensure freedom of movement and choice of place of residence." He further emphasized that in non-government controlled areas, "the leadership of the territories under the control of armed groups are also bound by the same obligations to the extent proportionate with national and public security measures" (*UN Daily News* 2016). He took note that there is "no efficient special arrangements for elderly, children, pregnant women or persons with disabilities" (*UN Daily News* 2016). Moreover after speaking with IDP sources in Ukraine, Bayani noted a particular lack of voting rights as well as initial discrimination with regard to access to education.

Recent Situation

<u>Where did the IDPs Move to?</u>

As seen in Figure 2, at the onset of the conflict and as of 2015 "three out of four IDPs have relocated close to their home areas and over half of the IDP population are still within Donetsk and Luhansk oblasts" (Brenzel, Betliy, and Kirchner 2015). The western regions of Ukraine which seem to have acquired the largest number of IDPs are Kyiv with 7.3% of the displaced population and Lviv as the most economically developed region within the country. The Western regions only contain 16% of the IDP population, but again as noted above, these numbers must be interpreted cautiously due to complications found in the government run registering process of IDPs (Brenzel, Betliy, and Kirchner 2015). Referring to the graphic in Figure 2, the Cherkasy oblast can be included in the list of Western regions housing IDPs. While these numbers were compiled in 2015 and IDPs might have moved from temporary housing near the "line of contact" to other locations in Ukraine, these data illustrate the magnitude of the IDP flows in just the first year of violent conflict in Donbas.

Figure 2

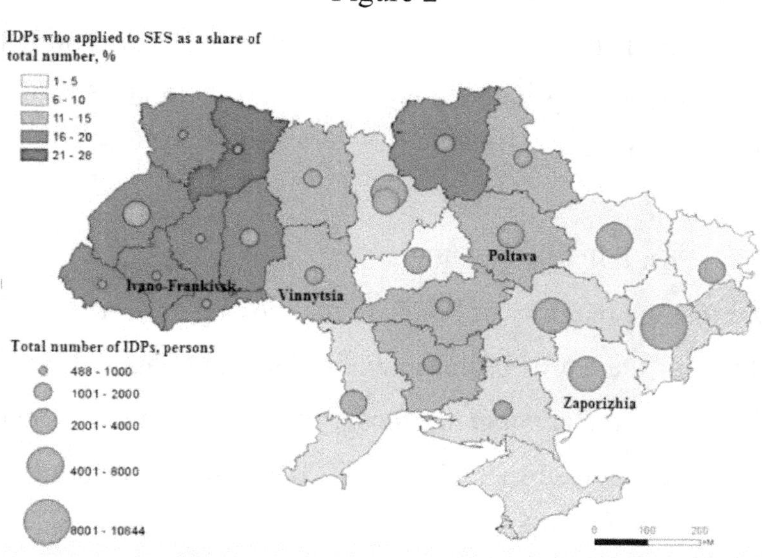

The Donbas Economic Situation Prior to IDP Movement

While the Donbas region was already a less well-off oblast economically speaking in comparison to other Ukrainian oblasts such as Kyiv and Lviv prior to the conflict, it continues to be recognized as representing Ukraine's industrial hub, rich with coal mining, metallurgy, and manufacturing. Potentially more important, it is an area from which many IDPs were forced to abandon well-paying secure jobs. Some individuals opted into fighting in the conflict so as to avoid displacement. Moreover, as noted by a Slovakian NGO monitoring the crisis in Ukraine, the Institute for Economic and Social Reform (INEKO), there was a remarkable impact on "local companies and companies with regional offices in these areas [as they] suffered serious disruption or destruction, which caused staff cuts or even closures" (INEKO 2015). Again, while this region was not quite on par economically with the oblasts of Kyiv and Lviv, it was still a highly functioning and productive region within Ukraine.

According to the Vienna Institute for International Economic Studies (WIIW) as of 2012, prior to the conflict, Donetsk and Lugansk, produced nearly 16% of the national GDP. Moreover while the Donbas region was responsible for importing 7.7% of national imports, it was also a primary player in producing exported goods and services for Ukraine as it maintained a 25.2% export ratio. The WIIW takes note in Figure 3 that as of 2012, while Ukraine's average GDP per capita measured in Euro purchasing power parity was EUR 6,800, the Donbas region maintained some of the higher purchasing power parities at a range of EUR 6,500 – 9,500. And lastly, prior to the conflict in the Eastern region of Ukraine, production was 60% higher in Donetsk and 85% higher in Lugansk (Havlik and Astrov 2014).

<u>Economic Situation Post IDP Movement</u>

There is evidence that the majority of IDPs are not moving to nearby Eastern regions. As Smal notes, that while "there are 30 times more IDPs in the Zaporizhia region than in the Ivano-Frankivsk region, the number of those who applied to the State Employment Service differs only by a factor of 6" (Smal 2016), which demonstrates a potential miscalculation as indicated by the number of those who desire and apply for employment aid.

Figure 3

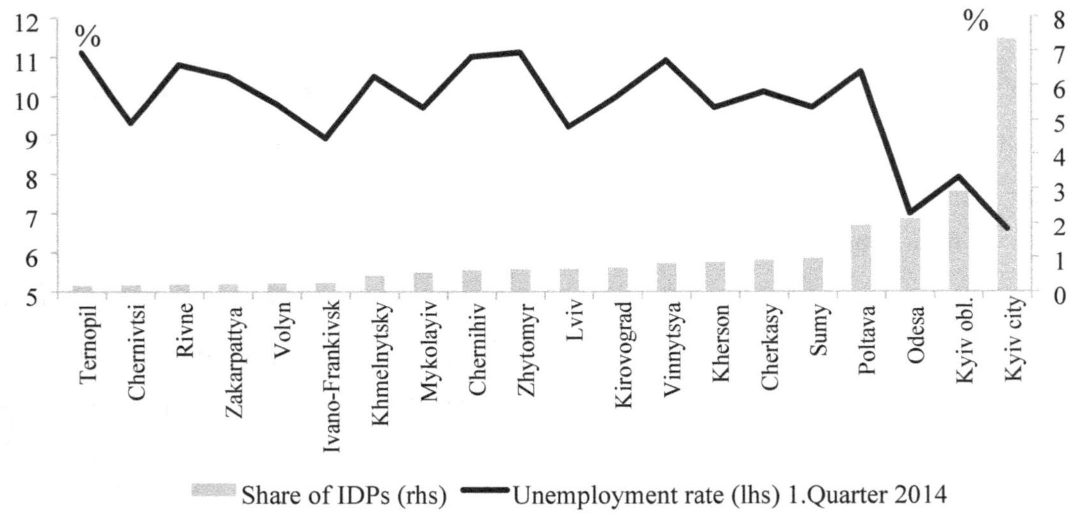

Share of IDPs (rhs) ━━Unemployment rate (lhs) 1.Quarter 2014

SourceUkrstatUNHCR

The graphic above demonstrates the relationship between unemployment and the number of IDPs who move to each specific region. The intriguing factor about the graphic is that it shows that there is a negative correlation between IDP population and unemployment. In other words, as the population of IDPs increases within an oblast, the rate of unemployment goes down. And as Brenzel, Betliy, and Kirchner (2015) note, "these findings have given rise to hope that the influx of migrants into regions might not be as harmful as they could have been."

Not only does unemployment drop within these regions, but there is a positive cycle between greater numbers of job vacancies being available upon the arrival of IDPs, and the higher the number of IDPs within an oblast, the more job vacancies become available.

Figure 4

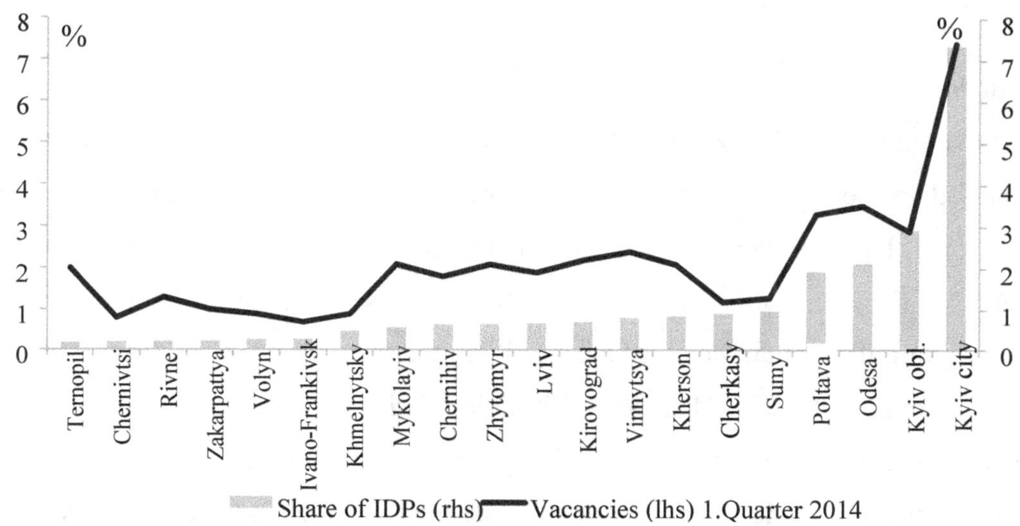

SourceSES

The gender differential in IDPs is quite remarkable in the case of Ukraine because according to the UNHCR, "the percentages of men and women in the total number of IDPs worldwide is nearly the same" (Brenzel, Betliy, and Kirchner 2015), while in Ukraine women make up approximately 62% of the IDP population. Women also outnumber men within the employable population and are on par with men within the unemployed population.

Most noteworthy about Ukrainian IDPs is that "according to the State Employment Service, the breakdown by education among IDPs substantially differs from the education level of the unemployed population in general: over 70% of unemployed IDPs have higher education, 19% have vocational education, and 11% have primary and secondary education" (Brenzel, Betliy, and Kirchner2015), while within the total population of unemployed Ukrainians fewer than 45% of overall citizens have achieved higher education. This factor has remarkable implications for the potential human capital which Ukrainian IDPs can provide to the regions to which they move, and therein the economic impact they might have upon these regions as well. In other words, contrary to general expectations of the future standard of living of IDPs including suffering and the worsening economic conditions, the socioeconomic background of Ukrainian IDPs indicates they could in fact impart a positive economic outcome on the regions to which they move.

Conclusion

Due to the ongoing militarized conflict in the eastern region of Ukraine, the population of internally displaced Ukrainians has grown to be one of the top 10 largest IDP populations in the world. However, the true Ukrainian IDP population has yet to be known due to challenges facing the government registration process, e.g. because men often avoid registering out of fear that they will then be recruited to fight in the Donbas.

Although internally displaced Ukrainians still struggle to obtain all the rights enjoyed by non-displaced citizens, e.g. freedom from discrimination, ability to vote, and access to education, their position is remarkable in comparison to other nations managing IDP populations. As noted by Brenzel, Betliy, and Kirchner (2015), not only is unemployment decreasing within the regions to which they move, but jobs vacancies are increasing as well. Moreover, Ukraine's situation of hosting an IDP population is unique in comparison to other nations' experiences insofar as the Ukraine's population of IDPs includes some of the most highly educated people of Ukraine. Furthermore, members of the non-profit organization Vis clarify that compared to other IDP crises throughout the world, there is less of an issue integrating into host communities in Ukraine due to an absence of cultural, ethnic, and linguistic differences between IDP and host communities (SAIS Group Meeting, Vinnytsia, 23 March 2017).

That being said, there has been slight push back on incoming IDPs. Host communities do not fully understand the situation of IDPs and therefore do not understand the government programs from which IDPs receive aid. Due to host community tensions and due to the lack of certain economic stability because of the ongoing conflict in the Donbas, the government of Ukraine needs to make economic stability and IDP aid joint policy priorities. Therefore, I offer the following recommendations:

Recommendations

<u>To the Government of Ukraine</u>

- **Detach IDP registration from social security and pension payments** so as to ensure accessible financial benefits throughout the country.
- **Support community efforts** to financially and communally aid IDPs.
- **Raise the level of awareness of host communities about IDPs** to decrease tensions, to facilitate integration of IDPs into communities, and to increase understanding within communities as to why IDPs are deserving of government financial aid.
- **Maintain and deepen the state's assistance programs for IDPs** due to ongoing conflict and lack of IDP capability to return home; the government needs to support the IDP community as they make long-term plans to remain in host communities.

<u>To International Institutions/Third Party States</u>

- **Continue to give financial aid to Ukrainian government** as the nation endeavors to recover from economic down-turn due to conflict.
- **Continue to advocate for Internally Displaced Persons** and work with government agencies to create a single policy regarding the IDP crisis, particularly in aiding in their housing and public services access.
- **Continue non-profit work** in financially aiding IDPs and local organizations that support IDP integration into host communities.

Part IV: Humanitarian Issues

Integration of the Internally Displaced – A Critical Challenge

Ashley Patton

Since the beginning of the conflict in Ukraine, millions of Ukrainians have been directly affected by the continuing violence, especially in the Donbas region in the east and in the Crimean Peninsula, resulting in a significant human cost. This chapter aims to assess the current situation of internally displaced persons (IDPs) in Ukraine, citizens of Ukraine who are suffering the negative consequences of the fighting and have been forced to flee their homes. In this assessment, I will generally focus on IDPs originating from the east, specifically from the Donetsk and Luhansk regions. While there are many commonalities in the situations that IDPs face, whether they originate from the Donbas or Crimea, there are also differences between these two groups, such as their needs and legal status, an issue noted by the Minister for Temporarily Occupied Territories and IDPs, Vadym Chermysh (SAIS Group Meeting, Kyiv, 24 March 2017).

I will first provide a brief explanation of the reasons that IDPs are forced to flee their homes, thus creating their status as IDPs. I will then briefly discuss integration of IDPs into their new communities, including stakeholders, barriers, and current programs in place to better foster integration. Lastly, I will provide recommendations to the Ukrainian state government, international organizations, and the local community for bettering how IDPs are managed, with the aim of creating more sustainable and effective policies and programs for more effective IDP integration into local communities.

Current Situation of IDPs

It is estimated that IDPs alone total upwards of 1.7 million people within Ukraine since the beginning of this conflict, which is a figure that both government and non-government entities use when discussing this population (SAIS Group Meetings, March 2017). The most recent government figure, as of March 20, 2017, from the Ukrainian Ministry of Social Policy (MoSP) records there have been 1,607,664 displaced from the Donbas and Crimea (MoSP 2017). However, many organizations working with these communities place this number much higher due to issues with tracking these individuals, such as registration issues, a hesitance of IDPs to register as such, and differences in data sets amongst different agencies. The International Displacement Monitoring Centre's most recent figures place Ukraine as the eighth highest displacement in the world, and the highest out of any European Country (IDMC 2016).

Who are the IDPs in Ukraine?

Figures on IDPs from a report released in June 2016 provide a good snapshot of demographics of Ukrainian IDPs, and while the exact figures are outdated, it allows us to better understand who is fleeing (There is currently no transparent, centralized system of IDP registration by the government that maintains updated figures). In Ukraine, a significant proportion of IDPs are women (62%), which differs from the global average where IDPs are fairly evenly split between male and female. Potential reasons for this discrepancy in Ukraine include men not wanting to register as an IDP in order to avoid the draft for the Ukrainian army and men staying in the east to care for family. In terms of age, over 40% of IDPs are under 35, and around 70% under 45. Statistics from the State Employment Service reported that more than 70% of IDPs have higher education, around 19% vocational education, and 11% primary or secondary education. In contrast, within the unemployed population of Ukraine, less than 45% of IDPs have higher education, around 35% vocational education, and 20% secondary education (Smal 2016).

Why are they displaced? Why can't they return?

One of the primary groups monitoring the current conflict in Ukraine is the Organization for Security and Cooperation in Europe (OSCE) Special Monitoring Mission to Ukraine (SMM). The SMM was not designed to deal with an open conflict, rather it was tasked to deal with events stemming from the protests on Maidan beginning in 2013. The OSCE now has a €1.5million mission, agreed upon by all 57 OSCE participating states, to both monitor and report on the situation in eastern Ukraine and to facilitate dialogue between parties (SAIS Group Meeting, Kyiv, 20 March 2017). A critical part of this mission is to produce daily, spot, weekly, and thematic reports surrounding their monitor assessments.

The most recent thematic report as of this writing, produced 16 February 2017 and covering May to September 2016, focuses on hardships faced by citizens in eastern Ukraine affected by the conflict, explaining the primary reasons for which IDPs are 1) migrating and 2) mostly unable to return. As the report explains, "[a]s long as the sides do not adhere to a sustained ceasefire, honour commitments made in the Minsk agreements and take steps to improve the humanitarian situation in Donbas, civilians throughout government-controlled areas and non-government-controlled areas of Donetsk and Luhansk regions will continue to face hardship, even life-threatening situations" (OSCE SMM February 2017, 2).

First of all, the report notes continuing violence within these regions, including the presence of weapons and armed positions within populated areas by both armed formations and the Ukrainian armed forces, increasing the risk of collateral attacks. In addition, in areas that are not fully controlled by either side, there is a lack of social services for civilians. The SMM noted several challenges that civilians continue to face in terms of their living conditions. The first challenge is access to adequate housing, including observed destruction, damage, and occupation of civilian properties and a restriction on the freedom of movement for civilians to physically access their properties. In the conflict-affected areas, civilians also lack access to basic utilities and social services, including access to safe water; energy, such as gas and electricity, to be used by civilians for lighting, heating, and cooking; and access to appropriate medical care (OSCE SMM February 2017).

The majority of IDPs in Ukraine often view their current situation as one that is temporary. However, they face many barriers in returning to their homes including sustained violence and no cessation of hostilities in their home regions, continued destruction of civilian property, the possibility that their homes have been occupied by foreign fighters, and political and ideological conflicts within the non-government controlled areas (NGCA) (UNHCR April 2016, 4). Because of this, it is critical that IDPs be able to successfully integrate and adapt to their host communities.

Integration of IDPs Into Host Communities

Integration of IDPs into host communities remains a priority throughout Ukraine, as the swift return home of IDPs remains less likely with the increase of violence and cease-fire violations throughout the Donbas since late January 2017 (ECHO 2016, 2).

<u>Stakeholders</u>

It is critical to understand the various stakeholders when discussing the integration of Ukrainian IDPs into local communities.

Government of Ukraine

At the national level, there are two government ministries within Ukraine that are specifically working on IDP issues. The first is the Ministry of Temporary Occupied Territories and Internally Displaced Persons (MTOTIDP). This ministry was established in April 2016, and its first budget was allocated in September of that year. It deals with five regions in particular, including Donetsk and Luhansk, which contain over 50% of Ukraine's IDPs. The state program focuses on social and physical infrastructure, economic recovery, and social cohesion, mostly between IDPs and local civilians. According to the MTOTIDP, its most important role is coordination between all actors (civilian, military, and international organizations) (SAIS Group Meeting, Kyiv, 24 March 2017). Also responsible for IDPs is the Ministry of Social Policy (MoSP), which is the ministry that maintains the registration of IDPs and works with international and local organizations on some aid and program implementation for IDPs. However, working with IDPs is not its main goal, rather it assists the MTOTIDP (SAIS Group Meetings, Kyiv, 24 March 2017).

International Institutions and Organizations

There are a variety of international entities working on IDP issues within Ukraine, both international organizations and multilateral institutions. For instance, the United States Institute for Peace (USIP) has a small program on IDPs, managed from a gender angle, currently being implemented in Ukraine (SAIS Group Meetings, March 2017). There are also international government institutions, such as the United States Agency for International Development (USAID) and the European Commission Humanitarian Organization, implementing projects that focus on IDPs. The OSCE Project Co-Ordinator in Ukraine is currently working on specific government policies to manage IDPs, rather than direct humanitarian work to address their situation, given limited staff and funding. Through their Human Security Programme, the OSCE focuses on policy recommendations for long-term strategies for integration (SAIS Group Meeting, Kyiv, 20 March 2017). The United Nations High Commissioner for Refugees (UNHCR) includes IDPs under its institutional mandate, and in Ukraine conducts such activities as research on IDP communities, providing direct relief and advocacy, and coordinating aid between international and local organizations (UNHCR: Ukraine).

While these examples are in no way inclusive of the international organizations that are working to ameliorate issues faced by IDPs in Ukraine, they provide an overview of the type of work being conducted by these institutions.

Local Level: Community, Government, and Grassroots Organizations
In meetings with all stakeholders, it became clear that the local, grassroots level is where the most significant work has been conducted in addressing issues related to IDPs.

First, local communities and governments are critical stakeholders in dealing with IDP issues. This is because the local level is where the greatest risks, burdens, and opportunities related to IDP integration into host communities are felt. In addition, the MTOTIDP maintained its role in creating an environment for dialogue, but said it is up to local communities to directly support IDPs (SAIS Group Meeting, Kyiv, 24 March 2017). Thus, the local community plays an important role in making decisions surrounding IDP policy, providing aid and support to IDPs, and ensuring IDP access to government representation.

Next, grassroots organizations and civil society organizations (CSO) have played a significant role in directly working on issues related to the integration of IDPs into their local community. This has ranged from instituting social services and implementing programs to distributing financial aid. This is also where the most direct access to and work with IDPs is conducted. For example, all economic assistance to Vinnytsia is through nongovernmental organizations (NGO) (SAIS Group Meeting, Vinnytsia, 23 March 2017). There are many grassroots organizations working with IDPs, so I will limit the examples provided in this chapter to those we met with during our research in Kyiv and Vinnytsia.

Crimea SOS, established as a partner to UNHCR in the summer of 2014, is an organization that focuses on assistance and programming for IDPs, dealing more specifically with those from the Crimean region (SAIS Group Meeting, Kyiv, 24 March 2017). The NGOs Vis and Spring of Hope are two grassroots organizations in Vinnytsia that focus on IDP issues within this town. Vis is an NGO with two ongoing projects, the first working directly with IDPs and communities (including a project with USAID on economic opportunities for victims) and a project on highlighting women's stories. Spring of Hope is a human rights organization founded on February 3, 2006 to deal with different social needs, and since March 2014 has implemented projects to deal specifically with issues related to IDPs, such as addressing post-traumatic stress disorder (PTSD) and economic integration into the community (SAIS Group Meeting, Vinnytsia, 23 March 2017). The Ukrainian Woman's Fund (UWF), based in Kyiv, is an organization that is a bit larger, with an annual budget around $1million, founded in 2000 by three women activists. Two of the organization's five strategic priorities address IDPs: economic empowerment and direct support to IDP communities. The UWF has also been a significant partner to program implementation conducted by other stakeholders (SAIS Group Meeting, Kyiv, 20 March 2017).

Lastly, stakeholders within the local community also include educational institutions, all the way from primary education facilities to adult education. Educational institutions within communities can act as a bridge between IDP communities and local civilians. One such example is Donetsk National University (DNU), which moved a large portion of the University from the Donetsk region to Vinnytsia in 2014, after violence in the Donbas made its location there unsustainable. This institution has provided many IDP students access to education and to opportunities for communication with other Ukrainian and international students (SAIS Group Meeting, 23 March 2017).

Individual IDPs

Even though this may seem like an obvious conclusion, including IDPs themselves as stakeholders in their integration is incredibly important. First of all, IDPs are playing an active role in working to ensure their integration into host communities, from finding employment to engaging with the local populations. In addition, IDPs must be made a critical part of the decision-making process at the policy level, surrounding decisions related to their future (SAIS Group Meetings, March 2017). In a UNHCR report on IDPs in Ukraine, "UNHCR re-affirms that internally displaced people must be at the centre of decision making regarding their own protection and welfare and expresses appreciation for all people who assisted with this process" (UNHCR 2015, 2).

Difficulties of IDPs and Barriers to Integration

There are a variety of difficulties and barriers that IDPs face when attempting to integrate into host communities. While the government of Ukraine has made recent strides to address issues of integration for IDPs, they fall short. And, despite international aid and phenomenal work being done by CSOs, IDPs still face many barriers to integration. These difficulties vary by individual situation, but I will provide a broad overview.

Legal Protection: Registration and Access to Legal Rights

First, IDPs face many barriers in attempting to register with the national government for their IDP status. While it varies by region, IDPs have reported a lot of trouble in gaining access to registration and documentation. Formal obstacles to registration include the acquisition of proper documentation to cross into the government-controlled areas (GCA) to register, valid identification documents, proof of permanent residence in a recognized conflict zone, limited mobility, fear of conscription, fear for the safety of family remaining in the NGCA, and fear of seizure or destruction of property left behind. Those displaced within an NGCA or from a conflict zone within a GCA that is not recognized are not eligible to register as IDPs (IDMC 2016, 3). There is also a reluctance among the displaced "to register as IDPs as they do not see any benefit in registration, considering that it may stigmatize them and lead to discrimination" (UNHCR 2015, 5). Strict requirements for registration, difficulties in obtaining proper documentation to maintain status as an IDP, and verification of IDP status for continued social payments constitute other restrictions (IDMC 2016, 4-5).

Another major issue that IDPs face in their communities is a lack of representation politically. As it currently stands, IDPs cannot vote for the president or parliament, only within their local elections (SAIS Group Meeting, 21 March 2017). However, issues even remain with the ability of IDPs to vote in local elections, and many IDPs are not afforded the right to vote at all (SAIS Group Meetings, March 2017). If

IDPs have no right to vote, they and their needs are not properly represented in the government.

Finally, the scope of legal aid for IDPs to handle the many legal issues they face is not always sufficient (MoSP and OSCE 2017, 4).

Freedom of Movement

IDPs continue to face significant barriers in traveling between GCAs and NGCAs. As one assessment of the impact of the Temporary Order on Control of the Movement of People, Transport Vehicles and Cargo along the Contact Line by UNHCR notes:

> Concerns raised include: (i) the pass permit system, including long waiting times, lack of transparency and difficulty in applying from the non-government controlled area; (ii) lack of knowledge of where and how to cross; (iii) long distances between checkpoints, including while passing through territory between checkpoints; (iv) long delays at government checkpoints, sometimes for many days; (v) lack of reception after crossing the line of contact. (UNHCR 2015, 2)

One IDP student, originally from Donetsk, explained it can take up to 24 hours for her to cross the Contact Line to visit family that remains in the NGCA. This creates further emotional strain (SAIS Group Meetings, March 2017).

Access to Housing and Utilities

Access to safe and affordable housing remains an issue for IDPs throughout Ukraine. While IDPs are eligible for free temporary accommodation provided by the government for up to six months after their registration, housing concerns include gaps in accommodation while displaced, the inability to repair former homes, and the refusal of landlords to rent to IDPs (UNHCR 2015, 2-3). IDPs noted that even though they may receive assistance for housing from the government, this does not include aid to help with the high cost of utilities, which places great burdens on families. In addition, in discussions with many IDPs, they felt that they should receive compensation for their lost housing, either destroyed or taken over, in the NGCAs (SAIS Group Meetings, March 2017). "As displacement becomes protracted, suitable housing must be provided that ensures that IDPs can live in dignity in accommodation appropriate to their needs and to their family requirements in regard to available space, privacy, facilities, and proximity to services, employment, and livelihood opportunities" (UNHCR February 2016, 9).

Another issue at the nexus of access to housing and the integration of IDPs into local communities is that some IDPs live within IDP collectives, further segregating them from interaction with the local population.

Access to Healthcare

Healthcare is to be provided free to Ukrainian citizens, but IDPs have complained about the high prices for medications and special treatment of certain diseases such as diabetes and HIV/AIDS, poor health conditions, and that "unofficial payments" in hospitals continue. IDPs also face issues with the physical access to healthcare facilities, as people living in remote areas have difficulties reaching care providers (UNHCR 2015, 4).

Access to mental healthcare also remains extremely important for IDP groups, especially for IDPs and children who face significant amounts of trauma and stress due to displacement and experiences within the conflict (SAIS Group Meetings, March 2017). "Social fragmentation, family separation, economic problems and an unclear future affects IDP's mental state, which can lead to tension and conflict, especially in areas with a high concentration of IDPs, such as collective centers" (UNHCR 2015, 6).

Access to Education

There are many issues that IDPs face in their access to education, including lack of proper documentation, high costs of school and extracurricular activities, social exclusion, and a deterioration of performance due to psychological trauma.[4]

Access to Information

Access to information, to both government information and information on international aid, remains an important barrier to the integration of IDPs. First of all, many IDPs have noted the confusion that stems from the lack of a central government structure to manage IDPs within Ukraine. With constantly changing IDP policy and legislation, it is difficult for IDPs to know where to receive information about government assistance, and to even

---

[4] See the chapter by Christina Connelly-Kanmaz for a more in-depth discussion on this topic.

understand what they are eligible for. Poor communication about international aid programs also exists, as IDPs believe there should be more clear information on these programs, including information on eligibility. Often the information that IDPs do receive is outdated, unreliable, and conflicting (UNHCR 2015, 5; OSCE and MoSP 2017, 4-5; SAIS Group Meetings, March 2017).

Employment and Livelihood

Despite the fact that IDPs within Ukraine tend to be well educated, one of the main barriers to integration that IDPs cite is finding and maintaining employment, especially due to discrimination from employers in local communities, resulting in reduced wages and incentive packages. Difficulties can also vary depending on where the host community is located. Where the cost of living in Ukraine is high, such as in Kyiv, "IDPs are particularly vulnerable, which can give rise to protection risks relating to marginalization, engagement in risky coping strategies and susceptibility to fraudulent schemes, etc." (UNHCR 2015, 3). The IDPs living in more rural areas note issues with the ability to travel to regions or cities that may have a greater availability of employment.

IDPs also face issues in adapting to the types of work available. For example, the Donetsk and Luhansk regions are very different from Vinnytsia, as the former are primarily industrial while the latter is based around agriculture. Naturally the IDPs in Vinnytsia are faced with the question of whether or not they could find a job they were good at, something that was not possible in many of these cases (SAIS Group Meeting, Vinnytsia, 23 March 2017).

IDPs complained about the quality of employment centers run by the government and the lack of information provided on jobs and vocational courses. In addition, finding childcare if both parents are working introduces another hindrance.

Access to Social Protection and Basic Needs

When IDPs are forced to flee their homes, they often flee with little to no personal belongings, and are required to establish their families within their host communities:

> Access to social services, addressing basic needs and 'making ends meet' is a daily struggle for a significant number of IDPs. While the Government has made efforts to support the displaced population by adopting relevant legislation and allocating available resources to provide financial assistance, the needs of the population…remain high. (UNHCR 2015, 7)

IDPs within remote areas, especially with a lack of information as previously described, often find that government and international assistance does not reach them. For various reasons, IDPs have also experienced great difficulties in receiving their social security benefits from the government.

Perception and Stereotypes of IDPs

In April 2016, UNHCR conducted a study of *Ukrainians' Attitudes Towards Internally Displaced Persons from Crimea and Donbas*, research conducted to better understand "the general attitude of the local population toward IDPs; to assess the prevalence of stereotypes and prejudices about the latter; and, to detail the perception of the impact IDPs have on city life as perceived by local residents" (UNHCR April 2016, 4). Generally, respondents to the survey believed that IDPs are not responsible for the situations they found themselves in, are entitled to the same rights as others, and are suffering within the life situation they are in, in need of help (UNHCR April 2016, 6). However, there was some telling information provided on more negative sentiments.

Within the western region of Ukraine, where respondents had less direct communication with IDPs, respondents "maintain more negative stereotypes about IDPs. In particular, the respondents in this sample emphasize the following features they attribute to IDPs: pro-Russian political views; unwillingness to work on equal terms; aggressiveness towards locals; arrogance; and the desire for special treatment fitting their circumstances" (UNHCR April 2016, 6). When respondents were asked whether they would hire an IDP as a tutor or nanny, hire a group of IDPs for apartment renovation, or provide premises for rent, only 50-60% answered positively. The respondents primarily cited fear, distrust, and personal biases as the main reasons (UNHCR April 2016, 6-7).

One important finding was that the majority of respondents found their opinions had not shifted over the two years of the conflict, citing neither improvement nor deterioration in their attitudes. This is an important insight given the current intractability of the conflict in Ukraine.

The study also found that for respondents, mass media is the main source where they receive information about IDPs (UNHCR April 2016, 6). Making current negative stereotypes surrounding IDPs worse is the significant presence and spread of propaganda within the information flow to the general Ukrainian population, especially Russian propaganda inside the eastern territories (SAIS Group Meetings, March 2017).

A Gendered Perspective of Interaction of IDPs with Host Communities

Before moving on from barriers to integration, I find it important to make a gendered assessment of interaction of IDPs within host communities, as many studies report a stark difference in how men and women interact within their new communities.

The UWF and USIP conducted a gender analysis of IDPs to find statistics on how displacement affects men and women differently. Initially, women IDPs find it very painful to leave their homes, crying for months, but realize the current situation is their new life, and thus they must help their family no matter the circumstances. In order to better integrate into local communities, women find it most helpful to speak with other women in the new communities, volunteer, and participate in public life.

For men, their perception of whether or not they were integrated into a community was based on whether or not they were working. Men said they coped with displacement by working hard to earn money, rather than engaging with others in the community. Many IDP men reported they had been rich and successful before displacement, and now they are poor. Male IDPs who have been unable to find jobs report severe frustration, which can lead to domestic violence and other issues within the household (SAIS Group Meeting, Kyiv, 20 March 2017). Our conversations with IDPs corroborated this information.

Examples of Current Work to Integrate IDPs

During our March 2017 research trip to Kyiv and Vinnytsia, Ukraine, we met with a variety of different stakeholders to the conflict, many of whom discussed their amazing work within IDP communities. I will highlight some examples of current work that is being conducted by different levels of stakeholders in working to integrate IDPs, as it is important to understand different models on how peers, IDPs and non-IDPs, are working together in local communities.

The UWF conducted a program that brings IDPs and local children together in communities, using sports as a form of reconciliation. Within this program, teams were formed from children in the local community to sail a catamaran, composed of two locals and two IDPs. In order for the catamaran to sail, all four sailors must work together simultaneously, requiring significant teamwork. Not only did the UWF find these children would work together, they also noted that the children would discuss their lives and stories, increasing conversation and understanding of the situations faced by the IDPs. The UWF noted great success with this program.

Understanding the prevalence and importance of PTSD within IDP communities in Vinnytsia, Spring of Hope established a PTSD organization under its umbrella, the Vinnytsia Regional Center for overcoming the consequences of PTSD. The aim of the initiative is to provide comprehensive reintegration assistance for trafficking victims and families that have been affected by the conflict, including IDPs. Based out of a room in their main organizational building, it conducts individual and group therapy sessions with qualified psychological associates for persons exhibiting symptoms of PTSD. It also functions as a site for dating and communication exchange for professionals working with PTSD. The Center works to develop and implement other programs and techniques to better rehabilitate and socialize persons suffering from PTSD. One IDP we spoke with, a male from the east, gave his testimony on the great success of this program and how it helped him to better interact with his new community and overcome psychological barriers to finding employment. Once he was able to work through some of his issues stemming from PTSD, he found he was much more successful in integrating into Vinnytsia.

The "women's stories" program out of the organization Vis is another great example of successful support for integration of IDPs into local communities. These stories are about narratives, specifically of non-separatist women IDPs. Initially, these stories were conversations IDP women were having about their experiences that turned into books after the need to share their stories with the greater community was understood. According to Vis, these projects bring understanding and peace in the community, and provide an opportunity for local NGOs to unite around these issues. The stories were recorded and performed throughout Vinnytsia, so IDP women could share their experiences to a greater audience. In addition, the performance of the stories had a great effect on deputies on the local council, which in turn caused them to give more money to IDPs within the city.

In terms of education, DNU, recently renamed to Vasyl' Stus DNU after a famous Ukrainian political dissident, is a very successful example. The students and faculty have come to work closely together to ensure the success of both the university and IDPs. In addition, students at DNU believe it is their role to act as a mediator and bridge between their home community in the east and their new community in Vinnytsia. As students with family in the east who are increasingly informed by propaganda from Russian sources, they have taken it on as their task and duty to talk about the correct history of Ukraine.[5]

Recommendations

<u>To the Government of Ukraine (GoU)</u>

- **Maintain updated information on IDPs and resources for IDPs in one centralized GoU Ministry**. Every region in Ukraine should have a subdivision office of this Ministry that is responsible for maintaining up-to-date information about IDPs within its region.

- **Implement a more efficient and transparent IDP registration system**, maintaining updated figures on demographics of IDPs so aid can be more effectively targeted. This registration system should be housed under the central IDP GoU Ministry.

- **Include IDPs in dialogue surrounding their integration into local communities.** The first step in doing this is **changing voting laws** so IDPs are able to register to vote in both local and national elections. The GoU should also

---

[5] See Christina Connelly-Kanmaz's chapter for more information on a successful project on media literacy conducted by journalism students at DNU.

employ a greater amount of IDPs in critical policy formation ministries in order to increase their representation.

- **Provide a subsidy to IDPs whose housing in NGCAs has been taken over or destroyed** in order to compensate their losses. This should be in addition to the aid that is already provided for housing and should include greater subsidies for utilities to IDPs.

- **Implement media and information campaigns in order to eliminate misconceptions and biases about IDPs.** This should include the introduction of programs and curriculum on IDPs and the conflict in state-sponsored education facilities, in order to enhance greater awareness of situations IDPs face and repudiate negative, false stereotypes.

- **Ensure better access to healthcare.** Within the mandated free healthcare system, IDPs should be granted greater access to reduced price or free health services, including but not limited to mental health care and special treatments for diseases.

To the International Community

- **Diversify where aid is sent**. International organizations and multilateral institutions should work to **better spread out the distribution of aid to IDP communities throughout Ukraine,** as opposed to providing certain CSOs or schools with uneven amounts of aid.

- **Better coordinate aid activities among international and local organizations.** This should include better communication with IDP communities and providing timely, clear information on the range of assistance programs provided to IDPs.

- **Place a greater focus on the long-term integration of IDPs into local communities** rather than emergency humanitarian assistance.

To the Local Community

- **Local government offices should create positions for IDPs to increase the amount of jobs for this group and allow greater representation of their**

needs. They must also work to better the quality of their employment centers and the information it provides.

- **Continue to implement integration programs for IDPs in host communities, especially through sports and art programs.** Local NGOs and CSOs, in collaboration with the international community and government, should hold semiannual best practices meetings to discuss program effectiveness.

- **Continue to foster dialogue between IDPs and the local government and population.**

- **Hold local media accountable for disseminating correct information about the IDP community.** This can include hosting workshops for media outlets to discuss the situations IDPs face, incorporating stories of successful IDP integration and their contribution to the community.

Human Rights in Ukraine

Kevin Toda

The crisis in eastern Ukraine has created a permissive environment for intentional violations of basic human rights and a chaotic environment that makes it extremely difficult for human rights to be protected. Both the Ukrainian government and the Russian-backed rebels have violated numerous human rights on both sides of the contact line. Violations range from killings, abductions, arbitrary detention, and torture to restriction on movement, expression and peaceful assembly. The lawlessness and chaos created by the conflict has limited the ability of the parties involved and the international community at large from mitigating the issues.

The first section of this chapter will outline the violations taking place in the conflict zone and around Ukraine. The second section will focus on the effects these violations have on the conflict and the negotiation process. The third section will touch on the Human Rights Action Plan and the positive steps that have taken place in order to mitigate violations. The final section will conclude and recommend policies for the Ukrainian government, the self-proclaimed Lugansk and Donetsk People's Republics (LPR and DPR), Russia, the EU and the international community at large. The focus of the paper will be on the Non-government controlled area in the eastern part of Ukraine (NGCA) and the government controlled area of Ukraine (GCA). While there are many similar issues occurring in Crimea, this chapter will not focus on the human rights violations in that region (see chapters by Anna Goodman and Christina Pushaw).

One final note: This chapter is based on reports from the Office of the United Nations High Commission for Human Rights (OHCHR), Amnesty International, Human Rights Watch, Council of Europe High Commissioner for Human Rights and interviews conducted in Kyiv and Vinnystia during March 2017. It is very difficult to verify all of the claims, as the majority of the violations come to the attention of the relevant authorities through eyewitness accounts. Some violations are directly observed by NGO observers and international monitors, while other accounts are corroborated several times over by multiple civilian witnesses. Verification is especially difficult in the NGCA where most international monitors are banned and almost no oversight exists.

Civilian Casualties

Since the fighting began in 2014, it is estimated that 2000 civilians have been killed, mostly as collateral damage of indiscriminate shelling. Others were executed, died of torture or lack of medical care in detention facilities. Civilians are sometimes apprehended to be used as bargaining chips in prisoner swaps (Amnesty International and Human Rights Watch and 2016). Once in detention civilians are subject to ill-treatment and sometimes torture. This issue will be discussed further in a later section (OHCHR 2016, 9).

Aside from a handful of checkpoints, the contact line area is littered with mines and unexploded ordinances that have killed and injured civilians and threaten to create more casualties. The majority of civilian casualties occur around the contact line where various artillery pieces are used indiscriminately by both sides on populated areas (OHCHR 2016, 25). Violence against civilians peaked in the summer of 2015 and has since declined but still remains.

Lawlessness

<u>Arbitrary Detention, Disappearances and Torture</u>

Hugh Williams of Human Rights Watch Europe and Central Asia has described the NGCA as a vacuum where no rule of law exists. The combined Russian, DPR and LPR forces operate with impunity, denying civilians their freedoms with no checks, balances or viable remedies. An influx of foreign fighters and Russian weapon supplies has exacerbated the lawlessness of the area (OHCHR 2017). Since the conflict started in 2014, there has been an increase in the number of abductions, arbitrary detentions and cases of ill-treatment of detainees on both sides of the contact line (Human Rights Watch 2017).

Amnesty International and Human Rights Watch released a joint report investigating cases of arbitrary detention and torture. The report included nine cases each of arbitrary, prolonged detention of civilians by Ukrainian and Russian-backed forces. Detention often involves beatings, threat of sexual violence, the threat of violence against the families of the detainees and the denial of adequate medical treatment (Amnesty International and Human Rights Watch 2016). The OHCHR report describes the use of arbitrary detention and torture as "deeply entrenched practices" in the NGCA. Because of the lack of accountability or checks and balances in the NGCA there is little recourse for civilians detained in this area. Often, the combined Russian, DPR and LPR forces do not release information on the detainees, thus leaving the relatives of the detainee unaware and unsure of their relative's fate (OHCHR 2016).

On the Ukrainian side, the reports mostly implicate the Security Service of Ukraine (SBU), who are reported to operate unofficial detention facilities in Kharkiv, Mariupol, Izyum and Kramtorsk. The Ukrainian government denies that any of these facilities exist except for one temporary facility in Kyiv. The government also denies any knowledge of SBU abuses of detainees. The SBU itself states that the reports are false and that the accusers are criminals trying to portray themselves as victims (OHCHR 2016).

Reports suggest that civilians are picked up either by pro-Ukraine paramilitary groups or the SBU itself, tortured to extract confessions about dealing with the DPR or LPR and then brought to SBU facilities where formal charges are brought against them. The UN Subcommittee for Prevention of Torture was unable to access detention centres in both the GCA and NGCA and therefore had to cut its report short but raised many red flags (Amnesty International and Human Rights Watch 2016).

Gender and Sexual Based Violence

The general lawlessness and chaos of war combined with the unchecked used of secret detention has led to increased reports of gender-based and sexual violence. There are many reported cases of men and women being raped or sexually assaulted while in detention, and the threat of rape and sexual violence against the acquaintances of prisoners has also been reported to be fairly common on both sides of the contact line (OHCHR 2016, 17). Because of the lack of capacity of law enforcement and the judicial system, not only are there few avenues of recourse for victims, but it is estimated that attacks are greatly underreported, even more so than usual. Additionally, humanitarian organizations that specialized in women's needs and sexual and gender violence are prevented from operating in the NGCA, exacerbating the problem further. Finally, the lack of employment and mental counselling for those who suffer from PTSD has led to an uptick in domestic violence (SAIS Group Meeting with Ukrainian Women's Fund, Kyiv, 20 March 2017).

Attacks on Basic Freedoms

<u>Expression and Assembly</u>

While the events of Euromaidan have increased the number of and raised the voices of civil society groups, many other voices have been silenced in both the GCA and the NGCA. In the GCA, anti-terrorism laws have been used to detain certain members of political parties, NGOs and members of the media critical of the current Ukrainian government. The OHCHR observed pro-Maidan protestors intimidating and preventing anti-Maidan protestors from peacefully expressing their views (OHCHR 2016, 25-28). The Ukrainian police have also refused to protect anti-Maidan protestors from such attacks. Communist supporters in the GCA have been subject to threats, attacks from right wing activists and subjected to numerous investigations by Ukrainian police without any charges being brought forward. The Ministry of Justice has even submitted a request to the Dnipropetrovsk circuit administrative court to prohibit the activities of pro-Communist parties. The Rada has also moved to ban any Russian-made movies in Ukraine (OHCHR 2016, 28-32).

Journalists, in particular, have been targeted by both groups in the conflict. In the GCA, the media face restrictions when covering issues related to the conflict. Many reporters admit that fear of detention and investigation has prompted widespread self-censorship. Publications are also used irresponsibly as a form of intimidation. A pro-Ukrainian website published the names and personal information, including telephone number and home address, of journalists supposedly working for the DPR. This list was not verified in any way and included names of people who were not journalists (OHCHR 2016, 32).

In the NGCA journalists and pro-Ukrainian ideas have been strictly limited. Journalists and people suspected of being pro-Ukrainian have been abducted and intimidated in the NGCA. This includes NGOs and international organizations that defend human rights and provide humanitarian assistance. There have also been reports from the NGCA that the combined Russian, LPR and DPR forces have targeted religious groups. For example, members of the Jehovah's Witnesses were arrested and labeled members of a prohibited sect. On 18 March 2016, the DPR "national council" passed a law stating that Protestant Christianity was a foreign imposition attempting to brainwash people. This has raised concern that future religious persecution could occur. The Ukrainian Orthodox Church reported from the NGCA that armed men forced priests to sign a cooperation agreement with the LPR and that the congregation has faced insults and intimidation from armed groups (OHCHR 2016, 25-28).

The OHCHR has received reports that "state" employees in the NGCA have been forced to join LPR and DPR parties, such as the "Free Donbas" movement (Svobodnyi Donbass), or face termination if they do not join (OHCHR 2016, 31).

<u>Movement</u>

Another violation of rights that has exacerbated other issues and created greater violations of other human rights is the restriction of movement in Ukraine. There are incredibly long lines at the contact line checkpoints, and the surrounding areas are filled with landmines. People have been killed by errant shells while waiting in line. Some report waiting up to 30 hours at the check points (OHCHR 2016). Both sides of the line are rife with corruption and many people are arbitrarily detained. Many humanitarian aid organizations are banned by the LPR and DPR, decreasing people's access to food, medical treatment, medicine, legal assistance and other forms of counselling and assistance. The Ukrainian Rada passed a law, contrary to the 16 October 2015 Supreme Administrative Court ruling, that states that IDPs and civilians residing in the NGCA may only receive government aid, social benefits and entitlements after being registered in the GCA. This means that many simply cannot access aid or are forced to travel long and potentially deadly journeys across the contact line (OHCHR 2016, 35).

The LPR and DPR have begun issuing civil registration documentation and passports that are not valid in the GCA but that are recognized by the Russian Federation. This has further limited people's ability to travel and access Ukrainian government services (OHCHR 2016, 36).

<u>Access to Justice</u>

Access to justice has been limited in several ways both intentionally and as a by-product of the conflict. In the NGCA, the Ukrainian government has removed all of its judiciary services. This has left a large vacuum for people living in the NGCA. In the place of Ukrainian courts, the DPR and LPR have set up an unrecognized, parallel justice system. This system is non-transparent, limited in capacity and under the control of the LPR and DPR authorities. The courts operated on an uncertain and ad hoc legal framework, subject to constant change. These courts lack even greater amount of resources and capacity than the relocated Ukrainian ones. Not only are people detained because of missing, lost or confiscated court files but also because of the lack of transparency in the parallel courts. Reports state that the parallel courts are often used to intimidate political opponents of the LPR and DPR. The Special Monitoring Mission to Ukraine (SMM) was unable to visit many of the combined Russia, DPR or LPR detention centres to verify their conditions or the number of people being held. The DPR claimed that 1,113 people were being held in custody as of July 2015. As of 6 July 2015, the LPR "prosecutor" claimed that 500 people were awaiting trial and were being held in LPR detention facilities (OSCE 2015).

The relocated Ukrainian courts are also plagued by numerous shortcomings that prevent the proper administration of justice. The relocated courts often lack capacity on several fronts. For one, they lack the funds normally allotted to them because of their transitory nature, the economic downturn in Ukraine and the prioritization of resources to other government services. This has greatly impacted not only the administration of, but also the access to justice. Many Ukrainians are denied their due process because of a lack of resources. The Ukrainian judicial system lacks the ability to provide legal aid and advice to citizens at an affordable rate. Secondly, amidst the chaos of the conflict and the relocation, many court documents and files have gone missing or have been destroyed. This has left many people stranded in limbo, indefinitely held without any valid reason or timeframe for release.

Even when verdicts and decisions are made, the Ukrainian courts have no ability to enforce their judgments in the NGCAs. The postal service also does not operate in the NGCA and so court notices and other administrative notices are unable to reach citizens.

Residents in the NGCA are forced to travel long and dangerous distances in order to access GCA courts.

The courts lacked a serious emergency plan and this has greatly hampered the judicial system's ability to administer justice. There has been a lack of accountability for all abuses on both sides of the contact line, and this does not seem to be a priority for the Ukrainian government. No cases of human rights abuses have been brought up in Ukrainian courts, even though the Ukrainian government has brought rebels to court for crimes against public safety and for violating the territorial integrity of Ukraine. No progress has been made on prosecuting the perpetrators of violence during the Euromaidan. Numerous extradition requests have been sent to Russia, and all have been ignored (OSCE 2015).

On a more positive note the Ukrainian government has tried to bring to justice members of the Ukrainian armed forces. So far 726 crimes have been investigated, 622 people charged, 381 indicted and the courts have ruled on cases regarding 272 people. However, the anti-terror legislation has been another obstacle in Ukrainians' right to fair trials and access to a fair judicial system. The anti-terror legislation is often exploited to create a permissive environment for further abuses of power (OHCHR 2016, 19).

Socio-Economic and Living Conditions

All of the violations discussed above, combined with the economic downturn in Ukraine, have led to worsening living conditions and increased vulnerability of the population. There has been a complete withdrawal of government and public services in the NGCA. LPR and DPR replacement institutions have been sparse and lack capacity. Access to employment has been another major issue in the NGCA, particularly for railway and coal workers, two major industries in the Donbas region before the conflict began. IDPs and unemployed people in the NGCA are highly susceptible to human trafficking and other exploitive working conditions. There has been no comprehensive plan for IDP resettlement, housing for those affected by the conflict or compensation for property damaged in the fighting (see chapters by Ashley Patton and by Dorothea Cheek). Both armies have confiscated, looted and damaged property on both sides of the contact line.

Medical conditions remain very low in the NGCA because of the lack of public services, resources and limited access of international actors that could provide necessary assistance. The reduced Ukrainian health budget, for example, only has enough resources for 30% of the population living with HIV or 66% of children with cancer. The stress of the conflict and lack of basic medical supplies has led to an increase in more serious illness (OHCHR 2016, 39). The World Health Organization estimates that 22,000 people living in the NGCA that require daily insulin are not receiving adequate supplies (HRMMU 2016). Conditions in the rural areas of the NGCA are even worse. There have been reports that patients are being charged for medical care, which is supposed to be free, because of lack of supplies, and elderly patients are even being turned away for the same reason (OHCHR 2016, 40).

There is very little support for mental illness and PTSD, especially for returning soldiers and children in the conflict region. When meeting with Ukrainian NGOs in Vinnytsia, organizers explained that children are dramatically affected and their development and socialization is severely hampered (see chapter by Christina Connelly-Kanmaz). Additionally, soldiers returning from the war have a hard time coping with trauma associated with the conflict which has resulted in an increase in domestic violence and trouble with employment.

Destruction of infrastructure, including roads, schools, hospitals, religious institutions and utilities, have all degraded the living standards in the NGCA and around the contact line. This is exacerbated by foreign fighters and an influx of weapons from Russia (OHCHR 2017).

Effects

Besides basic human decency why should the parties involved concern themselves with human rights? When the Ukrainian government violates the rights of its own citizens it loses legitimacy in the eyes of the population. If the government in Kyiv is not only guilty of corruption and the inability to protect its citizens but also arbitrarily detains them, tortures them and makes it extremely difficult for them to access public services, there are fewer and fewer reasons for the people to support them. The same applies to the LPR and DPR forces who have shown no signs of serious concern for human rights.

Russia, as a signatory of the Minsk Protocol, also bears responsibility to control its own forces and its LPR and DPR allies in order to enforce the agreement and at least progress toward a lasting agreement.

Violations on both sides of the contact line harden views and increase distrust, pushing the two sides further and further away from agreement. Trust-building and mutual understanding are essential components for solving any conflict. Retaliatory attacks or random sweeps to capture prisoners for swaps do not create a conducive environment for negotiation.

Another important consideration is the issue of justice versus peace. The government of Ukraine and the international community involved in the conflict should consider the future. How will violators be dealt with? A major reason many parties refuse to compromise or resign despite being willing to do so, is fear of prosecution. The Ukrainian government and international actors involved will have to determine whether certain parties will be granted amnesty in exchange for their surrender. It is unclear whether this will be acceptable to the victims of human rights violations and the Ukrainian population at large.

Human Rights Action Plan

On 21 September 2015, with the help of the OHCHR and the Commissioner for Human Rights of the Council of Europe, the Ukrainian Ministry of Justice adopted a National Action Plan on Human Rights. It was created to operationalize the National Human Rights Strategy declared by the Ukrainian government in 2014. The National Action Plan set out to address issues identified by the UN Human Rights Office, including current abuses and accountability for past abuses. The plan created benchmarks and standards as well as a directive for regular reports. The plan could not cover abuses carried out in the NGCA, but only violations in the GCA such as corruption, judicial reform, security abuses, denial of rights to minority groups and the mismanagement of resources. However, by 2016 the OHCHR assessment reported that a number of actions that were said to have been completed, were only done in name or partially completed (OHCHR 2016, 42).

Conclusion

As is always the case with human rights violations, the fate of victims and the prosecution of the perpetrators are found at the bottom of the priority list, especially during an ongoing conflict. Only with a serious cessation of the fighting can real work be done to halt the continued violations of human rights and for justice to be served for past violations. Only when the protection of the most vulnerable and the prosecution of violators is prioritized will any progress be made. It is up to the international community to pressure both sides to prevent violations, protect civilians, prosecute violators, and offer expertise and resources to ensure that human rights in Ukraine will be respected.

Recommendations

<u>To the Ukrainian Government</u>

- While it is difficult to affect change in the NGCA, **the current Ukrainian government can focus on the GCA and fully commit to seriously implementing the National Action Plan** as soon as possible.
- **Attempt to avoid shelling, occupying or confiscating property near the contact line.** Create a system of compensation to citizens when this is unavoidable.
- **Create a plan to increase access to public services, such as healthcare, the judiciary and housing**. Reach out to international organizations and other states to provide expertise, assistance and resources.
- **Avoid using anti-terrorism laws to indiscriminately violate the rights of citizens.** Benchmarks, reports and limits to the anti-terror legislation should be created to limit the ability of officials to abuse this power. Allow those detained due processes and contact to the outside world.
- **Investigate and prosecute those within the GCA that have violated the rights of citizens.** Establish an independent working group to investigate torture, extrajudicial killing and arbitrary detention in the SBU, Ukrainian forces and para-military groups.
- **Investigate hate crimes, sexual and gender violence.**

- **Help civilians cross the contact line to be better able access public services and to save lives.**
- **Avoid discrimination of citizens based on place of origin.**
- **Foster greater integration of IDPs and allow them greater access to public services.**
- **Respect the Minsk Agreement Ceasefire.**

<u>To the LPR and DPR Authorities</u>

- **Cease disappearances and arbitrary detentions**. When detentions are necessary, allow detainees access to the outside world and grant them due process. Eliminate the use of torture and ill-treatment of detainees.
- **Allow humanitarian organizations access to the NGCA** to better serve the people living in the area.
- Take care to **avoid attacks on civilians**. Control forces to avoid looting, confiscation and destruction of civilian property.
- **Allow safe passage for civilians across the contact line.**
- **Respect freedoms of expression, assembly, association and religion.**
- **Respect the Minsk Agreement Ceasefire.**

<u>To the Russian Federation</u>

- **Tighten control of Russian, LPR, DPR and foreign mercenary forces**, to cease all human rights violations and prosecute violators.
- **Allow international monitors to observe the conflict in the NGCA** and allow humanitarian organizations access to the area in order to provide services to the population.
- **Respond to Ukraine's extradition requests.**
- **Work with the Ukrainian government, the LPR and DPR forces and the OSCE to enforce the Minsk Agreement Ceasefire** by removing troops and halting the supply of ammunition and heavy weapons to the conflict zone.

<u>To the International Community: EU/OSCE/UN</u>

- **Continue to pressure both sides to obey international human rights.**
- **Pressure the authorities in the NGCA to allow humanitarian organizations access to the areas.**
- **Work to provide resources and expertise to the Ukrainian government in order to provide greater public services for their citizens**. Medical care and access to a fair and effective justice system are top priorities.
- **Continue to monitor the humanitarian situation as best as possible in the GCA and NGCA**. Regularly report findings and ensure validity of claims.
- **Help the parties implement the Minsk Agreement.**
- **Support the Ukrainian government in its effort to implement the Human Rights Action Plan.**

Assessing Barriers to Education for Children Affected by the Conflict in Eastern Ukraine

Christina Connelly-Kanmaz

Conflict often has the greatest effect on the most vulnerable, and there are no more vulnerable among us than children. In the case of eastern Ukraine's war with Russian-backed separatists in Donbas, children are experiencing the negative impacts in several ways—physically, emotionally, and psychologically. The interruption to their education due to fighting and displacement may have the most lasting impact on their lives and their futures, as well as the future of Ukraine. As of 2017, UNICEF estimates that the conflict in Donbas has resulted in nearly 1 million children in need and nearly 200,000 of those children live within 15 kilometers of the contact zone (UNICEF 30 January 2017). With severe damage to infrastructure, daily violations of the ceasefire agreement, and the psychological consequences of living amongst military violence, these children face enormous barriers in the pursuit of basic education. They are paying a heavy price for the wars of adults.

It is not only the children who remain within the Non-government Controlled Areas (NGCA) who face obstacles; by early 2017 the conflict has resulted in about 1.7 million Internally Displaced Persons (IDPs), though this official number is most likely a conservative estimate, and of that number, about 12% are children (IDMC 2015). These nearly 204,000 internally displaced children face numerous formal and informal barriers in attempting to access basic education. While their parents sometimes face difficulties in registering them in new schools, the children themselves must also deal with social obstacles to integration and psychological trauma that can impact their performance and ability to learn.

Despite these challenges, the Ukrainian government, civil society organizations, and international NGOs are responding to the crisis and intervening to ensure access to quality education for children within the NGCA and on both sides of the contact line, as well as the integration of IDP children into new schools throughout Ukraine. These responses are vitally important. Education is often overlooked in times of humanitarian crises, as basic needs such as food, water and shelter take priority, both in terms of effort and funding. Education should not be overlooked, however, and the international community must recognize its significance and respond with urgency. Education plays a vital role in a child's development and personal growth, as well as the economic and social development of the society in which she lives (Save the Children 2006). Interruptions to a child's education at critical moments in their development can have devastating consequences on their futures and thus impact their ability to make positive economic contributions to their country or participate in a liberal, democratic, civil society.

Finally, education can be a vehicle to fuel or prevent future conflicts. It can promote or destroy social cohesion, and it can be a conduit for teaching hate or promoting peace. When curriculum is co-opted and used for a political goal, this lays the ground for an unstable society and increases the likelihood of future conflict in a country. There is also an opportunity, however, to benefit from this conflict. It has highlighted the need to teach human rights, peacebuilding, and conflict prevention to school-aged children, and this can contribute to a cohesive society and promote a generation of future adults who can peacefully resolve conflicts before they escalate into war. Since 2014, there have been both positive and negative attempts to utilize basic education in Ukraine for higher goals. The history curriculum in particular is a contested issue and it has been rewritten on both sides of the conflict zone. There have also been new attempts to train teachers in human rights education and many other positive developments. The interventions being made by all parties, domestic and international, must continue, and this chapter lays out further recommendations to ensure access to quality education for all those affected by the fighting, as well as ways to ensure that classroom education is utilized to promote positive peacebuilding skills for future generations.

Barriers to Education for Those Near the Contact Line

At the immediate onset of fighting in the Donbas in early 2014, towns were inundated with shelling and gunfire which damaged public buildings, including schools. By 2016, one in five schools in the region had been damaged or destroyed as a result of heavy shelling. Schools on the frontline ceased normal functions, many being used as bomb shelters for the community. By early 2017, more than 740 schools have been damaged or destroyed, affecting nearly 200,000 to 250,000 children who live on both sides of the contact line (UNICEF 16 March 2017). The fighting has also badly disrupted services in the NGCA with heating, electricity, and water being shut down. This makes survival difficult and schooling impossible. In some towns, such as Mironovsky located in Donetsk Oblast, children spent the winter of 2014 under blankets in the basement of a local school without heat or electricity, listening to the sounds of gunfire outside (J. Cha, in-person interview, 15 March 2017).

School buildings have also been occupied by military forces on both sides. Armed formations in separatist-held areas often take over public buildings, (including schools), which inhibits children's access to education. The OSCE Special Monitoring Mission (SMM) observed military units positioned next to a school in the so-called Donetsk Peoples Republic (DPR) in Samiilove, and a headquarters located in a former school building (OSCE 2017). School staff said that school buildings were being used by military personnel and could no longer be accessed. The SMM also reported significant damage to school buildings due to shelling and gunfire. In the town of Dokuchaievsk, the school director told the SMM that 14 pupils had still been present in the school when it came under fire (OSCE 2017).

Entering the fourth year of this conflict, the situation remains unstable. The resurgence of fighting in February of 2017 forced thousands more children out of school in eastern Ukraine. Twenty-nine schools were destroyed, damaged, or temporarily closed in the first 3 months of 2017 alone (UNICEF 6 February 2017). In addition to destroyed infrastructure, another issue keeping children home from school is the fear of unexploded ordinances and mines in the streets. Many families choose to keep their children home from schools, rather than face this danger (UNICEF 6 February 2017).

Damage to infrastructure, lack of heat, water and electricity, and the inability to access buildings taken over by military personnel are all significant physical barriers to basic education. Worst still, the psychological damage to children who live in constant fear and in constant physical danger can impede their ability to learn. Not only is there an urgent need for safe-learning spaces, but there is also a need for immediate psychological support for the most vulnerable children who have witnessed fighting, lost a loved one, or have experienced shelling first-hand. Our research group met with several IDP women at the NGO Vis in Vinnytsia, Ukraine, and one woman shared a book published about IDP experiences which included illustrations by IDP children. She described how the drawings were dark and often contained themes of violence. She also shared how children she knew who experienced the fighting began to play violent war games, including one child who transported his Legos in a toy train describing them as "corpses" (Interview with unidentified IDP, Vinnytsia, 23 March 2017). These small anecdotes are a window into a larger problem. Without proper psychological support for these young children, they may be incapable of learning even once their physical needs are met.

Barriers to Education for IDP Children

In early 2017, there were around 204,000 IDP children who were forced to flee their homes and thus interrupt their schooling. These children face both formal and informal barriers to continuing their education. Based on a report on Out-of-School Children (OOSC) commissioned by UNICEF in 2016, the percentage of OOSCs rose from the pre-conflict number of 3% to 27% for primary school-aged children (6-9 years old) (GfK Ukraine 2016).

The OSCE SMM has reported complaints from IDPs that some unaccompanied and separated IDP children are not able to register as IDPs on their own and as a result are unable to access assistance, including the financial support and other documents necessary to enroll in school (OSCE 2017). When our research group spoke to IDPs in Vinnytsia, a woman shared the problems she faced when trying to register her children in schools in Odesa due to the fact that their IDP status guaranteed them half-priced school meals. The school was resistant to register her children because they wanted the family to pay full price for the meals; giving the family the required discount was a strain on school resources. The same IDP woman, who had moved with her family to 3 other cities within Ukraine before settling in Vinnytsia, described facing resentment and hostility from other parents as IDPs flooded classes and constrained resources (Interview with unidentified IDP, Vinnytsia, 23 March 2017). These informal social barriers affect IDP children's ability to learn in a safe, welcoming, secure and nurturing environment. For other families, the obstacle affecting continued access to schooling for some children came from the parents themselves. At the start of the conflict, many IDPs believed that they had only temporarily left their homes and therefore failed to enroll their children in the local schools in their new cities. In other cases, enrolling children in school simply did not take priority as families struggled to meet their basic food and shelter needs (Interview with unidentified IDP, Vinnytsia, 23 March 2017).

An additional barrier to continued education is access to essential documents, such as birth certificates and school records. A survey by UNICEF showed that some IDPs left behind important documents when they fled their homes. Given the significant amount of time it takes to renew these documents, some children were out of school for a long period of time (GfK Ukraine 2017). Older children who continued their schooling in the NGCA for a time and then left later in the conflict faced additional problems with their school documents. The certificates of completion of 9th grade issued by the separatist governments of DPR and Lugank People's Republic (LPR) were deemed illegal in the rest of Ukraine. As a result, these children had to retake all exams before entering a new school (GfK Ukraine 2017). This creates a significant added burden for students.

Poor knowledge of the Ukrainian language is another barrier faced by IDPs from both eastern Ukraine and Crimea. Study of the Ukrainian language was often limited in these regions in the pre-war period, and many of these children attended schools where they received their education in the Russian language, or in Tartar in the case of Crimea. In 2014, the NGCA school curriculum was altered to exclude the Ukrainian language altogether. This is a considerable problem for young children in particular who are just beginning school in the NGCA. They may face difficulties in learning in Ukrainian if they end up being displaced later on or when the Donbas comes back under government control and resumes education in Ukrainian. IDPs without a firm grasp of the Ukrainian language face extra difficulties in their new schools where Ukrainian is the main language of instruction.

IDP children who successfully register and enroll in new schools still suffer from psychological trauma which may affect their ability to successfully integrate into their new communities and classrooms. These social difficulties can distract from and impede learning. The OOSC survey indicates that those who experience interpersonal problems with teachers and classmates at school tend to skip classes (GfK Ukraine 2017). Most teachers in Ukraine are not equipped with the skills to deal with war-related trauma experienced by those who have witnessed violence and military conflict. IDP children also face difficulties interacting with local children. Speaking with IDPs in Vinnytsia, some shared how many of the community's good intentions often led to further difficulties; oftentimes IDP children were pulled out of class in front of their schoolmates and showered with gifts from charities, or singled out in groups and removed in the middle of the school day to receive psychological counseling. Despite the goodwill behind these actions, IDP children reported feeling uncomfortable as a result of this positive discrimination. These children want to fit in and feel normal, and actions that highlight their "otherness" impede their full integration into their new schools.

Responses from the Ukrainian Government

The Ukrainian government has taken some actions to respond to the educational needs of children near the contact line and IDP children. One action taken by the government is to ensure that IDPs can skip the line in order to register young children for kindergarten. Regular citizens must register at least one year in advance due to long lines and wait times. However, there is no specific state program aimed at addressing the problem of access to education for IDP children. The Ministry of Education and Science of Ukraine has delegated the responsibility of dealing with IDPs to regional, district, and municipal education bodies. With little oversight or central control, this has resulted in some of the problems mentioned earlier that IDPs shared with us about their personal experiences. There appeared to be no repercussions for a local administrator who does not want to accept the registration of an IDP family because they will not be responsible for paying full price for school meals or for any other reason. Complaints about this discrimination can take a long time to be heard and resolved, resulting in longer gaps in a child's education. There is also a lack of funding for schools experiencing an influx of new IDP students. This problem is amplified by the fact the IDPs have settled unevenly throughout Ukraine. According to UNHCR data Kharkiv, Dnipro and Zaporizhia oblasts host a disproportionately large number of IDPs compared to other oblasts (GfK Ukraine 2017).

The Ministry for Temporarily Occupied Territories and Internally Displaced Persons has an Action Plan directed at the implementation of certain principles of internal state policy on certain areas of Donetsk and Luhansk regions where public authorities temporarily do not exercise their powers. One aspect of this Action Plan includes ensuring the access to Ukrainian education for children residing within the NGCA. To carry this out, a special platform was created allowing for distance education to service children living in the NGCA who cannot leave and have no access to the study of Ukrainian history—a contested subject and one which is being rewritten by the separatists. There are also places being used for basic education close to the contact line within the GCA, and people from the NGCA can go to these places on certain days for consultation with teachers. In 2016, the government adopted a law to allow citizens from the NGCA to cross into the GCA for education. These schools service only about 180 students now, but, according to Minister Vadym Chernysh, this is "just the beginning" (SAIS Group Meeting, Kyiv, 24 March 2017).

The government of Ukraine has also implemented procedures to recognize the level of education obtained by students in the NGCA without recognizing the authority of non-state groups operating there so that those students can transfer to secondary schools and universities in the rest of Ukraine. The government is also preparing legal enactments to widen their capabilities and ensure that students have access to universities within the GCA by arranging free housing, improving the process of approving student documents, and arranging special allocations for IDPs at universities (SAIS Group Meeting, Kyiv, 24 March 2017).

Responses from Civil Society Organization and NGOs

There are many national and international NGOs and civil society organizations working to address the issue of access to education for students remaining within the NGCA, those near the contact line on either side, as well as for IDP children. We had the opportunity to speak with some of these organizations that are addressing the need to integrate IDP children into local communities through grassroots efforts. Natalia Karbowska of the Ukrainian Women's Fund shared how a group of women from Donetsk created their own kindergarten in their new city of Vinnytsia because of their strong desire to bring together IDP and local children. An organizer of another group which we met with brought IDP children and adults together through a music program meant to give children a traditional Ukrainian song to bring back home as a tool for understanding and peacebuilding when they return to their homes in the east.

On the international level, the Education Cluster co-led by UNICEF and Save the Children, is working in eastern Ukraine to support the authorities in ensuring access to education for children affected by the crisis. As of December 2016, the Ukraine Education Cluster helped 192,600 conflict-affected children and teachers to gain access to education in emergency programs implemented by Education Cluster partners (Ukraine Education Cluster 2016). Education Cluster partners ensure emergency repairs to school buildings, provide school equipment and school supply kits, oversee capacity building, and provide non-formal and life-skills education. They also provide mine risk education (Ukraine Education Cluster 2016).

The European Union (EU) and UNICEF launched the EU Children of Peace project in November 2015 to benefit schools and education facilities in Donetsk, Luhansk, Kharkiv, Dnipropetrovsk, and Zaporizhia oblasts. The project provides psychological support to build resilience and aims to develop life skills for children and their families affected by the conflict while helping them to integrate into their new communities. This project is meant to reach 300,000 children and their parents over its lifespan (UNICEF 18 November 2015).

Education for Good or Ill

In times of conflict curriculum can become politicized and schooling can become a conduit to fuel more fighting. This is happening in the NGCA, where separatist officials have rewritten the history curriculum that is being taught in schools to provide an alternate version of Ukrainian history. At the beginning of the conflict, the Ministry of Education in the separatist-controlled areas instructed history teachers to throw out their textbooks. These textbooks were considered problematic because they taught that the Ukrainian famine of 1932-33, which left nearly 3.3 million dead, was a result of Stalin-era policies forcing collectivization and exporting Ukraine grain abroad. Half way through the 2015 school year, the separatist Ministry of Education came out with

"Materials for the Questions of History Teaching." This new curriculum projects a softened view of the Soviet Union's historical interactions with Ukraine, downplaying the USSR's role in the famine and characterizing the famine as "unavoidable." This newly installed history curriculum also concentrates on ties between the Donetsk region and Russia (Kramer 2015). This attempt by the separatists to justify their uprising by indoctrinating children with a revisionist version of Ukrainian history may have a damaging, lasting impact even once the conflict is solved and children from the NGCA and the GCA return to school together.

Education is also being used as a tool for positive developments, however. This conflict has created awareness in Ukraine of the importance of teaching children peace-building, human rights, and media literacy. Education in how to recognize propaganda and fake news stories is an especially important skill in a country where Russia aggressively wages misinformation campaigns about events in Ukraine through the media (see chapter by Gabriella Huddart). These efforts are being made at the grassroots level by civil society organizations and international groups. Successful examples should be adopted by the government and implemented on a state level.

Our research team had the opportunity to meet with a group of journalism students from Donetsk University, which relocated to Vinnytsia after the conflict began, who have started a project training teachers on how to teach their students to recognize propaganda, hate speech, and fake news. With materials and assistance from StopFake.org, a group that specializes in debunking fake news about Ukraine, as well as the Academy of Ukrainian Press, these students reached a number of classrooms in Vinnytsia (SAIS Group Meeting at Donetsk University, Vinnytsia, 23 March 2017). Media literacy is an important skill in the midst of this particular conflict not only because of aggressive Russian propaganda campaigns, but also because false stories that are poorly fact-checked often make their way into mainstream Ukrainian media. It is important to teach this generation of Ukrainians resilience against this type of pernicious attempt at fracturing society.

Another heartening effort is the multi-national collaboration between USC Shoah Foundation; VAAD, the association of Jewish organizations and communities of Ukraine; and the German foundation Remembrance, Responsibility and Future (EVZ)'s

"Teaching Human Rights" program which hosted two seminars for educators from the conflict areas in Sloviansk, Ukraine in December of 2016. The seminars were conducted for vice principals, school psychologists and social workers from the Donetsk region who work with IDPs. The teacher's guide titled "Where do Human Rights Begin: Lessons from History and Contemporary Approaches" was meant to convey important skills for educators near the conflict zones to "reflect on their own situation, choices, and pedagogical strategies" (USC Shoah Foundation 2016). This training is important as it helps educators speak with children affected by the conflict and teaches students to value human rights and how to defend them. These are vital values to instill in this generation of Ukrainian youth in order to help avoid conflicts and human rights violations in the future.

Conclusion

Addressing the needs of children affected by this conflict will not only ensure their personal growth and development as individuals, but also help create a future society in Ukraine that is unified, cohesive, resilient, values human rights, and respects differences. Like most crises, this one is not easy to solve. Ukrainian officials and experts in the international community agree that the conflict raging in eastern Ukraine between separatists, with active support from Russia, and Ukrainian Armed Forces will not end any time soon. One clear message that emerged from our study trip is that there does not appear to be a single, unified vision of how to move forward in resolving this conflict. As time ticks by and the war rages on with daily ceasefire violations, hundreds of thousands of children are missing out on their right to be educated in nurturing and safe environments. This guarantees that the effects of this war will be felt for them personally long after it comes to an end. These missed educational opportunities and the resulting loss in human capital will have negative consequences for the economic growth of the Donbas region in the medium to long term. The Ukrainian government and the international community must urgently respond to the needs of students within the NGCA, those on both sides of the contact line, and the IDPs who have fled their homes. A concerted effort between all active parties, government, civil society and international organizations is needed, as well as an increase in funding specifically for this purpose.

Without immediate attention to this issue, the youth of today who represent Ukraine's future may suffer irreparably.

Recommendations

International standards dictate that every child has the right to education, as laid out in the 1948 Universal Declaration of Human Rights and the 1959 UN Declaration of the Rights of the Child. The war in eastern Ukraine has no end in sight, but children cannot wait for a political resolution to the conflict before their educational needs are met. Though the Ukrainian government and national and international civil society organizations and NGOs are making strides to ensure access to education for children affected by the conflict, there are a number of policies that should be implemented to ensure that each child has immediate access to safe, quality schooling that addresses their specific needs as children impacted by military violence. This will ensure not only personal growth, but will also contribute to a cohesive society and provide economic returns for both the individual and the nation.

To the Ukrainian Government

- **Immediately enact laws that remove all barriers to school registration for IDPs,** including **easing requirements for documentation** that may be inaccessible.
- **Ensure oversight that punishes any attempts to deny school registration to IDPs.**
- **Hire more teachers in areas with high volumes of IDPs** in order to reduce the strain on resources and to insure against resentment that it can create among local populations.
- **Provide for the special needs of IDP children**, including psychological support and additional tutoring in the Ukrainian language.
- **Enact a law obliging IDP parents to immediately enroll their children into new schools upon relocation** to cut short interruptions in schooling.

- **Waive fees for IDP children to participate in afterschool and extracurricular activities**, such as sports and clubs, to ensure integration into their new community.
- **Implement state-wide curriculum in peacebuilding, conflict resolution, human rights education, and media literacy.**
- **Forbid the use of school buildings by the Ukrainian Armed Forces as well as locating armed positions near schools.**
- **Invest the funds necessary to rapidly expand the reach of the virtual education effort** created by the Ministry of Temporarily Occupied Territories and Internally Displaced Persons so that it reaches all children living within the NGCA

<u>To the Trilateral Contract Group's subcommittee on Humanitarian Issues</u>
- **Establish an agreement with separatist forces to unsure that they cease occupations of school buildings within the NGCA.**

<u>To the Education Cluster in Ukraine</u>
- For children who are not able to attend school due to destroyed infrastructure or fear of mines and unexploded ordinances, **Interactive Radio Instruction should be implemented**. Radio delivery of high quality curriculum with local monitoring by trained individuals has proven successful in other situations.

<u>To the NGO/International Community</u>
- **Set aside funding to address the secondary costs of schooling such as lunch fees, uniforms, transportation, and supplies.**
- **Set aside funding to support the government of Ukraine in hiring extra teachers and trained psychologists.**

The Realities of the Conflict for Minorities:
The Experience of Crimean Tatars, Roma, and Jews

Anna Goodman

Almost every official in Ukraine is very proud of what they describe as their 'homogenous' country, a word in this context that signifies a general welcoming of various ethnicities and races into a society. And it is true that there are many ethnicities that have been welcomed with comparative ease. However, there are those that have not shared in that welcome. This paper looks at three specific groups: the Crimean Tatars, the Roma, and the Ukrainian Jews, exploring their history within the territory now identified as Ukraine and their relationship with Ukrainian society, investigating these dynamics were created and how they have been impacted by the conflict in the east.

Role in Ukrainian History

Of the three groups, the Roma are perhaps the latest arrivals and at the same time the least accepted. Most scholars agree that the Roma reached Ukraine sometime in the 15th century (*BBC News* 2016). Although many were kept as slaves in Romania during this time period, others were welcomed as pilgrims and penitents in Ukraine until 1500, when they were labeled as Turkish spies, hunted, and killed in the first Roma Genocide. During the Holocaust, Nazis killed over 500,000 Roma, and after the war there was no aid and no recognition on either side of the iron curtain of their losses until modern times. After the fall of the USSR, anti-Roma violence defied expectations and rose dramatically (*BBC News* 2016). Despite this, there are now estimated to be between 42,000–400,000 currently living in Ukraine, with their lack of appropriate documentation making it impossible to be certain as to their real numbers (US Department of State 2008).

The Jews have perhaps the second longest presence in the region of the three groups. They first arrived in Kyivan Rus from Palestine, Byzantium, and Persia in the 10th century AD. Throughout this early era, Jews were discriminated against due not only to their religion but also to their place as intermediaries between the Polish elite and the Ukrainian peasants. In later centuries, Jews suffered from extreme Judaea-phobia on part of the Russian authorities and were eventually confined to the "Pale Settlement" within Ukraine, although some intellectuals were part of a long-running experiment by Russian rulers to make ideal educated citizens. Despite this treatment, the region remained a major center of Jewish life. Unfortunately, with the rise of Stalin and the advent of World War II, Jews became the main targets of both the Nazis and their Ukrainian collaborators, who believed the Germans would liberate them from Stalin's strangle-hold. There was resistance on part of the Ukrainians, but the Nazis played up the ties between Jews and Bolshevism and gave others little choice, manipulating many Ukrainians towards violent measures. By 1943, almost all Jews in Nazi occupied Ukraine were dead. After the war, Stalin's hostility towards Jews led to purges of the remaining population. Discrimination against Jews continued throughout the Cold War but was lessened dramatically with Ukraine's independence (Petrovskiĭ-Shtern 2014, 1-59).

The population known as the Crimean Tatars is actually a heterogeneous group descended from the many waves of settlement that had been experienced by the peninsula since human habitation began. Crimean Tatars can be divided into two general categories; those descending from the Mongols, known as Nagois, and those descending from an amalgamation of coastal dwellers (including Greeks and Italian merchants, among others) known as the Tat-Tatars. The Crimean Khanate, a once independent kingdom based around a slave-trading economy, fell under the authority of the Russian Empire in 1783 with the decline of the Ottomans. Life got increasingly difficult, resulting in nearly one-third of the Crimean Tatar population emigrating. Eventually, on May 18th, 1944 Stalin had the entire Crimean Tatar population deported to the Central Asian territories. After Gorbachev came to power he gradually granted Crimean Tatars the right to return, officially denouncing Stalin's deportation policies. Upon their return, they democratically elected a parallel parliament called the Mejlis to ensure Crimean Tatar representation. By 1993, over 259,000 or over half of the Crimean Tatar population had returned to the peninsula (Williams 2015).

Pre- Conflict–Present Day (2000-2012)

Now that a foundation has been laid around the history of these three groups, it is important to understand the general trends in ethnocentrism and racism within modern day Ukraine to see where these three groups lie on the spectrum of treatment. Generally, since 2000 there has been a growing level of ethnic intolerance and impunity for perpetrators that is becoming "more systemic and brutal" within Ukraine. Only 5-10% of all hate crimes are labeled as such in reports, and many police do not collect statistics on these types of crimes at all (US Department of State 2008). It is not uncommon to hear about document checks targeting those with different skin colors and harassment that has resulted in illegal detentions accompanied by beatings or ill treatment. Aside from mistreatment from the role of the authorities, this growing intolerance has led to a difficulty accessing goods and services (ECRI 2012), attacks by Neo-Nazis and separatists (Human Rights Watch 2006), and blatant racist and ethno-centrist comments by both media and politicians, including the Central News Agency Union, which described one protest as "Negro-lovers gathered in Kyiv" (US Department of State 2008).

Further complicating things, Ukraine lacks a truly comprehensive set of civil and administrative anti-discrimination laws (Human Rights Watch 2006). For example, hate speech and the publishing of discriminatory pamphlets and newsletters are rarely prosecuted. Yet, despite this lack of a comprehensive approach, there are laws that address the treatment of national minorities. One example would be the 1992 Law on National Minorities, which gives general guarantee for the protection of ethnic groups (US Department of State 2008). However, the 1992 law only applies to citizens and there are no real regulations on its implementation. Another regulation is Article 161 of the Criminal Code, which says that incitement to ethnic or religious hatred is punishable. But direct intent must be proven, something that many justice systems find difficult, so many perpetrators are charged with mere hooliganism and receive a lesser sentence for their actions than if they had been charged with incitement (US Department of State 2008). In an attempt to further address the issue, a special unit was created to combat xenophobia in 2008 and a Law on the Principles of Preventing and Combatting Discrimination was created in 2012 (OSCE 2014). While these new changes have been able to legally prohibit direct and indirect discrimination, as with the previous laws, they lack clear and complete definitions and the institutional provisions necessary to ensure their effective implementation (OSCE 2014). Overall, there have been many attempts to address the issue through the creation of laws, regulations, and task forces, but issues of implementation prevent them from protecting the vulnerable populations in question.

Given their unique historical experiences within Ukraine, it should be no surprise that all three groups have come to be treated very differently by the general central European population of Ukraine. The Roma have come to be treated particularly harshly. Of the three groups, the Roma are generally the most frequent victims of outright police abuse (Human Rights Watch 2006). They also suffer from harsh government and societal discrimination (US Department of State 2008). For them, finding and maintaining employment is incredibly difficult. Only 21% of the official 42,000 were permanently employed at the time of the Department of State report in 2008 and there were no government programs aimed at improving Roma employability as of 2014 (OSCE 2014). Roma are also frequently evicted, kicked off of transportation, beaten by the general Ukrainian population, and suffer from numerous instances of police intimidation tactics. Some instances of 'hooliganism' against Roma include burning down settlements, throwing Molotov cocktails at them, and murder (OSCE 2014).

The main challenges facing attempts at integrating Roma into Ukrainian populations and adequately addressing their needs include three major factors. The first is that many of the Roma lack official documents/identity cards (OSCE 2014). The Ministry of Social Affairs is trying to help register the Roma, but no comprehensive policies to do so had been put in place as of 2014. The second factor lies in the difficulties Roma have in accessing education, healthcare, and employment. In terms of education, Roma children have been basically segregated into Roma-only schools, where the lack of any pre-K education and low levels of Ukrainian language proficiency have left them behind the curve. However, despite this Ukrainians have taken action and included Romani history and culture in their curriculum (OSCE 2014). Without adequate documentation, healthcare has become unaffordable in Ukraine (US Department of State 2008), to the point where life expectancy among the Roma is actually 10-15 years lower than the national average (Human Rights Watch 2016). Finally, there is a general low level of awareness of their rights and available redress mechanisms, so few are able to address their mistreatment (OSCE 2014).

The government has made efforts to address the situation. The Parliament's Human Rights Committee did hold a hearing on the situation of the Romani in 2005, and a Strategy on the Protection and Integration of the Roma National Minority into Ukrainian Society was designed (OSCE 2014). This is a good sign that the government has recognized that something must be done about the issue. However, there is still a long way to go.

On the other side of the treatment spectrum lays the relationship between Jews and Ukrainians, which is generally amicable. Jewish monitors of anti-Semitism found levels of physical and media attacks against Jews to be very low when compared to other areas in Europe and Russia (Kuzio 2016). Even Prime Minister Volodymyr Groysman comes from a Jewish background, as well as many of the oligarchs (Kuzio 2016). However, the key word there is 'generally.' There are still multiple instances of violence carried out against Jews in Ukraine, and discrimination and hate speech have an undeniable place in society. Some examples include four attacks on rabbis in 2008, one involving noxious gas, and vandalism in synagogues, cemeteries, and holocaust monuments (US Department of State 2008). Anti-Semitic hate speech is also relatively easy to find in Ukraine, with small publications and irregular newsletters containing anti-Semitic messages being spread throughout the populace. Jews have also suffered discrimination through difficulties in buying and leasing property (US Department of State 2008).

For Crimean Tatars, life since Ukrainian independence has been generally difficult for many of the returnees. Having been excluded from settling on the coast, many are forced to live in shacks along the margins of urban areas where it was difficult for white-collar workers to adapt. There, they are stuck living in settlements that are often ill-equipped to support an adequate standard of living, lacking water or electricity, resulting in a deterioration of health among the Crimean Tatar population. Moreover, Ukrainian citizenship laws excluded many returnees from gaining citizenship until 1999, until recently leaving them—like the Roma—unable to access medical treatment, schooling, pensions, voting, etc. They suffer constant anti-Tatar discrimination and social, economic, and political marginalization, with even government policies deliberately designed to exclude them from land ownership (Williams 2015).

Specific Conflict Impact

Of the three, the group that has perhaps been most impacted by the eruption of conflict within Ukraine have been the Crimean Tatars. Within the Crimean peninsula, Crimean Tatars have become the main targeted ethnic group by the occupying Russians as they are seen as a threat to the occupation. A significant sign of Russia's intentions can be seen in the April 26, 2016, declaration of the Mejlis of the Crimean Tatars as an extremist organization and its subsequent banning by "the Supreme Court" of Crimea. This meant that almost all Crimean Tatars—having participated in Mejlis activities or having some connection to representatives—were legally considered criminals and labeled as extremists among Crimean society. This gave the Russians an excuse to arrest almost any Crimean Tatar with impunity (Andreyuk, Asanova, and Avseyushkin 2016, 5).

Since the ban, numerous members of the community have been prosecuted either due to this excuse (usually labeled as extremism, incitement to hatred), due to criticism of the Russian Federation, or due to a connection with Hizb ut-tahir, a Muslim group legal in almost every country but the Russian Federation. In total, as of December 2016, there were 38 enforced disappearances, 15 of which have not been found—including 11 Tatars—and six of which were discovered dead—all of whom were Tatars. There have also been mass searches, most thinly disguised attempts to collect identification data on the majority of the Crimean Tatar population, detentions, arrests, torture and forced psychiatric examinations (Andreyuk, Asanova, and Avseyushkin 2016, 5).

Religious and cultural persecution against the Crimean Tatar has become pervasive throughout the peninsula. The government has imposed bans on public gatherings commemorating culturally important days, including the anniversary of the 1944 deportation (IPHR 2016, 115). Mosques have been raided or vandalized under guise of fighting extremism, with Russian security forces planting banned literature in mosques to allow them to initiate criminal cases (Andreyuk, Asanova, and Avseyushkin 2016, 12). Most madrassas have been shut down, with the few remaining being put under Russian control. Memorials to the 1944 deportation and other monuments of historical and cultural significance have been destroyed or defaced (IPHR 2016, 115). Finally, and perhaps most pervasively, the Russian state has disseminated propaganda painting the

Crimean Tatars as Muslim extremists and terrorists, inciting acts of discrimination-based violence and heightening tensions within the communities of Crimea.

Further, the Crimean Tatar population has been one of the main targets for expulsion and land grabs, mirroring their 1940s deportation. Of the 60,000 who have been forcibly displaced as of 2016, it is likely that half were Crimean Tatar. Moreover, the imposition of Russian citizenship has put some 95,000 members of the Crimean population in danger of being deported (IPHR 2016, 91). Prominent religious and cultural leaders have already been barred from being able to return to the Peninsula.

However, within the un-contested parts of Ukraine, Crimeans have found an increasing sense of welcome from the general population. According to one of the Crimean Tatars I was able to talk to, they have found their general treatment to be much friendlier than before, in response, they believe, to the solidarity Ukrainians feel with Crimean Tatars in the face of Russian aggression, a solidarity echoed in many of our meetings with politicians and advisors. Another individual observed that many Ukrainians are finally recognizing Crimea as the home of Crimean Tatars, and not just the location of their dachas and summer vacations. There were also specific programs created by IDP assistance organizations to support the transition and resettlement of orthodox Tatars to other regions within Ukraine, though many have recently been shuttered with the slowing flow of Crimean Tatars.

As for the Roma, the conflict has mostly led to mixed consequences for their population. On the negative side, the funding necessary for carrying out the Strategy on Protection, and the more recently created Roadmap of Security and Integration of the Roma minority until 2020, is not available, as it has been supplanted by the conflict effort. Moreover, many Roma have been displaced from east Ukraine by the separatists. I was able to uncover the existence of some organizations working on Roma issues during our trip; we were informed of one working on Roma women's issues. However, there was no knowledge of any organization with programing specifically addressing the needs of Roma IDPs. Thankfully, there have been government initiatives to aid the displaced Roma by facilitating the provision of Ukrainian passports to those leaving conflict areas, including 4,400 over the last two years. Moreover, groups like the Inter-Ministerial Working Group for the Implementation of the Roma Integration Strategy were formed to bring together state and local representatives as well as Roma to address issues like documentation and census taking, and attempts were made to create an association between Roma groups to strengthen their voice (OHCHR 2016).

Finally, the impact of the conflict on Jews in Ukraine is complex, including aspects of anti-Semitism and solidarity, as well as economic push factors. Perhaps one of the most significant results from the conflict is not a change in the treatment of the Jews in Ukraine, but instead is their willingness to remain in the country itself. Since the conflict began, between 6,000 and 8,000 Jews have been leaving Ukraine a year. Now, most of those who are left in Donbas are the elderly who can't, or won't, leave their homes. The majority of this diaspora is leaving for Israel at the encouragement of Israeli missions in Ukraine, who have set up transition shelters catering to Jewish IDPs where they can receive both humanitarian support and aid for a potential transition to Israeli nationality. While many fear anti-Semitic actions, this emigration is primarily due to economic concerns. Most see the opportunity to move to Israel as the chance to rebuild their lives and find jobs, which are sorely lacking in Ukraine (Englehart 2017). This is all serving to undermine the post-91 renaissance that Jewish communities in Ukraine have been building towards, leaving a rebirth of the pre-war Jewish society in doubt.

Jews are being also used as propaganda tools by both sides of the conflict. The general argument used by both separatists and pro-Ukrainians is that the other side is anti-Semitic and willing to target the remaining Jewish population. This is a method not only of gaining the support of Jews but also of undermining the perceived level of morality of the other side. On the pro-Ukrainian side, for example, many are putting the blame for anti-Semitic violence and harassment on thugs paid by Russia. Unfortunately, I was not able to come across anything confirming or discrediting these allegations, and no one on our trip cared to comment on this issue. In fact, one of the best examples of verbal gymnastics occurred in response to this particular question. Frustratingly, many speakers did their best to avoid the questions, repeating that Ukraine was a welcoming melting pot. Yet, despite this claim each side exhibits behaviors that belie this position as the protector of the Jewish people.

On the separatist side, there is prevalent Russian anti-Semitism in Donbas where it has become an important component of the official ideology of the separatist regime.

This is a reaction to the fact that the majority of Jews supported the Maidan movement. Separatist political leaders accuse Ukrainian leaders of being Jews who changed their names, believing this accusation will undermine their authority among Ukrainians. There is also a high level of anti-Semitism in public discourse within these regions. This has been one of the primary factors in causing Jews to flee Donbas, although the economic situation is the main force behind emigration out of Ukraine itself (Kuzio 2016).

On the Ukrainian side, many claim that the strong pro-Ukrainian stance of much of the Jewish population has led to an increase in efforts to reach out to the Jewish community. Poroshenko himself is working to promote the acceptance of Jews in Ukraine, through extending well wishes during high holy days—this past Passover included—and building memorials. However, these actions are generally undermined by efforts to minimize the tragedy of the Jewish experience in Ukraine during the Holocaust. There has been a trend towards both downplaying the genocide and highlighting the Ukrainian losses in order to obscure the real history. Moreover, there has been pressure towards emphasizing the Jewish heritage of perpetrators of Holodomor, implying their ethnicity had a role in the tragedy (Baltic Worlds 2011). The Ukrainian government has also consistently failed to call out hate speech used in popular media and political discourse. Most recently, at a march in January 2017 commemorating controversial nationalist Stepan Bandera, a hero to many Ukrainians for his part in WWII, thousands marched through Kyiv chanting "Jews out" (Hoffman 2017). The government has failed to condemn their words despite calls from the Jewish community. Both the extreme left and extreme right parties remain a threat to Jewish wellbeing in Ukraine. Svaboda, though its popularity has waned, enjoyed widespread support at the start of the conflict, leading many Jews to be concerned about potential pogroms. In general, although Jews are often treated better in Ukraine than in the rest of Europe (Kuzio 2016), there is still anti-Semitism within the country and a danger of extremists on either side acting upon that sentiment.

Conclusion

The treatment of these groups must be addressed. Along with the higher-level anti-corruption efforts, measures need to be taken to ensure that effort is put into altering police patterns of behavior. Hate crimes need to be labeled and prosecuted as what they are, not as hooliganism. Hate speech must also be taken to task, despite the difficulty in doing so, otherwise it will continue to proliferate and poison the potential for healthy, interethnic interactions and dialogues. For the Romani, the document checks, arbitrary detentions, and abuse must be halted and biases towards Romani criminality must be addressed in order to win the trust of the Romani community and begin to address the economic and social issues that keep them on the fringes of Ukrainian society. Finally, the Crimean Tatars have seen their relationship with everyday Ukrainians improve with the impact of the crisis, but their vulnerability in Crimea and in the occupied territories has increased exponentially. Though this may be a daunting list of efforts to some, they are undeniably necessary for Ukraine's transformation into a nation respecting the human rights of all of its citizens. I look forward to see how Ukraine's efforts in this domain progress.

Recommendations

<u>To the Ukrainian Government</u>
- **Compile and release official statistics on discrimination within Ukraine** to inform the populace of the true scope of the issue, allowing them the chance to address the issue themselves through daily life and civil society efforts.
- **Work to implement already-written policies criminalizing discrimination through campaigns to address corruption** at the lowest levels and trainings around minority rights and sensitivity. Address specifically the perception of Roma as criminals.
- **Offer official condemnation of anti-Semitic actions** in order to illustrate to the Jewish community that the government will protect them.
- **Recognize the controversial role in anti-Semitic violence that many of Ukraine's nationalist heroes played during WWII.**
- **Work with Jewish civil society organizations** to ensure that Jewish IDPs are not only supported but are given incentive to stay in Ukraine and not emigrate to Israel.

- **Create programs encouraging cross-ethnic exposure and understanding** in small towns and villages where Jews, Crimeans, and Roma do not have a presence. This will help combat instances of ethnocentric-based violence by breaking the stereotypes held by some Ukrainians toward persons belonging to minorities.

- **Actively** and not passively **preserve remaining Jewish historical sites.**

- Should Ukraine regain Crimea, **ameliorate land-owning laws to make it easier for Crimean Tatars to own property. Provide support for the return of Crimeans to the region**, and also for the reconstruction and cleaning of mosques and memorials destroyed or vandalized during the occupation.

- **Support efforts to spread awareness and offer aid to displaced Crimeans.**

- **Ensure the provision of enough resources towards efforts to provide documentation to the Roma, as well as the Strategic Plan and the Road Map.** This would allow Roma to more easily pursue education, employment, shelter, and healthcare, helping to integrate them more into Ukrainian society.

To Ukrainian NGOs

- **Reach out to Roma organizations to potentially coordinate and support Roma fleeing the conflict zones and their reintegration into society.**

- **Reach out to Jewish organizations to collaborate on inter-cultural understanding events**, potentially involving dialogues, radio shows, and community level discussions to disassociate anti-Zionism from anti-Semitism.

- **Continue to support efforts to disseminate information on human rights violations in Crimea**, including the targeting of Crimean Tatars.

The Status of Crimean Tatars Under Russian Occupation

Christina Pushaw

Historical Context

When the international community discusses the Ukraine crisis, the focus is often on the entrenched hybrid conflict in the Donbas region between pro-Russian forces and the Ukrainian military. Indeed, Russia's annexation of the Crimean Peninsula in March 2014 has often been called a *"fait accompli,"* even from the earliest days of Russian intervention (Seselgyte 2017). However, this paper argues that the "frozen" conflict in Crimea does not diminish the strategic and humanitarian significance of the region. Although the *de facto* return of Crimea to Ukrainian control is unlikely in the foreseeable future, regional and international stakeholders should not only continue to condemn Russia's occupation of the peninsula, but also draw attention to the alleged human rights abuses that disproportionately affect the native inhabitants of the peninsula—the Crimean Tatars.

Crimean Tatars, a majority-Muslim Turkic ethnic group, comprised the majority of Crimea's population until the middle of the 19th century (Troynitski 1905). During World War II, the Stalin regime propagated the notion that the Tatars and other minority groups were potential "fifth columns" of resistance to Soviet authority (Pohl 2010; Nekrich 1979). Indeed, several thousand Tatars likely served in anti-Soviet, German-aligned battalions, but Soviet leaders characterized the entire population—most of whom were loyal to the government—as potential traitors and Nazi collaborators (Kulbaev and Khegai 2000). Therefore, when Soviet secret service head Lavrentiy Beria ordered the mass deportation of over 200,000 Tatars from Crimea to remote regions of Central Asia in 1944, he justified the decision by appealing to national security concerns (The Kremlin 1944; Kinstler 2014). Conditions during the evacuation were so harsh that many Tatars died in the process, mostly due to dehydration and disease (Naimark 2002). Official Soviet statistics likely underestimated the deportation's casualties, placing the number of deaths at 5% of the population (RFE/RL 1991) and an even larger percentage died of starvation in the months after resettlement in Uzbekistan (Embassy of Ukraine 2015). Crimean Tatars never fully integrated with native Central Asian populations, and in seeking repatriation, they protested the Soviet government's restrictions on movement in the decades after the deportation. After the beginning of liberalizing reforms under Mikhail Gorbachev in the 1980s, and especially since the collapse of the Soviet Union in the early 1990s, Crimean Tatars began returning to their ancestral homeland in large migration waves (Williams 2001). Just before Crimea's annexation in 2014, Crimean Tatars constituted approximately 12% of the peninsula's population (Said 2014). After Ukraine's Maidan Revolution culminated in the ouster of President Viktor Yanukovych amid popular demands for Ukraine to break away from the Russian sphere of influence, the Russian government acted swiftly to assert control over the strategically important region of Crimea. Russian special forces seized the peninsula, the home of several Russian military installations including the Black Sea Fleet in Sevastopol. Russia met with no notable resistance from the disorganized Ukrainian armed forces, and faced only condemnation but no actual retaliation from a Ukrainian government in turmoil.

In contrast to most inhabitants of Crimea, Tatars disproportionately opposed Russian annexation. In fact, prominent Crimean Tatar political leaders condemned Russia's move as illegal (RFE/RL 2014). Most Crimean Tatars therefore boycotted the March 2014 referendum on Russian annexation, voicing concerns about Russian oppression of minorities and disregard for human rights (Shishkin and Troianovski 2014) that were also apparent in reports from UN monitors from the same time period (Donath 2014). Protests involving thousands of Crimean Tatars formed human chains to block roads, with participants holding signs declaring Crimea as part of Ukraine (Pravda.ua 2014). Representatives of the Kyiv-based NGO Crimea SOS referred to the initiative as a "so-called referendum," noting that Tatar families who felt unsafe began leaving Crimea as early as March 2014 (SAIS Group Meeting, Kyiv, 24 March 2017). Since the occupation, Crimea has been effectively isolated from the rest of Ukraine. Because of the military significance of the peninsula, the Russian government is especially wary of potential subversion and resistance among Crimea residents (SAIS Group Meeting, Kyiv, 24 March 2017). Today, Crimea is nearly completely integrated into Russian administrative structures. Diplomas, licenses and identification documents of Crimean residents are recognized in Russia, and for all intents and purposes, most Crimeans are treated as Russian citizens—though very few states have recognized the transfer of Crimea to Russian sovereignty as being legal under international law.

The situation of Crimean Tatars as a historically marginalized religious and ethnic minority is especially precarious at present, because the Russian government essentially prevents international human rights and independent media observers from operating on the peninsula. A spate of suspicious deaths, disappearances, and suppression of community leaders has devastated the Crimean Tatar community since 2014. Thousands have migrated to Ukrainian government-controlled territories to escape persecution and seek better opportunities. Today, grassroots organizations operating in mainland Ukraine provide most of the scant factual information on the condition of Crimean Tatars under Russian authority, and the Crimean Parliament (Mejlis) in exile also attempts to bring attention to the alleged human rights violations.

The purpose of this chapter is to assess the conditions of Crimean Tatars in annexed Crimea, as well as Crimean Tatar IDPs elsewhere in Ukraine.[6] This analysis will support policy recommendations to improve the legal, social, and political conditions facing Tatars in Crimea as well as those who have migrated to mainland Ukraine. The impact of Russian disinformation in Crimea vis-à-vis the Crimean Tatars will receive special attention, as state-backed media have constructed a similar narrative—regarding potential threats from the minority group—to that which justified the deportation and decimation of the Crimean Tatars in 1944. Ultimately, an evidence-based assessment to raise awareness of the actual situation of Crimean Tatars, as well as efforts to integrate this group into Ukrainian political life, will assist conflict resolution by addressing the informational component of Russian hybrid warfare.

In the framework of conflict management, analysis of political, social, and military developments on minority populations can provide a cornerstone for peaceful conflict resolution. The experience of the contemporary Crimean Tatars, which will be constructed in this paper from interviews with IDPs from Crimea, grassroots organizations active in Kyiv, and scholarly research, reveals the nature and effects of the annexation. Despite the dim prospects for reunifying Crimea with the rest of Ukraine in the near future, it is crucial for the international community not to ignore the plight of

---

[6] See also chapters by Ashley Patton and Anna Goodman regarding Crimean Tatar IDPs in Ukraine.

Crimean Tatars. Moreover, face-to-face negotiation and interpersonal connections form the foundation of conflict management, and those Crimean Tatars who are active in Ukraine's vibrant civil society can function as a vital conduit between the annexed peninsula and the rest of Ukraine.

Threats to Human Rights in Occupied Crimea

At the start of the Russian operation in Crimea, officials attempted to gain support—or at least, compliance—from the Crimean Tatar community. Days before the annexation on March 12, 2014, Russian President Vladimir Putin spoke with longtime Crimean Tatar National Movement leader Mustafa Cemilev, who is perhaps the most visible spokesperson and political activist representing the ethnic group (Olevskiy 2014). Putin requested that Cemilev endorse Russia's plans for occupation and garner support for the referendum from his constituents. In return, Putin promised Cemilev that Russian hegemony in Crimea would preserve the rights of the Tatar population, and indicated that Crimean would be enshrined as an official language of the region in addition to Russian and Ukrainian (Pravda.ua 2014). Cemilev rejected Putin's offer in no uncertain terms, emphasizing the Crimean Tatar community's support for Ukraine's territorial integrity as delineated in numerous documents signed by Russia between 1991 and 1999, including the 1975 Helsinki Final Act as reinforced in the 1991 Charter of Paris and the 1994 Budapest Memorandum (RBC.ru 2014).

The Crimean Tatars' political support for Ukraine, in the context of the rapidly developing conflict with Russia, allegedly caused a rise in discrimination, hate crimes, and human rights violations against the minority group. In Bahkchesaray, Crimean Tatars discovered graffiti of crosses on their homes, widely viewed as an attempt at intimidation of the mostly Muslim community (Izmirli 2014). On March 13, 2014, unidentified pro-Russian activists stripped the Crimean Parliament of the Ukrainian and Tatar letters that had been affixed alongside Russian-language signs, a symbolic declaration of hostility in a place where linguistic identification holds deep political significance.

The next day, the body of Reshat Ametov—a Crimean Tatar who had disappeared from Simferopol earlier in the month after protesting the Russian "invasion"—was discovered (Denber 2014). The suspicious circumstances surrounding Ametov's death, as well as reported signs of torture on his body, mobilized Crimean Tatars to oppose Russia's actions in greater numbers amid an atmosphere of heightened anxiety in the community. Crimea SOS published a graphic detailing the circumstances around Ametov's disappearance, alleging that he was "abducted by three men in military uniform from the so-called Crimean self-defense" unit, and that he was killed by a knife wound to his eye (Crimea SOS 2016). Tatars began sharing anti-Putin messages on social media, calling pro-Russian forces "torturous thugs" responsible for Ametov's murder (Izmirli 2014). This incident was only the first in a number of what Crimean Tatar activists call "enforced disappearances," which authorities in the occupied Crimea used as "instruments for systematic persecution," not only of Crimean Tatars (though they are disproportionately affected), but also of "persons with pro-Ukrainian views," including several Maidan protesters and NGO workers (Crimea SOS 2016).

When Crimea's Russian-backed government signed the annexation treaty with Russia on March 18, news outlets publicized the large pro-Russian rallies surrounding the referendum on the peninsula.[7] However, most Crimean Tatars did not participate in the celebration—the annexation was "the realization of their worst fears" (Williams 2015). Moreover, the return of their homeland to *de facto* Russian control represented a revival of the group's historical traumas: the 1944 deportation, and the first annexation of Crimea by imperial Russia in the 18th century. Crimean Tatar community leaders' characterization of the events of March 2014 as the "third annexation" is notable, because the Ukrainian government's sovereignty over the peninsula had been internationally recognized since Ukraine declared independence from the Soviet Union in 1991, and Crimean Tatars had not considered this period an "annexation" (Kozak 2016).

Several days after the annexation, Mejlis head Refat Chubarov called on the United Nations to send several hundred observers to Crimea, implying that he expected more frequent violations of human rights in the absence of international attention (Chubarov 2014). This absence should not, however, be blamed on international organizations. Notably, Astrid Thors, the OSCE's High Commissioner on National Minorities in 2014, as well as all of her predecessors in this position, had long supported the rights of Crimean Tatars (Baer 2015). However, Russian authorities denied her entry

---

[7] See Gabriella Huddart's chapter on the role of media in the Ukraine conflict.

to the peninsula when she attempted to conduct an official observation mission (Baer 2015). Chubarov alluded to the 1944 deportation as justification for the Crimean Tatars' widespread opposition to Russian domination, stating that his group was "collectively worried that under Russian rule, we can be deported again" (Kozak 2016). The narrative of Crimean Tatar political activists tends to be pro-Ukrainian not because of cultural affinity with Ukrainians, but because of historical persecution of the community under Russian rule. After the 2014 revolution, many Crimean Tatars perceived Ukraine as having a higher potential to build a democratic and pluralistic society that would respect minority rights, in comparison to Russia under Putin.

At present, several grassroots organizations operating throughout Ukraine function as networks for information sharing, political activism, and documentation of alleged human rights abuses against Crimean Tatars by Russian authorities. Crimea SOS, an NGO based in Kyiv with five satellite offices, has built a comprehensive media platform to publicize incidents of discrimination and to combat disinformation about the human rights situation on the occupied peninsula. Crimea SOS initiatives have already had tangible results. In summer 2016, Russian authorities in Crimea labeled Ilmi Umerov, an outspoken representative of the Mejlis who suffers from Parkinson's disease, as a "psychiatric danger" to justify detaining him for one month without due process (Crimea SOS 2016). Crimea SOS volunteers collected as much information as possible on the detainee and contacted partners in international organizations, raising concerns that Umerov was a victim of politically motivated prosecution. Volunteers organized protests on Kyiv's Maidan, drawing the attention of the Ukrainian government and international community, to successfully pressure Russian-backed Crimean authorities and secure the representative's release (SAIS Group Meeting, Kyiv, 24 March 2017). Attorneys from Crimea SOS have also brought a lawsuit against the referendum on annexation, although this symbolic action has had little real-world consequences (SAIS Group Meeting, Kyiv, 24 March 2017).

Despite some successes, civil society organizations still face serious obstacles in defending the rights of the Crimean Tatars living under occupation. Perhaps the most obvious issues are logistical consequences of annexation—effective Russian control over the peninsula and the administrative border prevents the free movement of individuals, while the lack of alternatives to Russian state-backed media precludes the free exchange of ideas. Given the Crimean Tatars' vulnerable status as an ethnic, religious, and linguistic minority group in a strategically significant location, the Russian government has also funded several community groups to represent the population on the peninsula in conformity with pro-Russian objectives (e.g. "Qirim Birgili," or "Crimea Union") (Williams 2015). Chubarov and other community leaders have condemned the approximately 5,000 Crimean Tatars who support such groups as "collaborators" who should be convicted of treason upon the return of Crimea to Ukrainian control (Chubarov 2016).

In this environment, representatives of Crimea SOS claim that the rights of Crimean Tatars have "disappeared" since 2014, and tensions between pro-Russian and pro-Ukrainian forces in a broad sense have disproportionately affected the minority group (SAIS Group Meeting, Kyiv, 24 March 2017). In addition to several mysterious deaths, at least eighteen Crimean Tatars (most of whom are politically active) are currently missing persons, and the community suspects the involvement of Russian authorities in these disappearances (SAIS Group Meeting, Kyiv, 24 March 2017). Thirty-one Crimean Tatars, as of this writing, were imprisoned on the peninsula and in Russia facing charges of "terrorism," which Russian officials tend to use to denote opposition political activities that they consider radical (Crimea SOS 2016). In 2016 alone, Crimea SOS reported three "enforced disappearances" of Crimean Tatar activists, six prison sentences with a total term of 38 years, and 32 new criminal cases prosecuting Crimean Tatars on charges of "terrorism," "espionage," "sabotage," "separatism," "incitement of ethnic hatred," and "illegal acquisition and storage of ammunition" (Crimea SOS 2016). All of these charges have been contested by Crimea SOS and other advocacy groups, who characterize the prosecutions as politically and racially motivated—particularly since most of the defendants are ethnic Tatar political activists. In addition, several of the accused have been detained in Russian prisons awaiting sentencing for over a year, which is a violation of their rights to due process. Dozens more have been subjected to searches without warrants, and at least seven people in Crimea were reportedly forced to undergo psychiatric examinations in violation of their civil rights (Crimea SOS 2016).

Given the Crimean Tatars' identity as a Muslim minority group, the characterization of activists as "terrorists" is an especially loaded term, which perpetuates religious discrimination. In reality, Crimean Tatars maintain Muslim traditions, but tend not to be fundamentalist in their beliefs and practices. No Muslim group from Crimea has ever been found responsible for a terrorist attack. However, the Russian state-backed outlets that comprise the entire mass media landscape on the peninsula often equate secular Muslim Tatars with radical Islamic terrorists from unrelated movements (Gvozdeva 2014).[8] In April 2016, Natalia Poklonskaya, the Russian general prosecutor in the occupied Crimea, declared the Crimean Tatar Mejlis an "extremist organization"—the official status that the Russian government has assigned terrorist groups like Islamic State and Al-Qaeda (Nechepurenko 2016). Despite widespread protests and condemnations from civil society and international observers, the Russian Supreme Court voted to uphold this designation in September 2016 (Crimea SOS 2016).

After the annexation, moreover, Russian security services implemented the same policies toward Muslims that had existed in Russia and Central Asia—strict monitoring of mosques, outlawing nonviolent political Islamic groups, and prosecuting Tatar activists on dubious grounds of "conspiring to commit terrorist activities" (Crimea SOS 2016). Crimean civil society leaders emphasize that although Ukraine, like Russia, is a majority Orthodox Christian country—and is likewise not free of xenophobia or religious discrimination—the Crimean Tatars' Muslim identity "had never been a factor before" when Ukraine controlled the peninsula (SAIS Group Meeting, Kyiv, 24 March 2017). Indeed, Ukrainian government officials and opposition politicians emphasized that, although Crimean Tatars are culturally distinct from the majority Ukrainian population, they should not be treated any differently in Ukraine, which political leaders from diverse ideological movements overwhelmingly view as a pluralistic society.

Internally Displaced Crimean Tatars in Mainland Ukraine

Due to the lack of human rights protections for Crimean Tatars in Russian-occupied Crimea, approximately 25,000 have migrated to the Ukrainian mainland since 2014.

---

[8] The author is a member of the Valdai Discussion Club, a Russian think tank closely linked to President Putin.

Their reasons for migration are diverse, but many Crimean Tatar IDPs left their homes to escape religious discrimination or the threat of retribution for anti-Russian political activities (SAIS Group Meeting, Kyiv, 24 March 2017). Volunteers from Crimea SOS characterized this migration wave as a "hybrid deportation," in which Crimean Tatars are not being removed from their homeland by force as in 1944, but are being driven out by state-sanctioned marginalization and fear (SAIS Group Meeting, Kyiv, 24 March 2017). Crimea SOS and other civil society organizations work closely with Crimean Tatar IDPs to assist them with meeting their basic needs and integrating into Ukrainian society. Specifically, Crimea SOS provides *pro bono* legal assistance to IDPs—whether they are from Crimea or elsewhere in Ukraine—to assist them in obtaining official status, which entitles migrants to social protection and support.

NGOs including Crimea SOS also offer humanitarian aid to Crimean Tatar IDPs, but due to a lack of state capacity, many people still live in "deplorable conditions" after migrating to mainland Ukraine (SAIS Group Meeting, Kyiv, 24 March 2017). Therefore, Crimean Tatar civil society representatives advocate stronger policies protecting the rights of IDPs, whether or not they are ethnic Tatars. To advance social acceptance of Crimean Tatar IDPs in particular, Crimea SOS has partnered with international organizations and received funding for social initiatives that transcend the typical categories of humanitarian assistance. For example, Crimea SOS helps organize athletic and artistic programs for Crimean Tatars living in mainland Ukraine, enabling them to participate in society while maintaining their distinct cultural traditions (SAIS Group Meeting, Kyiv, 24 March 2017). These initiatives also serve as a conduit for community building among displaced Crimean Tatars, enabling them to exchange information while increasing support and social capital—and potentially reaching relatives and friends in occupied Crimea.

Several Ukrainian civil society activists noted the Crimean Tatars' significant cultural differences; one NGO leader working mostly with ethnic Ukrainian IDPs from Donbas claimed that her organization would need "to learn the Koran" in order to assist Crimean Tatar IDPs most effectively (SAIS Group Meeting with Spring of Hope, Vinnytsia, 23 March 2017). She elaborated that Crimean Tatar men often contend with an especially pronounced cultural and religious stigma against seeking mental health care, which prevents them from accessing counseling and psychiatric resources to deal with the effects of the trauma they have experienced. However, she noted that NGOs focused on IDP integration have been relatively successful in promoting education and civic participation among Crimean Tatar women and girls (SAIS Group Meeting with Spring of Hope, Vinnytsia, 23 March 2017). This implies that Crimean Tatars—although they are a conservative community—tend to align with more secular religious practices, rather than the fundamentalist strains of Islam that Russian authorities in Crimea attempt to associate with Tatars. At times, Russian propaganda links the activism of Crimean Tatars to the religious extremism of Chechen rebels, even implying that Crimea could become "a new hotbed of radical Islam,"[9] but discussions with Ukrainian civil society representatives do not support this argument (Gvozdeva 2014).

The Ukrainian government has not yet developed a comprehensive policy to address the particular needs of Crimean Tatar IDPs. The Ministry of Temporarily Occupied Territories and Internally Displaced Persons has a broad mandate that encompasses all aspects of economic and political relations between Ukraine and the non-government-controlled areas. Minister Chernysh stated that a relatively small number of IDPs in Ukraine originated from Crimea, in comparison to the much larger groups of displaced ethnic Ukrainians from the Donbas regions (SAIS Group Meeting, Kyiv, 24 March 2017). For this reason, protecting the rights of Crimean Tatar IDPs is—perhaps understandably—not the highest priority for Ukrainian authorities with limited resources.

Conclusion

As the findings from local media, scholarly research, and field interviews demonstrate, the situation of Crimean Tatars in Crimea is more precarious than in mainland Ukraine. For a relatively peaceful return of Crimea to Ukrainian sovereignty, the following phenomena must occur simultaneously: a serious internal economic and political crisis in Russia, a rise in discontent and anti-Russian sentiment among the majority-Russian population of Crimea, and successful democratization in Ukraine. Therefore, these

---

[9] See chapter by Gabriella Huddart.

economic and political developments represent necessary preconditions for international law and institutions to reopen the question of Crimea's status.

The aforementioned trifecta is highly unlikely, but not impossible. First, as of March 2017, Russia's economy has been in a severe recession that coincided with the global drop in oil prices and the sanctions imposed by the EU and United States in response to the annexation of Crimea. If the Russian government fails to incorporate structural economic reforms, a serious crisis might threaten the stability of the state. Second, most non-Tatar residents of Crimea have generally supported the Russian occupation. Crimea has a large population of pensioners, government employees, and retired senior military officers, who were among the most vocal advocates of the annexation, as Russian pensions and public salaries are higher than Ukrainian ones. However, if a financial crisis in Russia were to occur in tandem with higher-than-expected GDP growth in Ukraine, non-Tatar Crimea residents might begin to oppose the Russian occupation. Third, Ukraine's political and economic trajectory is questionable at the time of this writing, but a trend toward reform, transparency, and market development could build the foundation for future prosperity.

Ukraine cannot defeat Russia in a conventional military campaign, but Ukraine has a real chance to prevail over Russia on the battlefields of economic, political, and social development—which would represent a much more consequential victory. Russian state media in Crimea portrays the current government of Ukraine, and much of the Western-leaning Ukrainian political class, as nationalistic and even fascist. Although these accusations are largely unfounded, Ukrainian leaders must not dismiss them outright. Indeed, if the Ukrainian political elites marginalize and oppress minority groups rather than embracing pluralism and creating policies to support social, economic and political integration, Ukraine will lose its moral authority vis-à-vis Russia. On the other hand, if Ukraine adopts an inclusive approach, it has a historic chance to become a transparent, pluralistic, and democratic state.

Recommendations

To the UN, OSCE, and CoE

- **Expand human rights monitoring in Crimea**. Both Russia and Ukraine are members of these organizations, which should insist on regular access, develop stronger reporting mechanisms, and agree on appropriate investigative proceedings for human rights violations in occupied Crimea.
- **Create a multinational task force on the rights of minority groups in Crimea**, with a base on the peninsula, under the auspices of the OSCE High Commissioner on National Minorities and the CoE.
- **OSCE and CoE could gain access to Crimea by appealing to Russia's security interests**:
    - **Propose to help Russia address concerns about Islamic radicalism** by helping monitor suspected extremists.
    - Help ensure that Muslim Tatars living under Russian occupation do not face marginalization, violence, or religious discrimination that might contribute to alienation and radicalization.

To USAID, UNDP, and Other International Development Agencies

- **Increase funding and personnel/capacity for Crimean Tatar grassroots organizations** operating in mainland Ukraine.
- **Prioritize media literacy training for partner NGOs** to better serve the population.
- **Media organizations** that report on daily developments in Crimea **require assistance for legal representation, translation, and digital media training** to reach the broadest possible audience.
- These organizations are a vital conduit for interpersonal contact between mainland Ukraine and annexed Crimea, and such direct communication is the most effective way to combat **Russian disinformation**.

<u>To the Government of Ukraine</u>

- To the Ministry of Temporarily Occupied Territories and Internally Displaced Persons: **assume full ownership of decisions related to IDPs.**
- To the Ministry of Social Policy and the Ministry of Economic Development and Trade: **engage in regular cross-team collaboration to provide input on IDP integration strategy.**
- **Establish an intra-governmental task force** to examine whether to devise a specialized and culturally sensitive integration strategy for Crimean Tatar IDPs.
- To the Ministry of Justice: **collaborate with the Ministry of Temporarily Occupied Territories and IDPs to develop and assess strategies to support the protection of minority rights in occupied Crimea**, alongside experts from international monitoring missions.
- **Ensure that religious and ethnic minorities are represented in Ukrainian public life**, and that discrimination is reported, investigated, and disciplined appropriately.

Part V: Role of International Actors

Challenges and Opportunities for the United Nations

Qifan Huang

The Ukrainian conflict, beginning in late 2013 when Viktor Yanukovych rejected the EU Partnership Agreement, has morphed into a complicated and multidimensional hybrid conflict. Starting as Euromaidan, a domestic political crisis, it has evolved to incorporate territorial aggression and secession movements that involve multiple state actors and international institutions. Many see it as the culmination of Russia's strategy to secure its peripheries and expand its frontiers following years of chaos in Abkhazia and South Ossetia in Georgia, but some attribute the conflict to mostly domestic grievances. In such a complicated scenario, where multiple narratives compete for subscription, it is even more important to examine the role of international organizations, particularly the United Nations, in resolving post-Cold War disputes. The inability of the current international system, based on a consultative process within the Security Council, to contain certain aspects of the conflict, especially Russia's annexation of Crimea and the ongoing fighting in the Donbas region, has raised doubt about whether the current international system is capable of resolving the crisis in the wake of a resurgence of conflicts around the world. Whether that is true or not, a careful analysis of the successes and failures of the engagement of the UN in resolving the conflicts in Ukraine is necessary. From that, valuable lessons could be learned, and appropriate policy recommendations could be proposed for future efforts on conflict resolution.

A Review and Evaluation of UN Actions

Review of UN Actions

The United Nations has followed the Ukrainian conflict since its early days. The Security Council held several meetings to discuss the situation in Ukraine in areas including the status of Crimea, the human rights violations during the conflict, the separatist movement in eastern Ukraine, and the downing of MH17, since February 2014. However, the results are meager compared to the efforts devoted to resolving the issue. As of March 2017, the Security Council has only passed two resolutions, one condemning the downing of MH17 (UNSC 21 July 2014) and another endorsing the Minsk II Agreements signed on

February 12, 2015 (UNSC 17 February 2015). These two resolutions were mainly ceremonial in nature in that the former one is a common gesture for the Council to call for an investigation of the matter, and the latter one a very brief statement of the Council's full support without offering any substantial action. Due to Russia's veto on a draft resolution on Ukraine (UNSC 15 March 2014) and its subsequent threat to veto any forthcoming resolution on the subject, the Council is essentially in a deadlock. Meetings continue to take place, but without a satisfactory way to bring Russia to the table no concrete action has been taken. Both Russia and Ukraine cited the need to protect universal values for justification of their own behavior, and a clear divide appeared in the Council: while the US, France and the United Kingdom have unequivocally blamed Russia for what happened in the eastern front of Ukraine, China and many other developing countries repeatedly referred to the importance of keeping the impartiality of the UN, and Russia has, of course, declined to have had any involvement in the issue.

The General Assembly passed a resolution to offer its support for the territorial integrity of Ukraine (UNGA 28 March 2014). It was at its roots a remedial effort by members of the Security Council after Russia's veto two weeks earlier and contained largely similar words. However, the resolution was not binding, and out of 169 member states that were present at the meeting, only 100 voted for the resolution, with 11 against and 58 abstentions. This is another reflection of the divide within the UN: a majority of those who abstained were developing countries not directly related to the conflict. Notably, the General Assembly has not passed any subsequent resolutions on Ukraine, even after the rise of the secessionist movements in the East.

Besides the two principal UN decision-making bodies, the UN High Commissioner for Human Rights has also established a monitoring mission to report human rights violations in Crimea and the self-proclaimed republics. Many of its reports detailing the human rights and minority issues in Ukraine, including in Crimea and Donbas, had also been discussed by the Human Rights Council.[10] Other specialized agencies, for example the Office of the UN High Commissioner for Refugees (UNHCR), have conducted field operations with regards to IDPs and issues surrounding the recent

---

[10] For example, see UN Document A/HRC/28/64/Add.1.

"blockade." These actions stand in clear contrast with the incapacitated decision-making processes surrounding "high politics" in UN headquarters in New York.

Evaluation of UN Actions

In general, the UN's response to the Ukrainian conflict has been lacking. It has more served as a platform for discussion of the matter than a dispute settlement mechanism. While it is acknowledged that, with Russian resistance in the Security Council, any proposed action would have to be cautious to avoid a Russian veto, there is still no reason for the UN not to act, especially in a time when it has not exhausted all measures to resolve the conflict. For example, it could have discussed whether the annexation of Crimea or other parts of the conflict in Donbas is, in essence, a dispute between Russia and Ukraine, which would have forced Russia to abstain in the voting process on matters related to the conflict according to Article 27(3) of the UN Charter. Granted that the article has not been invoked in the past 50 years and that there is doubt on whether that section applies to permanent members of the Security Council, it is still disappointing to see that the option has not even been considered by the UN.

Similarly, the General Assembly could have also reaffirmed its support for the territorial integrity of Ukraine, rejection of the annexation of Crimea, and condemned the actions of parties in Donbas. Sadly, it stopped short of action and did not pass any resolutions after an initial response, despite its full capacity to proceed. Although General Assembly resolutions are not legally binding, they nevertheless reflect the renewed political support for Ukraine and display the UN's commitment to the issue.

Some may argue that, due to the high number of abstentions in passing the only resolution, it is diplomatically difficult for the UN to continue to push for the discussion of the issue. However, the UN did not even attempt to establish a fact-finding mission to clear up member states' confusion on the actual happenings on the ground, especially in Donbas, which could have garnered more support for a diplomatic approach led by the UN to resolve the dispute and at least provided a starting point for subsequent actions. A fact-finding mission would also have been an effective way to establish whether Russia was directly involved in the conflict and provide grounds for invoking Article 27(3).

The bigger issue revealed by the UN's failure, or more appropriately, its unwillingness to exhaust all means of conflict resolution even within the boundaries of its own Charter, is that it reflects an underlying trend that has continued since the failure of its interventions in Rwanda and former Yugoslavia. Due to political concerns, the UN has avoided taking any substantial action or resorting to potentially murky and controversial approaches to resolve conflicts, even though a forceful change in the borders of a member state not agreed to by the parties is a clear-cut violation of the basic principles enshrined in the Charter. It has continued to put limitations on itself by yielding its mandate to other international actors. Some of these may have been based on a careful calculation of potential fallouts, but many were also forms of "self-censorship" that curtails its own effectiveness as an international platform for managing conflicts to accommodate interests of member states. The problem with this approach is that it is not a sustainable one: with each circumstance of surrendering its power, the accommodated actor gains more by winning the game of chicken, and other state actors and citizens of the affected states lose confidence in the current system. Frozen conflicts arise with regions proclaiming independence and achieving de-facto control with no feasible diplomatic outcome, and eventually, the UN will be derogated to merely a platform of communication without any sticks to enforce its mandate and cause it to lose public support.

Reception of UN Actions in Ukraine and its Implications for Policymaking

Indeed, the discontent towards the international system, particularly the UN, was obviously visible in Ukraine. Oksana Syrorid, Deputy Speaker of the Ukrainian Rada, commented extensively on the issue, describing the Security Council's failure to respond promptly to the secession of Crimea and its subsequent annexation by Russia as a degradation of the reputation of the international system and the undermining of the international legal and security order. She also criticized the UN's inadequate effort to monitor and prevent the conflict and described the Minsk Process supported by the UN as an appeasement of the world to Russia. Of course, her main criticism was targeted towards the Organization for Security and Cooperation in Europe (OSCE) which is mostly responsible for the Minsk Process, but her disappointment in the weak responses of international actors was apparent (SAIS Group Meeting, Kyiv, 22 March 2017).

Other actors, including a member of a research institution affiliated with the Ministry of Foreign Affairs of Ukraine and a former member of the US diplomatic mission to Ukraine, pointed out that the UN and other international organizations should pay more attention to the pacific settlement of the conflict because it is a challenge not only to Ukraine but also to the West and the post-WWII order upon which the various organizations were built. Holding the belief that the conflict is international rather than local or internal in nature, they advocate the utilization of the full scale of conflict management tools of the organizations to resolve the dispute.

Despite the general disappointment towards the inaction of the UN and the ineffectiveness of processes advocated by the UN, there is still significant support within Ukraine for resolving the conflict under the framework of international law and the UN. However, many have also pointed out the significance of time: backing for current mechanisms of conflict resolution loses strength every day as the international community chooses not to act, and unless prompt actions are taken, trust in the UN is doomed to disappear altogether, in particular among those directly affected by the conflict. One of the most memorable moments of the field trip happened during the discussion of the situation in Donbas with students at Donetsk National University, which moved out of the occupied territories and relocated to Vinnytsia: when a member of the SAIS delegation described his major in international law and organizations, a student commented "that won't help us much" (SAIS Group Meeting, Vinnytsia, 23 March 2017).

While the desire to see international action is strong, some Ukrainians have admitted that their efforts to get the UN and other international and regional organizations to respond have largely been ineffective. A representative to the Minsk Political Working Group, when asked about expectations of a political settlement of the conflict in Donbas, acknowledged that he could not see how the goal of forcing Russia to abide by international law can be achieved (SAIS Group Meeting, Kyiv, 22 March 2017). However, although the SAIS delegation did not have any meetings with the UN or its specialized agencies in Ukraine, other international organizations have proposed ideas for facilitating the UN's role in resolving the conflict, which will be discussed later.

Notably, some politicians described the initial hope of the Ukrainian government that resorting to the UN and other international organizations might bring an end to the conflict. When these hopes were unfulfilled, the attitude of the government towards the tackling of the conflict changed. It would be interesting to research in detail how the disparity between expectation and reality altered the decision-making of the Ukrainian government as well as the calculation of Russia in its involvement, but the limitations of the scope of this book would force that discussion to be left to future scholars.

What Could the UN Have Done Differently?

More could have been done in Ukraine. The UN must do more in Ukraine. Challenges for the organization could be turned into opportunities should the UN choose to act proactively. Indeed, various actors in Ukraine have proposed actions that are worth discussing here.

Enhancing Conflict Prevention Mechanisms

In assessing the conflict in Ukraine, especially Russia's annexation of Crimea, local stakeholders repeatedly pointed out that the failure of conflict prevention plays a significant role in the situation as of March 2017. As the situation unfolded since the beginning of Euromaidan in late 2013, the UN failed to closely monitor the situation and take necessary measures for conflict prevention. The Security Council hosted its first meeting on the issue as late as February 28, 2014, after receiving a letter from the Ukrainian government two days before.[11] It then held several meetings to no avail due to the opposition of Russia on any preventive actions, and the UN powerlessly witnessed the referendum in Crimea and the occupation of government buildings in Donbas.

While the inability of the UN to take any measures after the ousting of Viktor Yanukovych can be at least partially attributed to conflicting political interest among its member states, its failure to closely monitor and react to the Euromaidan and its fallout reflects the limitations of the current prevention mechanism of the UN. The organization

---

[11] See UN Document S/2014/132.

continues to recognize the need for preventive diplomacy after the 2005 World Summit (UNGA 25 October 2005), but there is still a substantial gap between theory and practice. A US diplomat commented on the cognitive inability for the world to accept Russia's breach of international law and norms, and inadequate prevention and early warning mechanisms are one of the contributing factors to that outcome.

There are many ways for the UN to improve its capacity in conflict prevention. It does not have a political mission that is capable of carrying out monitoring and early warning functions on the ground, and although it did work with other regional organizations, for example with OSCE in Georgia until Russia blocked the continuation of the OSCE mission in 2008, such collaboration in facilitating conflict prevention capacities could be more thoroughly developed. However, given the successes of UN regional offices in recent years in mediating and preventing the crises in Kyrgyzstan and Burkina Faso, plans for expansion of the mandate of UN regional offices in other regions of the world could be discussed and analyzed. Regional offices have the advantage of coordinating with multiple field offices to offer a multifaceted analysis of potential escalations of conflict, and they could also work with regional organizations to take on different roles in an integrated early warning system.

The UN could also change its mode of dealing with conflicts from a passive manner where the Security Council only moves to discuss issues upon receiving the request of member states, to a more proactive approach, utilizing the good offices of the Secretary-General to support high-level discussions among Council members that focus more on potential conflicts. Smaller ad-hoc missions could be deployed with a clear mandate to observe the situation and promote Track II and III dialogues between aggrieved groups without adding an excessive burden to the limited budget of the organization.

When political differences incapacitate the functioning of the Security Council, other bodies of the UN could attempt to build prevention mechanisms without having to pass through the Council. The General Assembly could seek to expand the mandate of its subsidiary body, the Peacebuilding Commission (PBC), or establish a similar commission or working group that focuses on conflict prevention, to circumvent the disagreements within the Council. Specialized agencies of the UN, due to the different decision-making procedures, also could explore options to prevent conflicts.

Make Better Use of Current Mechanisms to Contain Conflicts

The UN needs to make better use of existing mechanisms to contain the dispute. It is understandable if it has tried everything possible but failed, but not exhausting all possible measures demonstrates the unwillingness rather than the inability of the UN to resolve conflicts. Some mechanisms are readily available, some need explorations to "unknown territories," but shrinking its own authority by choosing not to act undermines the authority of the UN and its adaptiveness to a resurgence of conflicts around the world.

Several members of the government stressed the need for Russia to abide by international law, especially concerning the situation in Crimea, but are pessimistic on how to achieve that result. However, it is ironic that the UN has not even exhausted all measures to bring Russia to justice. Ukraine has filed suits to the International Court of Justice (ICJ) in January 2017, in which it claimed that Russia employed terrorism in the Donbas region, violating the International Convention on the Suppression of Financing of Terrorism and that Russia discriminated against the Crimean Tartars, violating the International Convention on the Elimination of All Forms of Racial Discrimination (ICJ 17 January 2017). Both treaties grant jurisdiction to the ICJ, binding Russia to accept the ruling from an international law perspective should the Court decide that it has jurisdiction over Ukraine's claims. However, none of the allegations concern the legality of Russia's alleged involvement in eastern Ukraine or its annexation of Crimea. This is primarily because violations against international law not governed by treaties must be brought to the Court on a voluntary basis by all parties in the dispute (UN 16 April 1946, Article 36), and it is highly unlikely, if not impossible, for Russia to agree to submit the matter to the Court.

The fact that the Court's jurisdiction is lacking for a case on contentious issues does not mean that it is incapacitated. The Statute of the Court also outlines that certain bodies can seek a non-binding advisory opinion without obtaining the consent of all parties (UN 16 April 1946, Article 65), which provides an alternative route for legal recourse. Although not binding, advisory opinions of the Court are still influential in international law and could exert pressure on offending parties, and similar courses have been pursued before by the General Assembly, for instance when it asked the Court to determine the legality of Kosovo's declaration of independence (ICJ 22 July 2010). In that case, Russia supported Serbia's motion to bring the matter to the Court (РИА Новости 8 December 2009) and upon the passing of the resolution (UNGA 8 October 2008), the Court delivered a result contrary to Russian expectation. Russia nevertheless accepted the results without denying the legitimacy of the Court (Sputnik 22 July 2010). An advisory opinion on the status of Crimea, the legitimacy of its referendum, and Russia's interference in the Donbas region, will help settle legal issues and deny Russia's claim that it got involved in Ukraine to uphold international law.

Seeking legal recourse under current mechanisms is a relatively easy step, but there are other roads to be taken if the UN decides to act. For example, it is legally permissible, or at least worth exploring, to utilize the General Assembly's "Uniting for Peace" resolution[12] and consider the possibility of deploying a peacekeeping mission or similar forces in the Donbas region to circumvent any possible Russian veto over the issue in the Security Council.[13] While politically difficult, it is not impossible: a similar mission, the UN Emergency Force (UNEF), was designated under the framework of the "Uniting for Peace" resolution and was deployed in Egypt in 1956. The Ukrainian government has displayed its willingness to accept the deployment in the East to enforce the ceasefire provisions of the Minsk Agreement, clearing the path for such a mission.

<u>Facilitating Coordination with Regional Organizations and NGOs</u>

Regional organizations have taken the lead role in the effort to resolve the Ukrainian conflict in a diplomatic manner. OSCE has deployed its Special Monitoring Mission (SMM) to observe the implementation of the Minsk Agreement, which was negotiated thanks to its good offices. It is also, as of March 2017, one of the only international platforms recognized by Russia to be neutral on the matter. The European Union, on the other hand, has taken a more definitive stand and has sided consistently with Ukraine. It

---

[12] See UN Document A/RES/377(V).
[13] For a legal analysis of deploying a peacekeeping mission in eastern Ukraine without the Security Council, see Zavoli, Ilaria. 2016. "Peacekeeping in Eastern Ukraine: The Legitimacy of a Request and The Competence of the United Nations General Assembly." *Journal of Conflict and Security Law:* 1-27. doi:10.1093/jcsl/krw008.

has contributed to facilitating communication between local and central authorities and has engaged extensively in the reform process. Compared to these actors, the UN has done surprisingly little: it has only received periodic reports from the OSCE mission, without actively participating in the coordination of the efforts of regional organizations.

The UN should enhance its collaboration with regional organizations in Ukraine. During the SAIS delegation's meetings with the EU, the OSCE Project Coordinator's Office in Ukraine, and the SMM, a common problem exposed was that the efforts of regional organizations were not well coordinated. For example, both the SMM and the EU delegation were working to improve the dialogue between Kyiv and local authorities, especially those close to the contact line, but their efforts were not coordinated enough to maximize each institution's comparative advantages. While it is understandable that they have their own priorities, an integrated approach, led by the UN, would be able to focus their work at the local level in their respective fields while minimizing duplication. The engagement of the UN could also inject legitimacy to the actions of regional actors, particularly when some of them are perceived by the local population and external actors as biased.

On the humanitarian front, the scattered efforts of regional actors in humanitarian assistance, education and medical care should be fit into a grand strategy coordinated by the UN. Some regional organizations, for example, the EU, have already reported collaboration with specialized agencies of the UN in some areas, but the leadership of the UN would be crucial to creating a mechanism that ensures the consistency of aid delivery.

The EU delegation also stressed the importance of utilizing powerful NGOs and civil societies to promote reconciliation between residents within GCAs and NGCAs. The UN should take that into consideration when proposing peacebuilding measures and work with them through Track II and III diplomacy to facilitate a stronger UN presence in Ukraine.

Conclusion

With the resurgence of conflicts, especially protracted conflicts, in the second decade of the 21st century, the role of international organizations, especially the United Nations, is becoming more important. However, rather than utilizing this opportunity to improve its organizational structure to adapt to the trend, the UN has displayed a tendency to act extremely cautiously, to the point that inaction becomes the safest reaction to rising conflicts. Ironically, the unwillingness of the UN to take political risks contributes to the increasingly politicized nature of international disputes: parties to the conflict accuse the other side of violating international law and blame the failure of conflict resolution on the non-cooperation of other parties, which further curtails the UN's capability to respond to emergencies.

What happened in Ukraine revealed the deficiency of the post-war international system and the way the UN operates in that system. Without change, the system is doomed to fail. This is a moment for political vision and bravery: the UN must take these challenges and make structural adjustments to how it handles conflicts of the same sort.

Recommendations

<u>To the United Nations</u>

- **Enhance the capacity of regional offices in conflict prevention.** Invest in its unique advantage and work with other actors to improve the monitoring and the early-warning of conflicts.

- **Take a proactive role in preemptive discussions of the escalation of potential conflicts.** Through the good offices of the Secretary-General, deploy small-scale fact-finding missions to monitor and report tensions between groups with grievances.

- **Explore mechanisms other than the Security Council for preventive diplomacy.** Existing mechanisms under the General Assembly, as well as specialized agencies, could play a more important role in these efforts.

- **Initiate procedures to request an advisory opinion from the ICJ on the legality of Russia's annexation of Crimea and its involvement in the Donbas region.** This will help settle the question from the perspective of international law and exert pressure for Russia to restrain its conduct not conforming to international law.

- **Explore the possibility of authorizing peacekeeping missions in the Donbas region without going through the Security Council.** Through the "Uniting for Peace" resolution, deploy security forces to ensure the implementation of the ceasefire agreement.
- **Enhance collaboration with regional organizations in political and humanitarian areas.** Such coordination would streamline global efforts in these fields and maximize the utilization of limited resources.
- **Work with NGOs and civil societies to promote reconciliation.** Through Track II and III diplomacy, the UN could start its post-conflict reconstruction process.

The European Union in Ukraine: One Voice or Many?

Rebecca Grenham

This chapter will examine the foreign policy of the European Union (EU) towards Ukraine and the ongoing conflict. It specifically examines the dynamics of foreign policy formulation within the EU, focusing on how both member states and supranational institutions jointly make foreign policy decisions, and the role of normative power in dealing with states in the 'neighborhood.' In some foreign policy domains, the EU behaves as a unitary actor, where both states and institutions speak with one voice and choose to advance certain policies. However, the EU is also a composite body of many states, each with differing foreign priorities. EU institutions must reconcile these differences and compose policies that all member states approve. This means that EU foreign policy can be highly effective if all states agree, but also incredibly inconsistent if national governments fail to reach agreements with one another (Hodson 2011). Given these constraints and compromises, the EU typically falls back to promoting its own values abroad and international norms.

This paper argues that, in Ukraine, member states were divided over what kind of relationship the EU should have with Ukraine and the Former Soviet Union (FSU) generally. These divisions resulted primarily from differences in member states' bilateral relations with both Ukraine and Russia. The compromise reached was to venture timidly into the FSU through cooperation and development programs, though without promising these countries eventual membership in the EU. This compromise, perhaps best exemplified in the Eastern Partnership (EaP), seemed to work until crisis erupted in Kyiv in 2014, and Russia showed that it was not willing to tolerate even a tepid step into its own 'neighborhood.' As the crisis ensued, member states grew more divided over how to best respond, and the Commission scrambled to create a blanket policy, and often fell back to its usual approach of supporting liberal values. This policy includes a mixture of sanctions toward Russia and development aid for Ukraine, and the chapter will demonstrate how both of these policies also arose out of compromises between member states.

The chapter first describes the process of EU foreign policy formation and accession to the union, which are both highly relevant to understanding operations in Ukraine at the time of writing. It then delves into varied attitudes towards both Ukraine and Russia amongst existing EU member states, examining how national governments, business, and public opinion influence broader policy. Next, it looks at the EaP and shows how it arose out of many compromises between member states. Finally, it analyzes EU policy since the beginning of the crisis in 2014, focusing on sanctions and structural reform programs.

Forming EU Foreign Policy

Analyzing how foreign policy is formed within the EU is critical to understanding specific policies. With the launch of the Treaty of Maastricht in 1992 came a Common Foreign and Security Policy (CFSP), which strove to create a clear external policy that protects EU values, promotes democracy and the rule of law, and keeps peace abroad (European Commission). To do so, the EU works primarily through the European Council, which facilitates discussion amongst national heads of state and ministries. In 2009, this framework was modified somewhat with the Treaty of Lisbon, which created a European External Action Service (EEAS) and a High Representative for Foreign Affairs, thus expanding the foreign policy capabilities of the EU and its institutions. However, national governments still play a large role in foreign policy formulation— arguably more so than in any other area under EU governance (European Commission).

There are naturally benefits and drawbacks of creating unified foreign policy by mediating the desires of individual member states. The major advantage is that, when all states agree on a program, it can prove incredibly effective, as the EU is large enough that its voice carries significant weight in the international arena (Hodson 2011). The EU can be a powerful actor, and is in a strong position to advance its interests and values abroad. However, if disagreement between member states persists, policy can be inconsistent and lack a clear vision. The challenge of coordinating foreign policy between 28 different member states, each with unique histories and special relationships with outside states, should not be underestimated. Issues of critical importance to some nations have little to no significance for others. Moreover, even if all do agree to address a common concern, they can remain divided over how to do so. In addition, since some states are adept at persuading other EU member states to pursue a common foreign policy that aligns with their own national interests, EU policies can serve the interests of some states but not others (Roth 2011). Essentially, the EU can either be a forceful or weak global actor, depending on the extent to which member states' priorities converge and the ability of EU institutions to introduce and implement common frameworks that national governments find agreeable.

As far as policies themselves, the EU typically relies on its normative power when dealing with outside powers. The EU does this because values play a central role in the community, and hence in theory all members can agree to promote certain norms. Though all member states have different strategic priorities, all have agreed to adhere to a specific set of values regarding governance, free markets, and human rights. Since the EU finds forging a common strategic policy in some areas difficult, it can theoretically always promote its own values abroad. Values-based foreign policy enables the EU to reconcile multiple national perspectives and act as a unitary actor in some areas. However, this rests on the ability of the EU to serve as a model of its own values abroad. Others must believe that EU states are successful liberal democratic economies. Moreover, others must want to be more like the EU, and attempt to mold themselves to function more like existing member states. This phenomenon is the basis of the EU's normative power. Though member states may argue over strategic issues, the EU itself can still rely on its ability to attract others in many situations.

The accession process exemplifies the EU's power to attract others and how the EU can act as both a unitary and composite body in foreign affairs. Accession is an example of normative power because the EU's ability to influence applicant countries is based almost solely on the power of attraction: other states want to be more like the EU, and hence will do what it takes to join (Grabbe 2006; Borzel and Risse 2009; Manners 2002). As a result, applicant countries typically undergo years of extensive structural—and often painful—reforms. The EU itself advises countries on what changes are needed and how to best implement them, providing financial donations as well as technical advice throughout the process. The EU can be successful at promoting reform, though often when it has a series of carrots and sticks that incentivize applicant countries to change, such as the pull of eventual membership or the ability to stall accession talks should the country fail to meet expectations (Grabbe 2006; Borzel and Risse 2009; Manners 2002). During the process, both existing member states and EU institutions play an important role. The European Council—comprised of heads of state and ministers from members—must agree to open negotiations with the applicant, while the Commission must conduct routine screenings outlining existing conditions, areas for improvement, and structural goals (European Commission). While the Commission is entrusted with most of the day-to-day work after negotiations begin, only member states can conclude negotiations after examining the candidate country's progress, and they must ratify the final accession treaty (European Commission). Enlargement shows how EU normative power operates, and it also highlights how the EU behaves as both a composite body and unitary actor.

Before continuing, it is important to note that, though promoting liberal democratic reforms through soft power may seem like a completely generous policy stemming from pure benevolence, it also serves EU interests. Creating a secure and safe region—without using force—helps the EU protect itself and its own way of life. Regarding its 'neighborhood' policy, the EU Commission states that: "As the EU has grown, the countries of Eastern Europe and the Caucasus have become our neighbors. Increasingly, their security, stability, and prosperity affect ours" (European Commission). Moreover, by helping other countries look more like the EU, the EU remains the dominant power in most of its bilateral relations with neighbors. The EU is not a passive actor by any means, but rather one that actively works in the region to preserve its privileged position. The significance of this is that EU action in the region does have geopolitical consequences (Copsey and Pomorska 2014; Kuzio 2016; Merry 2016).

Ukraine, Russia, and The European Union

Member states vastly differ in attitudes towards both Ukraine and Russia, which complicates EU relations with Ukraine. Poland is one of the most enthusiastic about Ukraine joining the EU, for a mixture of historical and strategic reasons (Copsey and Pomorska 2014; Roth 2011; Krasnodebsvka 2016). For Poland, having Ukraine in would facilitate already large labor flows between the two while adding another EU/NATO ally along its Eastern border (Krasnodebska 2016; Copsey and Pomorska 2014; Roth 2011). Moreover, several parts of Western Ukraine were part of Poland-Lithuania, so the two states do share historical and cultural ties. The Baltic States and a few others in Eastern Europe are also in favor of closer relations with Ukraine for similar reasons (Fix and Kirch 2016). These states argue that Ukraine can develop a successful market economy post-communism, as many of them managed to do so themselves (Krasnodebska 2016; Dragneva and Wolczuk 2015). Moreover, many are relatively 'hawkish' regarding Russia, and believe that the EU must take a strong, united stance to deter Russian assertiveness (Shagina 2017). Other states, such as Sweden, are less concerned with strategy but remain open to Ukrainian membership should Ukraine meet outlined criteria in key areas (Krasnodebska 2016). In short, some member states that support Ukraine fully support it joining the EU, while others are less enthusiastic about full membership but willing to consider the possibility.

Other states, however, are far more wary about the implications of close ties with Ukraine on relations with Russia (Shagina 2017). Italy, for example, tries to preserve relatively friendly ties with Russia, with some journalists even arguing that Italy has a 'special relationship' with Russia because countries are willing to respect the other country's claimed sphere of influence (Kirchgaessner 2015; Rosato 2016). France, which is more concerned with the Mediterranean than FSU, prefers to deal with Russia on a bilateral basis (Nougayrede 2015). This means that France is somewhat indifferent to EU policy regarding the East so long as it does not impede its own relations with Russia (Nougayrede 2015). French and Italian energy firms also enjoy close relations with Gazprom, and advocate for a national policy that does not endanger this relationship (Abdelal 2013). For example, during a series of "gas crises" in 2006 and 2009, when Gazprom shut off gas through Ukrainian pipelines completely due to contract issues, these firms pushed to find transportation routes outside of Ukraine while keeping Gazprom as a supplier (Abdelal 2013).

German policy towards Ukraine and Russia is perhaps the most mixed. On the one hand, there are many factors that push Germany to be rather friendly towards Russia—the two were allies for a long period before the First World War, Russia did withdraw troops from East Germany in 1989, enabling reunification, and German manufacturing benefits greatly from trade with Russia (Rees 2011; Manners and Whitman 2000; Pond and Kundnani 2015). Moreover, like Italy and France, Germany also receives most of its gas from Gazprom, and even built a direct pipeline from Russia to Germany in 2011 after the gas crises of 2006 and 2009 (Abdelal 2013). Since the end of the Second World War, in fact, German foreign policy has rested on its ability to broker ties between East and West (Rees 2011; Manners and Whitman 2000). However, this policy was largely based on promoting liberal values and so Germany will take a stand against action seen to violate international norms (Manners and Whitman 2000). Moreover, Germany is concerned with security in the East, and is not willing to ignore this region all together (Fix and Kirch 2016). To further complicate German foreign policy, the public is wary of conflict escalation while political parties differ widely on their attitudes towards the USA and Russia, making policy even more layered (Gressel 2015; Ziener 2015).

Official policy aside, public opinion regarding Russia and Ukraine is also highly split within the EU. In 2010, though nearly 70% of Bulgarians, Lithuanians, and Croats supported Ukraine joining the EU, 81% of Austrians were opposed, along with nearly 70% of Germans and over half of Italians (Eurobarometer 2010 poll). Hence, it is unrealistic to expect these citizens to engage in a full-scale confrontation with Russia on Ukraine's behalf as well. Similarly, when asked if the EU should have a military defense force to manage international crises, almost one third of Austrians and Germans disagreed (Eurobarometer 2005). In 2008, almost 15% of the entire EU was against forming a common security/military policy, and by 2015 18% were still opposed (Eurobarometer 2008). Efforts to formulate common foreign and defense policy, particularly in the FSU, have met substantial resistance from a variety of actors, including national parliaments, businesses, and ordinary citizens.

The Eastern Partnership: A Polish-Swedish Plan or Grand Compromise?

After enlargement and accession of many post-communist states in 2004, the EU began to promote closer ties with nations in its region. Under the 2002 European Neighborhood Policy (ENP), the EU decided to pursue closer ties with countries in the Mediterranean and the FSU by promoting economic growth and development along with EU values, such as democracy, human rights, and rule of law. The Eastern Partnership (EaP) is an example of neighborhood policy in action. After first being proposed by both Poland and Sweden, it was launched as a formal EU program in 2008. The EaP strives to strengthen ties with six former Soviet states (Armenia, Azerbaijan, Belarus, Georgia, Moldova, Ukraine) through development aid and political cooperation. The program includes three parts: 1) an Association Agreement (AA), or general framework that outlines cooperation between the EU and the specific country; 2) a Deep and Comprehensive Free Trade Agreement (DCFTA) between both the EU and the signatory nation; and 3) visa liberalization, which waives the visa requirement for citizens of these countries when staying less than 90 days in the Schengen area. Though the program does not include EU membership for these states, most onlookers consider it an important step towards the EU and eventual membership. The partnership rests on the assumption that recipient countries will work to make themselves more like the EU, like states negotiating membership do (Merry 2016).

When first launched, the Eastern Partnership was fairly controversial (SAIS Group Meeting, Washington DC, March 2017). Both Poland and Sweden pursued the plan for similar yet distinguishable reasons. Poland saw the Eastern Partnership, and specifically Ukrainian involvement in it, as a means to protect itself from becoming an EU and NATO outpost and promote community values (Copsey and Pomorska 2014, Roth 2011, Krasnodebska 2016). In fact, Poland even went so far as to hint that the EaP was a step towards EU membership, as the program would weave Ukraine more tightly into the EU's orbit (Copsey and Pomorska 2014; Roth 2011). Sweden, on the other hand, saw it as a means to promote liberal values and also preserve its neutrality, which requires stability along its borders (Krasnodebska 2016). Other states worried about the impact that the policy would have on Russia. France, for example, privately expressed concern about potential backlash from Russia, while Germany liked the idea of promoting reform in the FSU but was not comfortable offering EU membership (Gressel 2015; Nougayrede 2015). The EaP, then, was a compromise. It offered association agreements but not accession, visa liberalization but not free movement of people, and free trade but not access to the single market. On the one hand, the EaP was bold in that it ventured into the FSU, from which the EU has normally abstained. However, its goals are tamer than those other programs within the neighborhood, such as accession talks in the Balkans.

Implementation of the EaP reflects a mixture of unitary and composite decision-making. The Commission is still entrusted with much of the bread and butter work of the program, including introducing reforms, drafting agreements and protocol, and general advising (SAIS Group Meeting, EU Commission, Kyiv, 24 March 2017). However, member states still can influence its progress, as they must ratify Association Agreements. The Dutch referendum of 2016, where voters rejected the agreement, shows that member states are still an active part of EaP implementation. Therefore, in implementation the EaP is a hybrid of national and supranational decision-making, which has important implications for its success on the ground.

The EaP, though too tame for some member states, soon became highly controversial. Russia specifically did not trust the program, fearing that it was a step into what it saw as its own sphere of influence (Kuzio 2016; Merry 2016; Rees 2011; Rieker and Gjerde 2016). In fact, after its launch Russia began further developing plans to start a Eurasian Economic Union (EEU), or a customs union to consist of former Soviet states (Pop 2016). The success of this program depended on Ukrainian involvement in it, and Russia began pushing Ukraine to join (Dragneva and Wolczuk 2015). Ukraine was wary of joining, as it had spent most of its post-Soviet years trying to keep itself outside of a Russian-dominated regional program (Dragneva and Wolczuk 2015). Russia began a 'trade war' with Ukraine, where it limited Ukrainian imports into Russia, which had a large negative impact on the Ukrainian economy (Dragneva and Wolczuk 2015). At the same time, Vladimir Putin offered then-Ukrainian President Viktor Yanukovych a tempting financial loan and cheaper gas imports in exchange for extending a Russian naval base lease in Crimea (Dragneva and Wolczuk 2015; Treisman 2016). Though many in Ukraine were itching to sign the Association Agreement, Yanukovych refused, prompting protests and political turmoil that soon engulfed the entire country (Dragneva and Wolczuk 2015).

EU Policy since the Start of the Ukraine Crisis

When the crisis first erupted, the EU was unsure of how to proceed. The EU initially tried to remain as aloof as possible, choosing to respect the rights of citizens to protest and express gratitude that many Ukrainians wanted to build stronger bonds with the EU (Kuzio 2016). The EU also condemned Yanukovych for using violence against protestors (Kuzio 2016). However, disagreements amongst states soon began to arise as the conflict persisted, with some member states advocating for more confrontation with Russia, especially as fighting began in the Donbas (Pond and Kundnani 2015; Kuzio 2016; Shagina 2017). Others states were wary of becoming too involved. EU institutions, like the Commission, continued to voice support for democratic measures and finding a non-violent solution to the protests (January 30, 2014). Over time, the EU started to formulate a comprehensive policy based on Russian sanctions and Ukrainian development, which both stemmed from compromises between member states.

With the annexation of Crimea and the outbreak of bloody conflict in the Donbas, the EU saw the need to form a clear policy toward Russia, though one that also accommodated the wishes of all member states (SAIS Group Meeting, Washington DC, March 2017). The resolution was to introduce sanctions that hit some individuals, demonstrating support for Ukraine (Shagina 2017). These sanctions were somewhat measured due to divisions between member states. For example, none of these initial sanctions targeted Russian officials, but only those declaring authority in Crimea after the referendum (Shagina 2017). However, after the shooting down of Malaysian Airlines Flight 17, which sparked public outcry in many member states such as the Netherlands, the sanctions grew more comprehensive. They grew to include the Russian oil sector, Russian banks, and introduced an embargo on weapons trade (Shagina 2017; *BBC* 2014). Thus, the EU did create common policy, which it was also able to adjust unilaterally as further issues arose.

The sanctions try to bridge demands from multiple member states, and as a result are more extreme than some would like but not harsh enough for others. Notably, the sanctions do not touch gas, nuclear energy or space technology (*BBC* 2014). Gas, though a key component of EU-Russia trade, was not targeted due to most of Europe's heavy dependence on Russian gas imports. Therefore, the sanctions are more tepid than some would like. However, others argue that the sanctions are excessive and want them removed (SAIS Group Meeting; Kyiv, March 2017). This is partly because some states feel the economic effects of the sanctions more than others (particularly after Russia introduced counter-sanctions on many agricultural goods), yet some are more willing to withstand the economic pain (SAIS Group Meeting, Kyiv, March 2017). Like the EaP, sanctions are also a compromise, as the EU itself had to build a cohesive policy out of vastly different national agendas. The sanctions highlight both the EU's ability to act as a unitary actor (by being able to introduce them) but also as a composite body, as serious disagreement persists amongst member states.

The EU has also fallen back on its typical policy in the neighborhood of promoting structural reforms that strive to make Ukraine more liberal, democratic, and market-friendly. The Commission is leading most of the process, though some states like Germany and Poland are individually involved as advisors (Gressel 2015). The EU's role in promoting structural reforms does resemble policies in accession countries; however, the EU has fewer incentives to offer Ukraine since membership is not on the agenda. Instead, most incentives are financial the EU has donated money itself, encouraged IMF loans, and worked with the European Investment Bank (EIB) and European Bank for Reconstruction and Development (EBRD) to do the same (SAIS Group Meeting, EU Commission, Kyiv, 24 March 2017). However, even here compromises were made—the EU itself donated relatively little to Ukraine as compared to amounts given to member states in the past, largely because of challenges in rallying support from member states (SAIS Group Meeting, Washington DC, February 2017). The EU has also had a significant presence in humanitarian efforts in the Donbas. For example, ECHO, the humanitarian wing of the External Action Service, strives not only to provide aid but also to address critical issues in the region, such as water security (SAIS Group Meeting, EU Commission, Kyiv, 24 March 2017). Ukraine has verbally committed to implementing reforms, yet progress is slow, raising questions as to how feasible some reforms are, how dedicated Ukraine is to reforming, and how effective EU policy is without the promise of membership.

Lastly, the EU does remain a vocal supporter of the Minsk process, and two member states (France and Germany) are part of the Normandy Quartet (see chapter by

Linan Peng). Though neither country acts on behalf of the EU at these talks, the process does shape overall EU policy towards Ukraine since these countries both influence EU projects.

Conclusion

EU policy in Ukraine consists of decisions made at both the supranational and national level, which means that the EU behaves as a unitary actor at times and a composite body at others. The EU has pursued both sanctions and development aid to help Ukraine, and both of these policies ultimately reflect compromises made between member states. On the one hand, EU policy does seem somewhat tepid, as sanctions do not target some key Russian industries like gas, while Ukraine is expected to implement massive structural reforms without the powerful incentive of future membership in the EU.

However, though it may be easy to criticize EU policy, it has done far more than many thought. For example, agreeing on sanctions alone was an achievement, while using the EBRD and EIB as tools to aid development does help promote structural reform in Ukraine. Moreover, since some states are more actively involved in Ukrainian development and the Minsk process, this gives EU institutions the ability to focus on development and humanitarian support, which is an area of expertise. Hence, considering the limitations the EU faces in foreign policy, it has acted with relative consistency and vigor and achieved quite a lot given some very real constraints.

Recommendations

<u>To the European Union</u>

- **The EU should continue to promote reforms in Ukraine** through a series of mechanisms, including the EIB and EBRD.
- The EU should recognize that once visa liberalization and other components of the EaP pass, it will have little to offer Ukraine in exchange for reforms. Therefore, **it should begin to brainstorm further ways to keep Ukraine engaged in the reform process**, even if these do not include membership, such as further economic cooperation or access to EU consultation.

- **EU member states should show a united front in multilateral settings in supporting further funds to Ukraine**, as well as the existing OSCE special monitoring mission and other humanitarian efforts.
- **The EU should focus on further humanitarian work in the Donbas**, as there is massive need for this and its efforts thus far have been successful.

Conclusion

P. Terrence Hopmann

At the time of our SAIS Conflict Management trip to Ukraine in March 2017, the outcome of the multiple conflicts in Ukraine remained very much uncertain. The Russian annexation and incorporation of Crimea into the Russian Federation had become a *fait accompli,* although not recognized as legal by all but a few states in the international community; Crimea has thus effectively become a "frozen" conflict, similar to those in neighboring regions of Georgia and Moldova. But violence continued to rage along the "line of contact" in the two Donbas regions of Donetsk and Luhansk, in spite of two cease-fire agreements negotiated by the parties in Minsk, Belarus. At the time of our visit, approximately 10,000 persons had been killed in the fighting, including both combatants and civilians, and about 1.7 million inhabitants of the region fled to other parts of Ukraine as IDPs, while some one million also fled to Russia as refugees, bringing normal life largely to a halt in those regions. In spite of the continued fighting along the line of contact, the basic line dividing separatist and Russian forces on one side and Ukrainian national forces on the other has not changed materially since the Minsk II agreement of February 2015.

As Mark Brass describes in his chapter, there is no short-term prospect for a military victory by either side. Even the most "hawkish" Ukrainian analysts do not believe that Ukraine can win the conflict militarily, and at most they would like to receive more sophisticated weaponry to pursue what one leading defense analyst described as "active defense," an ability to deter a more visible Russian military intervention with anti-tank and anti-aircraft weapons. Any significant offensive push, though, by the Ukrainian army would most likely be met with a counter-escalation by Russian forces, leading to a war that few if any Ukrainians believe they could win. At the same time, most believe that Russia would be unlikely to initiate a major escalation without such a provocation, as that would necessarily entail the introduction of Russian armored vehicles and air support and remove any doubt about the level of Russian engagement in the conflict. Although a few analysts believe that there is some chance for a Russian push across southern Ukraine to create a land bridge to Crimea, most tend to believe that the military situation is likely to remain violent and unstable, but with a low probability of major escalation or change in the *status quo* on the ground.

The Minsk diplomatic process, at the same time, has tried to bring an end to fighting along the "line of contact," as Linan Peng describes in her chapter, but as of March 2017 their efforts have been to little avail. The Minsk agreements have sought to create a stable cease-fire in order to permit local and regional elections in the break-away regions that could take place under a new Ukrainian constitutional amendment that would grant a significant degree of autonomy to these regions within a federal system. However, the negotiations in Minsk have been stymied by a classic "chicken and egg" problem, namely that the separatists and their Russian backers argue that devolution of power to the regions must come before there is a stable cease-fire, whereas the Government of Ukraine argues that the measures necessary to implement greater regional autonomy, especially local and regional elections, cannot take place in the presence of massive violence, so that a fully implemented cease-fire must come first. The problem, as Peng notes, is that there is no party available in the region to enforce compliance with the terms of the Minsk agreements, so that violations take place on a regular basis. Meanwhile, the Minsk negotiations seek to create confidence-building measures on specific, concrete issues where common interests exist, such as water pipelines that crisscross the conflict zone. The Special Representative of the OSCE Chairperson-in-Office serves as a third-party facilitator in the Trilateral Contact Group (TCG), in which Russia and Ukraine are the other full participants, while representatives of the self-proclaimed Donetsk and Lugansk Peoples' Republics are present as "observers." The TCG, in turn, reports both to the OSCE Permanent Council in Vienna and to the so-called Normandy Quartet of France, Germany, Russia and Ukraine.

Under the terms of the Minsk Agreements, the cease-fire and other provisions are to be monitored by the OSCE's Special Monitoring Mission (SMM), a force at the time of our trip with over 700 unarmed monitors stationed throughout Ukraine, but predominantly in the eastern regions. As Angelica Valdez reports, the SMM is limited in its effectiveness because its mandate does not include any peacekeeping or peace-enforcement role; their job is primarily to report the facts as they observe them, and their daily reports indicate that there are literally hundreds of violations occurring every day throughout the conflict zone. Since their mandate derives from the OSCE, a consensus-based organization with 57 participating states including Russia and Ukraine, the SMM must maintain strict neutrality or face the likelihood that its mandate will not be renewed as required on an annual basis. Therefore, although it cannot identify the violating party explicitly, it is apparent from their reports that there are widespread violations by all parties, but the SMM cannot take any action against the culpable parties. In spite of these many limitations to its effectiveness noted by Valdez, its mere presence may have deterred further significant escalation by either side, thereby reinforcing the unstable and violent situation on the ground, but nonetheless preventing the parties from engaging in any major escalatory steps that would widen or deepen the existing violence.

Given that an end to the violence seems far into the future and that most Ukrainian analysts see no prospect of immediately regaining their "temporarily occupied territories," most hopes for an eventual resolution rest on the belief that a more politically open, transparent government in Kyiv will be able to produce sufficient economic gains with reduced corruption and an improvement of the humanitarian situation so that belonging to Ukraine will, over the long-run, be more attractive than ties with Russia to residents of the Donbas region, and perhaps even Crimea. If so, Ukrainians hope that residents of these regions will eventually cease their separatist conflict and negotiate a political settlement with Kyiv. In other words, their goal is to make belonging to the Ukrainian state a magnet that will attract the separatists to return to Ukraine through a political/diplomatic path rather than bringing them back by force of arms. At the same time, most Ukrainians are painfully aware that this is a tall order that presents many challenges to the country.

The first set of challenges is in the realm of political reform. Ross Hurwitz argues that Ukraine, though more democratic than most other post-Soviet states, still falls well short of an ideal, liberal democracy. For the first 20 years of independence, the presidency tended to alternate between incumbents from the more pro-Russian eastern Ukraine and those from the more pro-European western Ukraine, thereby reinforcing an identity divide that split the country rather evenly. However, with the flight of President Yanukovych to Russia in February 2015, his Party of Regions largely fell out of favor in Ukraine, and President Poroshenko was elected in May 2015 with 56% of the vote, a decisive victory compared to that of most of his predecessors. However, two years later, we found that much of his support had withered away, largely due to a widespread belief that governance by Ukraine's wealthy oligarchy had not changed, and that pervasive corruption had not yet been dealt with adequately. Even the president's closest former advisors with whom we met expressed disappointment with the performance of the new government.

Yet the opposition is very much divided, as Hurwitz observes, with six political parties holding 154 seats in the 450 member Rada (parliament) along with 47 unaffiliated deputies. Furthermore, these opposition parties hold very different positions, even on the conflict. For example, the Party of Regions is trying to reconstitute itself as a European-style Socialist Party, led by Yanukovych's former Foreign Minister Leonid Kozhara; while condemning the invasion of Crimea by Russia as a blatant act of aggression, his party also advocates political reconciliation with Russia to bring an end to fighting in the Donbas region. At the other end stands the Self-Reliance Party led by Deputy Rada Speaker Oksana Syroyid, who opposes the Minsk process and favors Ukraine taking matters in the Donbas into its own hands, not to seek military victory, but to pressure its leaders to negotiate more seriously. Mikheil Saakashvili, former president of Georgia, who held the post of Governor of Odesa rayon after leaving Georgia, came to Kyiv to form a political movement focusing on the fight against corruption; the degree to which his movement has taken hold in Ukraine, however, seemed questionable to many other Ukrainian politicians we encountered. Finally, Yulia Tymoshenko, the populist leader who has moved back and forth between the position of prime minister and serving time in prison during the Yanukovych years, had at the time of our visit emerged as the most popular opposition figure in Ukraine. Taken together, however, the absence of a clear political agenda for the opposition and significant infighting among the opposition parties means that the long-term stability of the Ukrainian government remains in doubt, and this political uncertainty creates a major obstacle for the government in Kyiv to become the "beacon" to which many hope that people in eastern Ukraine will eventually be drawn.

Another factor impeding eventual reintegration of the Donbas into Ukraine, as Gabriella Huddart writes, is the pervasive role of Russian media and propaganda within that region. Russian media has largely emphasized the wildly exaggerated view that the

Euromaidan movement was dominated by right-wing "fascists" from western Ukraine, playing on animosities that divided Ukraine, especially during and after World War II. As Huddart emphasizes, Ukraine has tried to counter this Russian propaganda, but much of this effort falls short, in part because of the high saturation of the market in the east by Russian media and also because the relatively free press in Ukraine makes it more open to a diversity of views. However, she also emphasizes that too often the Government's Ministry of Information Policy has resorted to its own counter-propaganda that appears to mimic the Russian media and cyber campaign rather than highlighting the relatively democratic and open media market in Ukraine.

On a more positive note, Chloe Colbert emphasizes the increasing role of women in Ukraine, especially in the political life of the country. The role of women in supporting the Euromaidan demonstrations has frequently been documented, but Colbert also notes that many have taken their place as combatants on the front lines in the Donbas. Ukrainian women have also been among the largest group of leaders and activists in civil society organizations, especially those assisting the huge number of IDPs in Ukraine. But it is in the political life of Ukraine where female political leaders, such as Yulia Tymoshenko and Oksana Syroyid, have emerged and acquired significant popular following. However, Colbert also notes that the frequent belief that women primarily play the role of peacemakers is, at least in part, contradicted by the Ukraine case, where women have fought in battle and led political movements that are frequently highly nationalistic and opposed to peace processes that they believe fail to realize Ukrainian national interests. She thus emphasizes that there is no single "women's narrative" of the conflict, and that Ukrainian women play a wide variety of roles about the violent conflict in their country.

The ability of Ukraine to attract separatists in the east to want to return to Ukraine may depend most importantly, however, on the success of the Ukrainian economy. Economic difficulties in the Donbas basin were among the many drivers of conflict in the first place. Once a center of Soviet industrial might, the breakup of the Soviet Union and the changing global economy has made the heavy industry and coal production in Donbas no longer in high demand. Alex Simon notes that the separatist movement gained strength as a result of the economic decline in Ukraine as a whole, and in Donbas in particular, in the early years of the decade. At the same time, economic conditions in the breakaway regions have worsened considerably since the outbreak of fighting and have made the region heavily dependent on Russia for its economic survival. This dependency notwithstanding, the Donbas regions have also retained vital infrastructure links that cut across the "line of contact," especially water pipe lines, the electricity grid, and energy lines; even coal mined in the east is shipped across the line of contact for processing and then either returned to the Donbas or shipped abroad. Simon explains that these economic ties have been disrupted by the blockade against goods entering the non-government controlled areas by train, initiated by "volunteers" in January 2017 and endorsed by the Ukrainian Government in March. This form of economic warfare, according to Simon, is unlikely to create sufficient "hurt" among separatists to force more serious negotiation, but in fact it is likely to intensify the animosity between the two sides as well as worsen economic conditions for both.

On a somewhat more positive side, Dorothea Cheek notes that the huge influx of IDPs from the eastern regions into the rest of Ukraine has not had the disastrous economic consequences that many analysts feared. Because many of these IDPs are better educated and come with valuable skills, despite the serious obstacles they face, many have been able to obtain good jobs and contribute to the economic growth of the country as a whole. In fact, Cheek finds that unemployment has generally decreased in regions to which IDPs have moved, and many IDPs have been able to contribute significantly to the economy of the regions where they have settled.

One of the most fundamental issues that Ukraine must confront in order to become an attractive "home" for separatists in the east is the fight against entrenched corruption. As Karina Panyan argues, this corruption is in part a legacy of Soviet-era corruption that has been hard to break. At the same time, post-Soviet privatization provided numerous opportunities for Ukrainian oligarchs to amass massive fortunes and, thereby, to dominate post-Soviet politics throughout the country. Panyan notes that a National Anti-Corruption Bureau created in 2014 is an important step in the right direction, but she also argues that its powers are limited by the absence of a clear definition of corruption and its inability to indict and prosecute corrupt officials, as it is restricted to collecting and providing information for government prosecutors. However, in the presence of an inefficient or even corrupt judicial system that itself needs to be reformed, this is not sufficient to eliminate some of the most deeply entrenched corruption. The result is a great deal of cynicism throughout the country about the role of government, not only in the breakaway regions, that must be countered if Kyiv is ever to be an attractive symbol of unity for all residents of Ukraine.

In conflicts that have divided Ukraine, it is important to remember that the victims are often innocent civilians whose lives are disrupted in many ways by the violence, a disruption that also makes post-conflict reconciliation more difficult to achieve. Kevin Toda emphasizes the extensive human rights violations that have accompanied the conflict, in which over 2,000 civilians have been killed as of early 2017, due to direct exposure to ordinance used in violation of the Minsk cease-fire or to land mines that have been placed widely throughout the conflict zone. In addition, people have been detained arbitrarily, been tortured, or have even disappeared; although cases have occurred on both sides, the largest portion appear to be within the non-government controlled territories, where information has also been difficult to obtain. Journalists have been threatened and frequently killed for doing their job, and the movement of people throughout the conflict zone has been greatly restricted. In 2015, the Ukrainian Ministry of Justice adopted a National Action Plan on Human Rights, supported by the UN Office of the High Commissioner for National Minorities and the Commissioner for Human Rights of the Council of Europe. However, like the National Anti-Corruption Bureau, the declared goals have been identified but actual implementation falls far short of the stated goals. Since human rights violations also create distrust and animosity, the failure to address these concerns more effectively could undermine efforts at post-conflict reconciliation or even reduce the interest by residents of the Donbas to accept Ukrainian sovereignty over their territory at any time in the foreseeable future.

Undoubtedly the largest humanitarian consequence of the conflicts in Ukraine has been the huge numbers of persons who have had to flee their homes, either as internationally displaced persons (IDPs) within Ukraine or as refugees within the Russian Federation. The number of IDPs living in the government controlled areas of Ukraine exceed 1.7 million in early 2017 according to official statistics, of whom a majority (62%) are women. As Ashley Patton emphasizes, most fled because of the violence they experienced at home, but also because of the economic problems that worsened dramatically in the non-government controlled territories after fighting broke out. Although many IDPs are professional and have been able to find work in their new areas of residence, as described by Cheek, almost all have experienced significant obstacles to integration in their new communities. As Patton enumerates, some have faced legal difficulties with voting registration and other legal rights, some have faced problems due to the shortage of housing for such large numbers of IDPs, access to health care has sometime been limited, many less skilled individuals have faced difficulties to find employment, and some Russian-speakers confront language problems when resettling in areas that are predominantly Ukrainian speaking. We witnessed a dramatic illustration of both the resilience and difficulties for the IDPs when we visited the newly created branch of the Donetsk National University in the western Ukrainian city of Vinnytsia. Here a majority of faculty and students from the university moved together from Donetsk city in the Donbas to re-establish their university in Vinnytsia. With the assistance of the International Renaissance Foundation, they have converted old factories into classrooms and offices and have continued to operate as a fully functioning university that comprehensively covers the full range of the academic curriculum. Their enthusiasm and resilience in their new location represents a spirit to continue life as it was before, while also demonstrating clearly that the conflict dividing Ukraine is not primarily about the issue of language, as is often depicted; here educated Russian-speaking scholars and students have shown that they too are Ukrainian regardless of their city of origin and native language.

On the other hand, the transition to a new setting has not been so easy for many school-age children affected by the conflict, as Christina Connelly-Kanmaz demonstrates in her chapter. Over 200,000 of the IDPs are children, many of them severely affected by the trauma of having experienced war in their previous homes, and they carry with them haunting memories of the violence they experienced. Younger children are also faced with the difficulty of integrating into local schools where Ukrainian is the language of instruction. Parents have faced problems with registering their children for school and obtaining essential records from their original schools. Children living in or near the conflict zone face even greater problems, as school buildings have been damaged, destroyed, or occupied by military forces, and military action frequently occurs near their schools and homes. Both the Government of Ukraine and multiple civil society and international non-governmental organizations have mobilized to aid these displaced children now living in government controlled areas, but the effort to meet the educational needs of such a large population of children is daunting, and additional help is still needed to see that these children are able to obtain their right to education.

Persons belonging to minorities have also been serious victims of the conflicts in Ukraine, whether or not they are also IDPs. As Anna Goodman points out, Jewish, Roma, and Tatar minorities have all been affected by the conflict. Jews have long played an important role in Ukrainian history, but Ukrainian Jews became massive victims of Stalin's "Holodomor" or forced starvation, his later purges, and above all the mass slaughter of virtually all Ukrainian Jews under the Nazi occupation, in which much of the killing was carried out by Ukrainian collaborators. Although the Jewish population of Ukraine today is relatively small, all continue to live under the specter of the Holocaust, reinforced by renewed violence in their homeland and even fear of the small, but outspoken neo-Nazi movements that have appeared in western Ukraine in opposition to Russia. The Roma population too suffers from systematic discrimination in Ukraine, as is the case also throughout much of Central Europe. Roma have always been subjected to hate crimes, and in times of widespread violence these became more prevalent, although it is also often difficult to distinguish between hate crimes and other acts of violence in an unstable situation like that in Ukraine.

However, the largest minority group to suffer from the fighting in Ukraine is undoubtedly the Crimean Tatars, a mostly Muslim people who were indigenous to Crimea but were deported to Central Asia by Stalin late in World War II. As Christina Pushaw writes, the Tatars were allowed to return to Crimea during the Gorbachev presidency in the Soviet Union, and expanded after the breakup of the Soviet Union. Since most of those who came to Crimea had never lived there before, having been born in Central Asia, they gradually began to restore their political rights and social status within the autonomous Ukrainian region of Crimea, with the special assistance of the OSCE's High Commissioner on National Minorities. They established their own Mejlis (parliament) alongside the Crimean parliament, all within what they believed to be sovereign Ukrainian territory. Therefore, most strongly opposed the Russian occupation that took place in early 2014, and the vast majority boycotted the Russian-sponsored referendum on the transfer of Crimea to Russian sovereignty. Since that transfer, however, as Pushaw reports, many fled and those who remained in Crimea have been marginalized and have experienced human rights violations such as being detained as political prisoners or placed in psychiatric "hospitals." Due to their Islamic faith, generally very moderate, Russian authorities have nonetheless accused them of being terrorists without any apparent evidence. Mosques have been monitored closely, and many Tatars have been prosecuted for allegedly planning to commit terrorist acts. Finally, they suffer from the fear of having been forgotten by the international community and even by the Ukrainian government, as national and international attention has focused mostly on the ongoing conflict in the Donbas rather than the "frozen" conflict in Crimea. Civil society organizations in Kyiv, supported by international donors, have tried to maintain awareness of what is happening to Tatars in Crimea and elsewhere in Ukraine, and they have organized activities to aid Tatar IDPs to integrate into their communities, often a more formidable task than that faced by IDPs from the Donbas. But, despite these efforts, Crimean Tatars risk becoming the most disadvantaged community of all as a consequence of the violent change of governance in Crimea, compounded by the risk that their suffering will be largely forgotten by those managing the conflict in Donbas.

As Ukraine struggles to cope with internal conflict and political and economic insecurity, the international community has an important role to play. The primary international actor in Ukraine has been the Organization or Security and Cooperation in Europe (OSCE), a 57-country organization founded in 1975 by the Helsinki Final Act, and strengthened after the Cold War by new security tasks found *inter alia* in the 1990 Charter of Paris for a New Europe and in the humanitarian field in the Copenhagen Document on the Human Dimension of Security. After playing a major role in managing conflicts in Eurasia and Central Europe during the post-Cold War transition, many participating states came to believe that the OSCE no longer had a major role to play in European security until the Ukraine crisis came along, which in many ways reinvigorated the OSCE. As Linan Peng indicates, the OSCE has played the major third party role in the Minsk peace process, led in 2017 by the Special Representative of the OSCE Chairperson-in-Office, Ambassador Martin Sajdik (SAIS Bologna, 1974) of Austria. Monitoring of the Minsk II Agreement has been the responsibility of the OSCE Special Monitoring Mission, as discussed by Angelica Valdez and Mark Brass. Finally, advice and assistance on many aspects of democratic development, electoral processes, and internal reform has been provided by the office of the OSCE Project Coordinator in Ukraine, supported by the Office of Democratic Institutions and Human Rights (ODIHR), based in Warsaw.

The Commission of the European Union (EU) has also played a significant, if sometimes divided role in assisting Ukraine to manage its conflicts, as discussed by Rebecca Grenham. It was, of course, President Yanukovych's rejection of the EU's Association Agreement that sparked the Maidan demonstrations and the ensuing conflict in Ukraine, so it should hardly be surprising that the future relationship between Ukraine and the EU remains a widely-debated topic within the country and in Brussels. As Grenham points out, however, EU member states often have different interests and relationships with Ukraine, with members such as Poland and the Baltic states favoring speedy Ukrainian accession to the EU, whereas some Western European states that had formed the original core of the EU are generally more cautious, some even expressing a preference for ending sanctions that were imposed upon Russia because of its annexation of Crimea and its support for separatists in the Donbas. The EU's compromise, as Grenham emphasizes, has been to promote liberal, democratic and market-friendly policies in Ukraine, as well as to provide humanitarian assistance to victims of the conflict. Although reforms in these areas might make Ukraine eventually eligible for membership in the EU, present policies essentially push that issue off into the future while focusing first on efforts to end the violent conflict and responding to its many humanitarian consequences.

Finally, the United Nations has also played a role in conflict management in the Ukraine conflict, as analyzed by Qifan Huang. The Security Council has endorsed the Minsk II agreement and condemned the downing of the Malaysian airplane over non-government controlled territory. However, Russian vetoes in the Security Council have largely stymied more active UN engagement in direct conflict management. Ukraine has filed suits in the International Court of Justice, accusing Russia of multiple violations of international accords, but it seems unlikely that Russia will agree to participate in this process. On the other hand, the UN General Assembly has passed resolutions endorsing the territorial integrity of Ukraine within its original boundaries. Therefore, Huang argues that it might be appropriate for the General Assembly to resurrect the "Uniting for Peace" resolutions to enable the UN to engage more actively in a conflict involving one of its permanent five members without facing the possibility of a veto. He suggests that such a resolution might endorse deployment of a peacekeeping mission with greater authority for peace enforcement than is allowed in the limited mandate of the OSCE's SMM. However, given the past limitations on the capacity of the UN to seek a resolution of the primary underlying issues of the conflict, Huang emphasizes that to date the UN has focused mostly on humanitarian operations relating to the conflict, cooperating with other international organizations such as the OSCE and international NGOs and local civil society organizations. In this regard, the role of the UN High Commissioner for Refugees has been particularly important in assisting the large number of IDPs in Ukraine, as noted as well by Patton. In short, Huang argues that the UN could play a greater supporting role in managing the conflict in Ukraine without being stymied by a Russian veto if it identified more creative ways to engage in conflict management in politically sensitive regions such as Ukraine.

In conclusion, the situation that our SAIS Conflict Management group observed in Ukraine in March 2017 was very fluid. Although the situation in Crimea appeared to have become more or less "frozen," the Donbas conflict remained highly unstable. While the basic line of contact had not changed for more than two years, it still had not reached a "mutually hurting stalemate," nor had the parties discovered a "mutually enticing opportunity" to escape from the conflict (Zartman 2008), both of which might have facilitated a more serious negotiation to seek a resolution of the fundamental drivers that created these conflicts in the first place. At the time of our visit, the focus of all engaged parties was mostly on management of the conflict, preventing escalation—especially an overt Russian-Ukrainian military confrontation—or a worsening of the domestic situation in Ukraine, rather than seeking resolution. The dominant consensus that emerged, albeit with many variations, was that the military situation remained static but unstable, although it was unlikely to yield a convincing "victory" by either party. Therefore, the focus of conflict management necessarily concentrated on caring for the victims of the conflict, especially IDPs and persons belonging to minorities, while attempting to restore faith in a transparent political process and economic development of Ukraine, which many Ukrainians believe will, over the long-run, make Ukraine a democratic and prosperous country to which all of its citizens will want to belong. Achieving that goal will necessarily require time and a great deal of effort by all parties involved, but the entire international community has a stake in aiding Ukraine in this process so as eventually to realize peace, national reconciliation, and unity within a single, independent and sovereign state.

List of Briefings and Interviews

Washington, DC Briefings

February-March 2017

- **Ambassador Valeriy Chaly**, Ambassador of Ukraine to the United States (February 8, 2017, Embassy of Ukraine, Washington, DC)
- **Ambassador William Taylor**, Executive Vice President, US Institute of Peace; former US Ambassador to Ukraine (February 16, 2017, SAIS)
- **Dr. William Hill**, Professor at the National Defense University; former Head of the OSCE Mission to Moldova, and a former US Foreign Service officer (February 21, 2017, SAIS)
- **Dr. Anders Aslund,** Atlantic Council; Swedish economist and diplomat who served as economic advisor to the Government of Russia (1991-94) and of Ukraine (1994-97) (February 28, 2917, SAIS)
- **Ambassador John Herbst**, Director, Dinu Patriciu Eurasia Center at the Atlantic Council; former US Ambassador to Ukraine (March 8, 2017, SAIS)
- **Ms Caroline Vicini**, Deputy Head of the Mission of the European Commission in Washington (March 14, 2017, SAIS)

Ukraine Briefings

Kyiv and Vinnytsia
20-24 March 2017

Monday, 20 March - Kyiv
- Meeting with **Natalia Karbowski**, Director for Strategic Development, Ukrainian Women's Fund
- Meeting with **Ambassador Vaidotas Verba** and **Jeffrey Erlich**, OSCE Project Coordinator in Ukraine
- Briefing by **Alexander Hug**, Deputy Head of the OSCE Special Monitoring Mission (SMM)
- Briefing by **Florian Poetter,** Political Advisor, Office of the Special Representative of the OSCE Chair-in-Office (currently Austria) to the Minsk process
- Reception at US Embassy Residence hosted by **George Kent**, Deputy Chief of Mission (SAIS '92) with embassy staff and SAISers in Kyiv

Tuesday, 21 March - Kyiv
- Meeting with **Mikheil Saakashvili**, founder of the Movement of New Forces in Ukraine, former President of Georgia and Governor of Odesa Oblast, Ukraine
- Meeting with **Sergei Sobolev**, Fatherland Party, political associate of Yulia Timoshenko
- Briefing by **Grigoriy Perepelytsia**, Director, Foreign Policy Research Institute, Diplomatic Academy, Ministry of Foreign Affairs of Ukraine

Wednesday, 22 March - Kyiv
- Tour of Government area led by Prof. Leonid Kistersky, Director, Institute for International Business Development, Kyiv
- Meeting with **Leonid Kozhara**, President, Socialist Party of Ukraine and former Foreign Minister, and **Professor Alexei Plotnicov**, VicePresident
- Meeting with **Ambassador Olexander F. Motsyk**, Ukrainian Representative to the Minsk Political Working Group (former Ukrainian ambassador to the US)
- Meeting with **Oksana Syroyid**, Deputy Speaker of the Verkhovna Rada (Self Reliance Party)

Thursday, 24 March - Vinnytsia
- Coffee at Donetsk National University Co-Working Club
- Introduction, **Professor Tatiana Orekhova**, Vice-Rector for International Affairs, Donetsk National University in Vinnytsia
- Working Groups (with students, faculty and researchers from Donetsk National University in Vinnytsia)
- Meetings with IDP groups at the NGO **"Vis"**
- Meeting with **"Dzerelo nadyy" (Spring of Hope)**, NGO that supports IDP's in Vinnytsia oblast

Friday, 24 March - Kyiv
- Meeting with **Vadim Chernysh**, Minister for the Temporarily Occupied Territories and Internally Displaced Persons of Ukraine, and **Norbert Ruetsche**, Senior Advisor to the Minister (Federal Department of Foreign Affairs of Switzerland)
- Meeting with **Oleh Rybachuk**, Anti-Corruption Campaign
- Meeting with **Manar Merzouk**, Head, Directorate-General for European Civil Protection and Humanitarian Aid Operations – ECHO, and **Fabio Della Piazza**, Head of Political Section, Delegation of the European Union to Ukraine, European Commission Office in Ukraine
- Meeting with **Crimea SOS**, NGO supporting Crimean Tatars

Bibliography

РИА Новости. 08 December 2009. "Россия поддержала позицию Сербии по Косово в Международном суде." *РИА Новости.* Accessed 1 April 2017. https://ria.ru/international_justice/20091208/197915491.html.

991st Plenary Meeting. *Decision No. 1117: Deployment of an OSCE Special Monitoring Mission to Ukraine.* Permanent Council Journal No. 991, Agenda Item 1. 21 March 2014.

Abdelal, Rawi. 2013. "The Profits of Power: Commerce and Realpolitik in Eurasia." *Review of International Political Economy* 20:3.

Abrams, Neil, and M. Steven Fish. 2016. "Dethroning Ukraine's Oligarchs: A How-To Guide." *Foreign Policy.* http://foreignpolicy.com/2016/06/13/dethroning-ukraines-oligarchs-a-how-to-guide/.

Agence France-Presse. 23 March 2017. "Ukraine Central Bank Warns of Steep Hit from Trade Blockade." Agence France-Presse. Accessed 29 March 2017.

Altshuller, Maria. 2017. "Ukraine Another Forgotten War: The Lack of a Western Response to the Ukrainian Conflict." *Harvard International Review* 38 (2): 7-8.

American Association for the Advancement of Science (AAAS). 2014. *Satellite Imagery Assessment of the Crisis in Crimea, Ukraine: Part One, Sevastopol.*

Amnesty International and Human Rights Watch. 21 July 2016. *"You Don't Exist" Arbitrary Detentions, Enforced Disappearances, and Torture in Eastern Ukraine.*

Andreyuk, Eugenia, Emine Asanova, and Yan Avseyushkin. 2016. "Crimea Situation Report." Crimea SOS.

Aslund, Anders. 9 July 2015. "Russia's War on Ukraine's Economy." *Project Syndicate.* Accessed 28 March 2017. https://www.project-syndicate.org/commentary/russia-war-on-ukraine-economy-by-anders-aslund-2015-07.

Baer, Daniel. 19 November 2015. "United States Mission to the OSCE: Response to the Report by OSCE High Commissioner on National Minorities Astrid Thors." *OSCE Permanent Council to Vienna.* http://www.osce.org/pc/203231?download=true.

Baltic Worlds. 2011. "Both Victim and Perpetrator: Ukraine's Problematic Relationship with the Holocaust." *Baltic Worlds.* Accessed February 2017. http://balticworlds.com/ukraine's-problematic-relationship-to-the-holocaust/.

Barroso, Jose Manuel Durao. 30 January 2014. "Remarks by President Barroso Following his Meeting with Donald Tusk, Prime Minister of Poland." http://europa.eu/rapid/press-release_SPEECH-14-79_en.htm.

Barroso, Jose Manuel Durao. 5 March 2014. "Remarks by President Barroso on Ukraine." *European Commission.* http://europa.eu/rapid/press-release_SPEECH-14-184_en.htm.

BBC News. 2009. "On the road: Centuries of Roma History." *BBC News.* Accessed February 2017. http://news.bbc.co.uk/2/hi/europe/8136812.

BBC News. 11 August 2014. "Ukraine Conflict: Turning up the TV Heat." *BBC News.* Accessed 6 April 2017. http://www.bbc.com/news/world-europe-28706461.

BBC News. 15 September 2014. "How Far do US-EU Sanctions On Russia Go?" *BBC News.* http://www.bbc.com/news/world-europe-28400218.

BBC News. 19 February 2017. "Russia accepts passports issued by east Ukraine rebels." *BBC News.* Accessed 23 April 2017. http://www.bbc.com/news/world-europe-39018429.

Bell, Bethany. 15 June 2015. "Ukraine Crisis heightens threats to media – OSCE." *BBC News.* Accessed 20 April 2017. http://www.bbc.com/news/world-europe-33137779.

Bjerga, Alan, and Volodymyr Verbyany. 13 October 2016. "That Boom You Hear is Ukraine's Agriculture." *Bloomberg Businessweek.* Accessed 28 March 2017. https://www.bloomberg.com/news/articles/2016-10-14/that-boom-you-hear-is-ukraine-s-agriculture.

Borzel, Tanja, and Thomas Risse. May 2009. "The Transformative Power of Europe: The European Union and the Diffusion of Ideas." *KFG Working Paper.* Free University Berlin.

Brenzel, Hanna, Oleksandra Betliy, and Robert Kirchner. 2015. "Economic Issues of Internally Displaced People in Ukraine." German Advisory Group, Institute for Economic Research and Policy Consulting, *Policy Paper Series [PP/06/2015]* http://www.beratergruppe-ukraine.de/wordpress/wp-content/uploads/2015/12/PP_06_2015_en.pdf.

Central Election Commission. "Extraordinary Parliamentary Election 2014: Basic Electoral Statistics." http://www.cvk.gov.ua/pls/vnd2014/wp001e.

Cha, Joniel. 15 March 2017. Washington, DC. In-person Interview.

Chaisty, Paul, and Stephen Whitefield. 6 February 2015. "Support for Separatism in Southern and Eastern Ukraine is Lower than You Think." *The Washington Post*. Accessed 22 April 2017. https://www.washingtonpost.com/news/monkey-cage/wp/2015/02/06/support-for-separatism-in-southern-and-eastern-ukraine-is-lower-than-you-think/?utm_term=.e2c2f871dc27.

Christie, Edward Hunter. 22 June 2016. "The Design and Impact of Western Economic Sanctions against Russia." *RUSI Journal* Vol. 161, Issue 3.

Chubarov, Refat. 25 September 2014. "Repressions against Crimean Tatars are becoming life-threatening." *The Kyiv Post*. https://www.kyivpost.com/article/opinion/op-ed/refat-chubarov-repressions-against-crimean-tatars-are-becoming-life-threatening-365895.html.

Clem, Ralph S. 7 March 2014. "Why Eastern Ukraine is an integral part of Ukraine." *The Washington Post*. Accessed 22 April 2017.

Copsey, Nathaniel, and Karolina Pomorska. May 2014. "The Influence of Newer Member States in the European Union: The Case of Poland and the Eastern Partnership." *Europe-Asia Studies* Vol. 66.

Crimea SOS. 2016. "December 2016: Serious Violations of Human Rights in Crimea." Graphic. *Crimea SOS/Find & Free*. http://krymsos.com/en/reports/analitichni-zviti-po-krimu/grubi-porushennya-prav-lyudini-v-krimu-za-2016-rik/.

Crimea SOS. 2016. "Enforced Disappearances in Occupied Crimea as of December 2016." Graphic. *Crimea SOS*. http://krymsos.com/en/reports/analitichni-zviti-po-krimu/infografika-po-zniknennyam-v-okupovanomu-krimu/.

Davis-Cross, Mai'a, and Ireneusz Pawel Karolewski. January 2017. "What Type of Power has the EU Exercised in the Ukraine-Russia Crisis? A Framework of Analysis." *Journal of Common Market Studies* Vol. 55.

Denber, Rachel. 18 March 2014. "Crimea: Disappeared Man Found Killed, Urgent Investigation Needed." *Human Rights Watch*. https://www.hrw.org/news/2014/03/18/crimea-disappeared-man-found-killed.

Donath, Mirjam. 19 March 2014. "U.N. human rights team aims for quick access to Crimea – official." *Reuters: The Thompson Reuters Foundation*. http://news.trust.org//item/20140319210920-t5yh9/.

Dougherty, Jill. 2014. "Everyone Lies: The Ukraine Conflict and Russia's Media Transformation." Harvard Kennedy School Shorenstein Center on Media, Politics and Public Policy *Discussion Paper Series #D-88*.

Dragneva, Rilka and Kataryna Wolczuk. 2015. *Ukraine Between the EU and Russia.* Palgrave Pivot.

E.C. Europa. "Ukraine - Trade - European Commission." 2017. *Ec.Europa.Eu.* http://ec.europa.eu/trade/policy/countries-and-regions/countries/ukraine/.

The Economist. 8 December 2016 "The Motherlands Calls: Russian Propaganda is State-of-the-Art Again." *The Economist.* Accessed 5 April 2017. http://www.economist.com/news/europe/21711538-1930s-moscow-beacon-international-movement-russian-propaganda.

The Economist. 21 January 2017. "The Other War: Ukraine's Conflict is also Financial." Accessed 28 March 2017. http://www.economist.com/news/business-and-finance/21714931-russia-may-extract-3bn-ukraine-ukraines-conflict-russia-also.

Election Law of Ukraine, No. 4061-VI, Enacted November 17, 2011.

Embassy of Ukraine in the Kingdom of Thailand. 15 May 2015. Declaration "To the 71st Anniversary of Crimean Tatars Deportation." http://thailand.mfa.gov.ua/en/press-center/publications/2447-do-71-rokovin-deportaciji-krimsykih-tatar.

Engelhart, Katie. 2016. "Why Record Numbers of Ukrainian Jews are Fleeing to Israel." *Vice News.* Accessed February 2017. https://news.vice.com/article/why-record-numbers-of-ukrainian-jews-are-fleeing-to-israel.

Eurobarometer. *Public Opinion Polls.* Years 2005, 2008 and 2010; Topics: Enlargement—Ukraine; Common Military.

European Commission. "Foreign and Security Policy." https://europa.eu/european-union/topics/foreign-security-policy_en.

European Commission. "European Union Neighborhood Policy and Enlargement Negotiations." https://ec.europa.eu/neighbourhood-enlargement/policy/steps-towards-joining_en.

European Commission against Racism and Intolerance (ECRI). 2012. "ECRI Report on Ukraine: Fourth Monitoring Cycle." ECRI. Accessed February 2017. https://www.coe.int/t/dghl/monitoring/ecri/Country-by-country/Ukraine/UKR-CbC-IV-2012-006-ENG.pdf.

European Commission European Civil Protection and Humanitarian Aid Operations (ECHO). February 2017. "ECHO Factsheet – Ukraine." https://ec.europa.eu/echo/files/aid/countries/factsheets/ukraine_en.pdf.

Fix, Liana and Anna-Lena Kirch. January 2016. "Germany and the Eastern Partnership After the Ukraine Crisis." *Notes du Cerfa.* Institut français des relations internationales.

"Forbes Profile: Petro Poroshenko." *Forbes.com*. https://www.forbes.com/profile/petro-poroshenko/.

GfK Ukraine. 5 May 2016. "Out of School Children in Ukraine: A Study on the Scope and Dimensions of the Problem with Recommendations for Action." https://www.humanitarianresponse.info/system/files/documents/files/out_of_school_children_report_eng.pdf.

Giles, Keir. 2016. "Russia's 'New' Tools for Confronting the West: Continuity and Innovation in Moscow's Exercise of Power." *Chatham House, The Royal Institute of International Affairs.*

Gorchinskaya, Katya. 2015. "Looking West: Lviv Models Itself As Ukraine's Future." *Radiofreeeurope/Radioliberty*. http://www.rferl.org/a/ukraine-lviv-elections-model-of-future/27323230.html.

Grabbe, Heather. 2006. *The EU's Transformative Power*: *Europeanization Through Conditionality in Central and Eastern Europe*. Palgrave Macmillan.

Gressel, Gustav. 19 May 2015. "Germany and the Eastern Partnership—The View from Berlin." *Commentary*. European Council on Foreign Relations.

Gvozdeva, Evgeniya. 22 May 2014. "Russia/Ukraine: Crimea as a Hotbed of Radical Islam in Post-Soviet Space." *European Strategic Intelligence and Security Center: Briefing*. http://www.esisc.org/upload/publications/briefings/russia-ukraine-crimea-as-a-new-hotbed-of-radical-islam-in-post-soviet-space/Russia%20Ukraine.pdf.

Haughton, Tim. 2011. "Half Full but also Half Empty: Conditionality, Compliance and the Quality of Democracy in Central and Eastern Europe." *Political Studies Review* Vol. 9.

Haukkala, Hiski. 2016. "A Perfect Storm, or What Went Wrong and What Went Right for the EU in Ukraine." *Europe-Asia Studies* Vol. 68, issue 4.

Havlik, Peter, and Vasily Astrov. 2014. "Economic Consequences of the Ukraine Conflict." *The Vienna Institute for International Economic Studies*. https://wiiw.ac.at/economicconsequences-of-the-ukraine-conflict-dlp-3381.pdf.

Hiemstra, Janthomas. 2016. "E-Declaration Is A Real Breakthrough In Ukrainian Reforms." *UNDP in Ukraine*. http://www.ua.undp.org/content/ukraine/en/home/ourperspective/ourperspectivearticles/2016/10/31/e-declaration-is-a-real-breakthrough-in-ukrainian-reforms.html.

Hoddenbagh, Jonathan. 2016. "Macroeconomics, Introduction." Syllabus and Slides. School of Advanced International Studies, Johns Hopkins University.

Hoffman, Rafael. 2017. "Calls for Government to Condemn Anti-Semitism in March in Ukraine." *Hamodia*. Accessed March 2017. http://hamodia.com/2017/01/04/calls-government-condemn-anti-semitism-march-ukraine/.

Hopmann, P. Terrence. 1996. *The Negotiation Process and the Resolution of International Conflicts*. Columbia, SC: University of South Carolina Press.

Horga, Ioan and Ana-Maria Costea. 1 September 2014. "The Ukraine Crisis: Between National Preferences/Interests of EU Member States and EU Security." *Eurolimes*.

Human Rights Watch (HRW). 2006. "Ukraine World Report 2005." *Human Rights Watch*. Accessed February 2017. https://www.hrw.org/world-report/2006/country-chapters/ukraine.

Human Rights Watch (HRW). 25 January 2017. "Ukraine Armed Conflict-Related Abuse in Detention: Impunity on Both Sides." *Human Rights Watch*. Accessed 11 March 2017. https://www.hrw.org/news/2017/01/25/ukraine-armed-conflict-related-abuse-detention.

INEKO. 2015. "Unemployment in Ukraine: Prevailing Trends and Measures to Reduce It." *Institute for Economic and Social Reforms*. www.ineko.sk/file_download/934.

Interfax. 20 February 2017. "Russian recognition of DPR/LPR documents incompatible with Minsk process - U.S. Embassy to Ukraine." *Interfax*. Accessed 5 April 2017. http://eds.a.ebscohost.com.proxy1.library.jhu.edu/ehost/detail/detail?sid=abbe7a72-33fe-4249-9e08-cde6180a9dc5%40sessionmgr4009&vid=1&hid=4202&bdata=JnNpdGU9ZWhvc3QtbGl2ZSZzY29wZT1zaXRl#AN=121337848&db=tsh.

Interfax. 28 March 2017. "Minsk process to become pointless unless parties agree to tie military, political components of Donbas settlement." *Interfax*. Accessed 5 April 2017. http://eds.a.ebscohost.com.proxy1.library.jhu.edu/ehost/detail/detail?sid=e96ee0f5-5cb6-4ba7-ad45-212e418730ad%40sessionmgr4008&vid=0&hid=4202&bdata=JnNpdGU9ZWhvc3QtbGl2ZSZzY29wZT1zaXRl#AN=122096792&db=tsh.

International Court of Justice. 22 July 2010. "Accordance with International Law of the Unilateral Declaration of Independence in Respect of Kosovo." *International*

Court of Justice. Accessed 1 April 2017. http://www.icj-cij.org/docket/files/141/15987.pdf.

International Court of Justice. 17 January 2017. "Ukraine Institutes Proceedings against the Russian Federation and Requests the Court to Indicate Provisional Measures." *Application of the International Convention for the Suppression of the Financing of Terrorism and of the International Convention on the Elimination of All Forms of Racial Discrimination (Ukraine v. Russian Federation).* Accessed 1 April 2017. http://www.icj-cij.org/docket/files/166/19310.pdf.

Internal Displacement Monitoring Center (IDMC). 2015. "Ukraine IDP Figure Analysis." Accessed 31 March 2017. http://www.internal-displacement.org/europe-the-caucasus-and-central-asia/ukraine/figures-analysis.

Internal Displacement Monitoring Centre (IDMC). 2016. "IDMC's Global Internal Displacement Database." Accessed 2 April 2017. http://www.internal-displacement.org/database.

International Crisis Group. 18 July 2016. "Ukraine: The Line." *Europe Briefing No. 81.*

International Crisis Group. 5 February 2016. "Russia and the Separatists in Eastern Ukraine." *Europe and Central Asia Briefing No. 79.*

International Monetary Fund. August 2015. "Russian Federation: 2015 Article IV Consultation, Press Release and Staff Report." *IMF Country Report No. 15/211.*

International Partnership for Human Rights (IPHRI). September 2016. "International Crimes in Crimea: An Assessment of Two and a Half Years of Russian Occupation." http://iphronline.org/international-crimes-crimea-20160927.html.

Isachenkov, Vladimir. 17 March 2017. "Kremlin Says Ukraine Cuts Off Rebel East with its Own Hands." *Associated Press.* Accessed 28 March 2017. http://bigstory.ap.org/article/a2593c1dfdf44fa1ac55aabc6a296020/kremlin-says-ukraine-cuts-rebel-east-its-own-hands.

Izmirli, Idil. 21 March 2014. "Crimean Tatars Fear for Their Safety After Crimea's Annexation to Russia." *Eurasia Daily Monitor - Jamestown Foundation.*

Jacobsen, Katherine. 2017. "New Fears In Ukraine's Coal Country." *Best Countries.* https://www.usnews.com/news/best-countries/articles/2017-03-28/blockade-threatens-to-worsen-ukraines-frail-economy.

Jones, Charles I., and Peter J. Klenow. 2016. "Beyond GDP? Welfare Across Countries and Time." *American Economic Review* Vol. 106, No. 9: 2426–2457. http://klenow.com/Jones_Klenow.pdf.

Karlsen, Geir Hågen. 2016. "Tools of Russian Influence: Information and Propaganda." In *Ukraine and Beyond: Russia's Strategic Security Challenge to Europe*, edited by Janne Haaland Matlary and Tormod Heier, 181-208. Springer International Publishing AG Switzerland.

Kelley, Judith. 2004. "International Actors on the Domestic Scene: Membership Conditionality and Socialization by International Institutions." *International Organization* Vol. 58.

Kinstler, Linda. 2 March 2014. "The Crimean Tatars: A Primer." *New Republic.* https://newrepublic.com/article/116814/crimean-tatars-primer-why-population-opposes-putin.

Kirchgaessner, Stephanie. 10 June 2015. "Putin's trip to Rome underscores Russia's special relationship with Italy." *The Guardian.* https://www.theguardian.com/world/2015/jun/10/vladimir-putin-russia-trip-rome-italy.

Koeth, Wolfgang. 2016. "Leadership Revised: How Did the Ukraine Crisis and the Annexation of Crimea Affirm Germany's Leading Role in EU Foreign Policy?" *Lithuanian Annual Strategic Review* Vol. 14.

Kozak, Tatiana. 31 October 2016. "Tatars Mark One Year of Blockading Crimea." *Transitions Online.* http://www.tol.org/client/article/26407-tatars-mark-one-year-of-blockading-crimea.html.

Kramer, Andrew E. 29 April 2015. "Ukraine Separatists Rewrite History of 1930s Famine." *New York Times.* Accessed 2 April 2017. https://www.nytimes.com/2015/04/30/world/europe/ukraine-separatists-rewrite-history-of-1930s-famine.html?_r=0.

Kramer, Andrew E., Mike McIntire, and Barry Meier. 14 August 2016. "Secret Ledger in Ukraine Lists Cash for Donald Trump's Campaign Chief." *New York Times.* Accessed 4 April 2017. https://www.nytimes.com/2016/08/15/us/politics/paul-manafort-ukraine-donaldtrump.html.

Kramer, John M. 1977. "Political Corruption in the U.S.S.R." *The Western Political Quarterly* 30 (2): 213-224.

The Kremlin. 11 May 1944. "State Defense Committee Decree No. 5859ss." *Library of Congress.* http://www.loc.gov/exhibits/archives/l2tartar.html.

Kulbaev, T. S., and A. U. Khegai. 2000. *Deportation* (Russian). Almaty: Deneker.

Kuzio, Taras. 21 November 2012. "Russianization of Ukrainian National Security Policy under Viktor Yanukovych." *Journal of Slavic Military Studies* Vol. 25.

Kuzio, Taras. 24 August 2016. "Ukraine Between a Constrained EU and an Assertive Russia." *Journal of Common Market Studies* Vol. 55, Issue 1.

Kuzio, Taras. 2016. "Two Myths About Nationalism and Anti-Semitism in Ukraine." *The Washington Post.* Accessed February 2017. https://www.washingtonpost.com/news/monkey-cage/wp/2016/08/01/ukraine-is-seeing-nationalism-and-anti-semitism-from-both-right-and-left-wing-forces/?utm_term=.6ac9bd4d0888.

Lund, Michael S. 1996. *Preventing Violent Conflicts: A Strategy for Preventive Diplomacy.* Washington, DC: United States Institute of Peace Press.

Machitidze, Ivanna. 2016. "The Eastern Partnership Project: Does Poland's Voice Still Matter?" *Centre for European Studies Working Papers* Vol. 8.

Makarenko, Olena. 28 January 2017. "Ukrainian Soldiers Initiate Trade Blockade with Occupied Donbas Territories." *Euromaidan Press.* Accessed 28 March 2017. http://euromaidanpress.com/2017/01/28/ukrainian-soldiers-initiate-trade-blockade-with-occupied-donbas-territories/.

Manners, Ian. 2002. "Normative Power Europe: A Contradiction in Terms?" *Journal of Common Market Studies* Vol. 40.

Manners, Ian and Richard C. Whitman, eds. 2000. *The Foreign Policies of the European Union Member States.* Manchester University Press.

Marjanovic, Marko. 21 February 2017. "Ukraine Is Selling More Arms to Russia Than Ever Despite 'Sanctions.'" *Checkpoint Asia.* Accessed 4 April 2017. https://www.checkpointasia.net/index.php/2017/02/21/ukraine-is-selling-more-arms-torussia-than-ever-despite-sanctions/.

Menon, Rajan, and Eugene Rumer. 2015. *Conflict in Ukraine: The Unwinding of the Post-Cold War Order.* Cambridge: Massachusetts Institute of Technology.

Meleshevych, Andriy. 2016. "Cost Of Parliamentary Politics In Ukraine." *Kyiv-Mohyla Law and Politics Journal* 2: 147-170.

Merkel, Wolfgang. 2004. "Embedded And Defective Democracies." *Democratization* 11 (5): 33-58. doi:10.1080/13510340412331304598.

Merry, E. Wayne. 2016. "The Origins of Russia's War in Ukraine." In *Roots of Russia's War in Ukraine*, by Elizabeth A. Wood, William E. Pomeranz, E. Wayne Merry, and Maxim Trudolyubov. Washington, DC: Woodrow Wilson Center Press.

Ministry of Social Policy of Ukraine (MoSP). 20 March 2017. "Official Web Portal." Accessed 1 April 2017. http://www.msp.gov.ua/news/12738.html.

Ministry of Social Policy of Ukraine and Organization for Security and Co-operation in Europe Project Co-ordinator in Ukraine (MoSP and OSCE). 7 March 2017. "Issues for long-term integration of female IDPs in hosting communities (Vinnytsia, Lviv and Kyiv regions)." http://www.osce.org/ukraine/303186?download=true.

Moore, Elaine, Roman Olearchyk and Neil Buckley. 2 September 2015. "Ukraine: Costs of conflict." *Financial Times*. Accessed 28 March 2017. https://www.ft.com/content/22f59e84-4d9a-11e5-9b5d-89a026fda5c9.

NABU. "History of the NABU." National Anti-Corruption Bureau of Ukraine. Accessed 4 April 2017. https://nabu.gov.ua/en/history-nabu.

Naimark, Norman M. 2002. *Fires of Hatred: Ethnic Cleansing in Twentieth-century Europe*. Cambridge: Harvard University Press.

NATO. 7 January 2016. "Sanctions after Crimea: Have they worked?" *NATO Review*. Accessed 6 April 2017. http://www.nato.int/docu/review/2015/Russia/sanctions-after-crimea-have-they-worked/EN/index.htm.

Nechepurenko, Ivan. 26 April 2016. "Tatar Legislature is Banned in Crimea." *The New York Times*.

Nekrich, Aleksandr (trans. George Saunders). 1979. *The Punished Peoples: The Deportation And Fate of Soviet Minorities at the End of the Second World War*. New York: W.W. Norton.

Nicoll, Alexander. 2015. "Ukraine Ceasefire Remains a Work in Progress." *Strategic Comments* 21 (2): 9-11. doi: 10.1080/13567888.2015.1042654.

Nitoiu, Cristian. April 2016. "Towards Conflict or Cooperation? The Ukraine Crisis and EU-Russia Relations." *Southeast European and Black Sea Studies* Vol. 16.

Nougayrede, Natalie. 19 May 2015. "France and the Eastern Partnership: The View from Paris." *Commentary; European Council on Foreign Relations*.

Organisation for Economic Co-operation and Development. 2014. "Background Brief: The Rational for Fighting Corruption." *OECD – CleanGovBiz*. Accessed 4 April 2017. https://www.oecd.org/cleangovbiz/49693613.pdf

Olearchyk, Roman. 5 June 2016. "Donetsk Faces a Creeping Russification." *Financial Times*. Accessed 28 March 2017. https://www.ft.com/content/1425647c-297f-11e6-8ba3-cdd781d02d89

Olearchyk, Roman. 21 December 2016. "Ukrainian Bonds Rally after Budget Vote Boosts IMF Loan Hopes." *Financial Times*. Accessed 28 March 2017. https://www.ft.com/content/1ed93816-6e6d-3004-8214-80391c23ea43.

Olevskiy, Timur. 12 March 2014. "Who told you that you need to protect us? – Mustafa Cemilev on the discussion with Vladimir Putin" (Russian). *TV Rain*. http://tvrain.ru/articles/kto_vam_skazal_chto_nas_nado_zaschischat_mustafa_dzh emilev_o_besede_s_vladimirom_putinym-364892/ .

Oliker, Dr. Olga. "Russian Influence and Unconventional Warfare Operations in the 'Grey Zone:' Lessons from Ukraine." Address, Statement Before the Senate Armed Services Committe Subcommittee on Emerging Threats and Capabilities, 222 Russell Office Senate Building, Washington, DC. *Center for Strategic and International Studies*. Accessed 6 April 2017. https://csis-prod.s3.amazonaws.com/s3fs-public/congressional_testimony/170329_oliker_testimony_russia_unconventional _warfare.pdf?6Qwf1dWtXshRBOdR72cjT9baSNXvubTL.

Onyshko, Olha. 16 March 2017. Film Screening of *Women of Maidan*. SAIS, Washington, DC.

OSCE. 2014. "Situation Assessment Report: on Roma in Ukraine and the Impact of the Current Crisis." *Organization for Security and Cooperation in Europe*. Accessed March 2017. http://www.osce.org/odihr/124494.

OSCE. 2015. "Civil Society and the Crisis in Ukraine." *Organization for Security and Cooperation in Europe: Special Monitoring Mission to Ukraine*. accessed 21 April 2017. http://www.osce.org/ukraine-smm.

OSCE. 12 February 2015. "Package of Measures for the Implementation of the Minsk Agreements." *Organization for Security and Cooperation in Europe*. Accessed 5 April 2017. http://www.osce.org/ru/cio/140221?download=true.

OSCE. 22 December 2015. "Access to Justice and the Conflict in Ukraine." *Organization for Security and Cooperation in Europe*. Accessed 11 March 2017. http://www.osce.org/ukraine-smm/212311?download=true

OSCE. 8 March 2016. "Two Countries – One Profession." *Organization for Security and Cooperation in Europe*. Accessed 20 April 2017. http://www.osce.org/fom/184881.

OSCE. 21 September 2016. "Framework Decision of the Trilateral Contact Group relating to disengagement of forces and hardware." *Organization for Security and Cooperation in Europe*. Accessed 5 April 2017. http://www.osce.org/cio/266266.

OSCE. 19 October 2016. "Disengagement: OSCE is monitoring how sides in eastern Ukraine deliver on agreement." *Organization for Security and Cooperation in Europe.* Accessed 3 April 2017. http://www.osce.org/ukraine-smm/275521.

OSCE. December 2016. "OSCE Special Monitoring Mission (SMM) To Ukraine: The Facts." *Organization for Security and Cooperation in Europe.* Accessed 2 April 2017. http://www.osce.org/ukraine-smm/116879?download=true.

OSCE. 2017. "Gender Equality." *Organization for Security and Cooperation in Europe.* Accessed 21 April 2017. http://www.osce.org/secretariat/gender.

OSCE. 2017. "Combating Human Trafficking." *Organization for Security and Cooperation in Europe Project Co-ordinator in Ukraine.* Accessed 19 April 2017. http://www.osce.org/project-coordinator-in-ukraine/combating-human-trafficking.

OSCE. February 2017. "Thematic Report: Hardship for Conflict Affected Civilians in Eastern Ukraine." *Organization for Security and Cooperation in Europe - Special Monitoring Mission to Ukraine.* http://www.osce.org/ukraine-smm/300276?download=true

OSCE. 1 February 2017. "Statement by the Trilateral Contact Group and the Representatives from certain areas of Donetsk and Luhansk regions calling for ceasefire." *Organization for Security and Cooperation in Europe.* Accessed 3 April 2017. http://www.osce.org/cio/296916.

OSCE. March 2017. "SMM Status Report as of 23 March 2017." *Organization for Security and Cooperation in Europe.* Accessed 2 April 2017. http://www.osce.org/special-monitoring-mission-to-ukraine/306911?download=true.

OSCE. 23 April 2017. "Spot Report: One SMM patrol member dead, two taken to hospital after vehicle hits possible mine near Pryshyb." *Organization for Security and Cooperation in Europe.* Accessed 27 April 2017. http://www.osce.org/special-monitoring-mission-to-ukraine/312971.

Petrovskiĭ-Shtern, Ĭokhanan. 2014. *Jews and Ukrainians.* Oxford, UK: The Littman Library of Jewish Civilization.

Phillips, Sarah D. 2008. *Women's Social Activism in the New Ukraine: Development and the Politics of Differentiation.* New Anthropologies of Europe. Bloomington: Indiana University Press.

Piechota, Grazyna PhD, and Robert Rajczyk PhD. 2015. "The Role of Social Media during Protests on Maidan." *Communication Today* 6 (2): 86-97.

Pleines, Heiko. 2016. "Oligarchs and Politics in Ukraine." *Demokratizatsiya* 24 (1): 105-127.

Pohl, Otto J. 18 May 2010. "The False Charges of Treason Against the Crimean Tatars." *International Committee For Crimea.* http://www.iccrimea.org/scholarly/pohl20100518.pdf .

Pond, Elizabeth and Hans Kundnani. March/April 2015. "Germany's Real Role in the Ukraine Crisis." *Foreign Affairs.*

Pop, Adrian. 2016. "From Cooperation to Confrontation: The Impact of Bilateral Perceptions and Interactions on the EU-Russia." *Eastern Journal of European Studies* Vol. 7.

Pravda.ua. 18 March 2014. "Crimean human chain stands for the unity of Ukraine" (Ukrainian). *Pravda.ua.* http://www.pravda.com.ua/rus/news/2014/03/18/7019399/.

Pravda.ua. 14 March 2014. "Putin 'promised' Crimea three languages and the rehabilitation of Crimean Tatars" (Russian). *Pravda.ua.* http://www.pravda.com.ua/news/2014/03/14/7018790/.

Prentice, Alessandra, and Anton Zverev. 25 July 2016. "Ukraine, after war, becomes trove for black market arms trade." *Reuters.* Access 4 April 2017. http://www.reuters.com/article/us-ukraine-crisis-arms-insight-idUSKCN1050ZE.

Radio Free Europe/Radio Liberty. 6 March 2014. "Crimean Tatars Boycott Referendum." *RFE/RL Incorporated.* http://www.rferl.org/a/crimean-tatars-boycott-referendum/25288044.html?z=16879&zp=1.

Radio Free Europe/Radio Liberty. 1991. "Report on the USSR." 3: 14-26. *RFE/RL Incorporated.*

Ramani, Samuel.3 August 2016. "Ukraine's Ministry of Truth – A Flop of Epic Proportions." *Huffington Post.* Accessed 6 April 2017. http://www.huffingtonpost.com/samuel-ramani/ukraines-ministry-of-trut_b_7918872.html.

RBC.ru. 13 March 2014. "Let them just try: Head of the Crimean Tatars Spoke with Putin" (Russian). *RBC.ru: Politics.* http://kavpolit.com/articles/rbk_pust_tolko_poprobujut_glava_krymskih_tatar_po g-1628/.

Rees, Wyn. 2011. *The US-EU Security Relationship: The Tensions Between a European and Global Agenda.* Palgrave.

Rieker, Pernille and Kristian Lundby Gjerde. 2016. "The EU, Russia, and the Potential for dialogue—Different Readings of the Crisis in Ukraine." *European Security* Vol. 25(3).

Rosato, Angelantonio. 15 July 2016. "A Marriage of convenience? The future of Italy-Russia relations." *Commentary: European Council on Foreign Relations.* http://www.ecfr.eu/article/commentary_a_marriage_of_convenience_the_future_of_italyrussia_relations.

Roth, Mathias. 1 July 2011. "Poland as a Policy Entrepreneur in European Energy Policy: Towards Greater Solidarity vis-à-vis Russia?" *Geopolitics* Vol. 16.

Said, Hashem. 14 March 2014. "Map: Russian Language Dominant in Crimea." *Al-Jazeera America.* http://america.aljazeera.com/multimedia/2014/3/map-russian-the-dominantlanguageincrimea.html.

Samadashvili, Salome. 2015. "Muzzling the Bear: Strategic Defence for Russia's Undeclared Information War on Europe." *Wilfried Martens Centre for European Studies.*

Save the Children. August 2006. "Rewrite the Future: Education of Children in Conflict-Affected Countries." *International Save the Children Alliance.* https://resourcecentre.savethechildren.net/sites/default/files/documents/3351.pdf.

Schimmelfenning, Frank. 2001. "The Community Trap: Liberal Norms, Rhetorical Action, and the Eastern Enlargement of the European Union." *International Organization* Vol. 55.

Schofield, Matthew. 9 November 2015. "Ukraine's Military has Rebounded Despite Budget and Battle Woes." *McClatchy.* Accessed 28 March 2017. http://www.mcclatchydc.com/news/nation-world/world/article43759791.html,

Seselgyte, Margarita. 8 March 2014. "A fait accompli in Crimea – a new frozen conflict in the Eastern Neighbourhood?" *European Geostrategy.* https://www.europeangeostrategy.org/2014/03/a-fait-accompli-in-crimea-a-new-frozen-conflict-in-the-eastern-neighbourhood/.

Shagina, Maria. January 2017. "EU Sanctions Policy Towards Post Soviet Conflicts: Cases of Crimea, Eastern Ukraine, South Ossetia and Abkhazia." *UNISCI Discussion Papers.*

Sharkov, Damien. 19 June 2015. "Russian Sanctions to 'Cost Europe €100bn.'" *Newsweek.* Accessed 28 March 2017. http://europe.newsweek.com/russian-sanctions-could-cost-europe-100-billion-328999?rx=us.

Shishkin, Philip and Anton Troianovski. 17 March 2014. "Crimean Tatars Appear to Boycott Voting." *The Wall Street Journal*. https://www.wsj.com/articles/SB10001424052702304747404579443341954329348.

Skard, Torild. 2014. *Women of Power: Half a Century of Female Presidents and Prime Ministers Worldwide* [Maktens kvinner. English]. Bristol: Policy Press.

Smal, Valentyna. 30 June 2016. "A Great Migration: What is the Fate of Ukraine's Internally Displaced Persons?" *Vox Ukraine.* Accessed 2 April 2017. https://voxukraine.org/2016/06/30/great-migration-how-many-internally-displaced-persons-are-there-in-ukraine-and-what-has-happened-to-them-en/.

Solovey, Yuliya. 9 December 2016. "Four Ways to Reduce Gender-Based Violence in Ukraine." *IREX*. Accessed 6 March 2017. https://www.irex.org/insight/four-ways-reduce-gender-based-violence-ukraine.

Sputnik. 22 July 2010. "UN Court Decision on Kosovo Will Not Change Moscow's Stance - Ministry." *Sputnik International.* Accessed 1 April 2017. https://sputniknews.com/russia/201007221599913010/.

Strasser, Fred. 18 March 2016. "Women and Peace: A Special Role in Violent Conflict." *United States Institute of Peace.* Accessed 16 April 2017. https://www.usip.org/publications/2016/03/women-and-peace-special-role-violent-conflict.

Strasser, Fred. 2017. "From Nazis to ISIS: Women;s Roles in Violence." *United States Institute of Peace*. Accessed 16 April 2017. https://www.usip.org/publications/2017/03/nazis-isis-womens-roles-violence.

Tanas, Olga. 1 February 2017. "Russia Nears End of Recession as GDP Shrinks Less Than Forecast." *Bloomberg Markets.* Accessed 28 March 2017. https://www.bloomberg.com/news/articles/2017-02-01/russia-nears-end-of-recession-as-gdp-shrinks-less-than-forecast.

Treisman, Daniel. May/June 2016. "Why Putin Took Crimea." *Foreign Affairs.*

Troynitski, N.A. 1905. *First General Census of Russian Empire's Population* (Russian). Saint Petersburg.

Ukraine Education Cluster. 03 December 2016. "Education Cluster Dashboard." Accessed 31 March 2017. https://www.humanitarianresponse.info/system/files/documents/files/ukr_dashboard_national_2016_12_03.pdf.

UN Daily News. 9 September 2016. "UN Expert Calls on Ukraine to Step Up Its Efforts to Protect the Rights of the Internally Displaced." *UN News Centre.* http://www.un.org/News/dh/pdf/english/2016/09092016.pdf.

UNIAN News. 20 May 2015. "Ukraine ranks 7th in EY's corruption perception rating." *Unian.info.* Accessed 4 April 2017. https://www.unian.info/society/1080288-ukraine-ranks-7thin-eys-corruption-perception-rating.html.

UNICEF. 18 November 2015. "Children of Peace initiative: EU provides € 800,000 to support education for children in eastern Ukraine." Accessed 2 April 2017. https://www.unicef.org/ukraine/media_28440.html.

UNICEF. 30 January 2017. "Current Appeal Ukraine." Accessed 1 April 2017. https://www.unicef.org/appeals/ukraine.html.

UNICEF. 6 February 2017. "Thousands of children out of school after classrooms hit by heavy shelling in eastern Ukraine." Accessed 2 April 2017. https://www.unicef.org/infobycountry/media_94570.html.

UNICEF. 16 March 2017. "Sirens and Bomb Shelters: Going to School in Eastern Ukraine." Accessed 1 April 2017. https://www.unicef.org/infobycountry/ukraine_95099.html.

Unidentified IDP. 23 March 2016. Vinnytsia, Ukraine. In-person Interview.

United Nations. 18 April 1946. "Statute of the International Court of Justice." *International Court of Justice.* Accessed 1 April 2017. http://www.icj-cij.org/documents/?p1=4&p2=2.

United Nations Commission on Human Rights. 11 February 1998. "Report of the Representative of the Secretary-General, Mr. Francis M. Deng, submitted pursuant to Commission resolution 1997/39. Addendum: Guiding Principles on Internal Displacement." http://www.un-documents.net/gpid.htm.

United Nations General Assembly. 3 November 1950. "Uniting for Peace." *A/RES/377(V).* Accessed 1 April 2017. http://undocs.org/A/RES/377(V).

United Nations General Assembly. 24 October 2005. "2005 World Summit Outcome." *A/RES/60/1.* Accessed 1 April 2017. http://undocs.org/A/RES/60/1.

United Nations General Assembly. 8 October 2008. "Request for an Advisory Opinion of the International Court of Justice on Whether the Unilateral Declaration of Independence of Kosovo Is in Accordance with International Law." *A/RES/63/3.* Accessed 1 April 2017. http://undocs.org/A/RES/63/3.

United Nations General Assembly. 28 March 2014. "Territorial Integrity of Ukraine."
A/RES/68/262. Accessed 1 April 2017. http://undocs.org/A/RES/68/262.

United Nations Human Rights Council. 27 January 2015. "Report of the Special
Rapporteur on Minority Issues, Rita Izsák, Addendum, Mission to Ukraine."
A/HRC/28/64/Add.1. Accessed April 1, 2017.
http://undocs.org/A/HRC/28/64/Add.1.

United Nations Office of the High Commissioner for Refugees (UNHCR). April—June
2015. "Summary of Participatory Assessments with internally displaced and
conflict affected people in Ukraine."
http://unhcr.org.ua/attachments/article/1526/PA%20Summ_proof.pdf.

United Nations Office of the High Commissioner for Refugees (UNHCR). February
2016. "Key Protection Concerns and UNHCR Recommendations: Ukraine."
http://unhcr.org.ua/attachments/article/1231/2016_02_Key%20Protection%20Con
cerns%20and%20UNHCR%20Recommendation%20-%20UKRAINE.pdf.

United Nations Office of the High Commissioner for Refugees (UNHCR). April 2016.
"Ukrainians' Attitudes Towards Internally Displaced Persons from Donbas and
Crimea: Summary of Opinion Polls."
http://unhcr.org.ua/attachments/article/1605/Public%20Survey_36_ENG_www.p
df.

United Nations Office of the High Commissioner for Refugees. "UNHCR: Ukraine."
Accessed 14 April 2017.
http://unhcr.org.ua/en/?option=com_content&view=article&layout=edit&id=1516

United Nations Human Rights Office of the High Commissioner (OHCHR). 21
September 2015. "Statement by Ivan Šimonović, Assistant Secretary-General for
Human Rights, at the Workshop on the development of the National Human
Rights Action Plan." Accessed 4 April 2017.
http://www.ohchr.org/EN/NewsEvents/Pages/DisplayNews.aspx?NewsID=16575

United Nations Human Rights Office of the High Commissioner (OHCHR). 2016.
"Committee on the Elimination of Racial Discrimination the Report of Ukraine."
Accessed April 2017.
http://www.ohchr.org/EN/NewsEvents/Pages/DisplayNews.aspx?NewsID=20370
&LangID=E.

United Nations Human Rights Office of the High Commissioner (OHCHR). 2 June 2016.
"Report on the human rights situation in Ukraine 16 February to 15 May 2016."
Accessed 16 March 2017
http://www.ohchr.org/Documents/Countries/UA/Ukraine_14th_HRMMU_Report
.pdf.

United Nations Human Rights Office of the High Commissioner (OHCHR). 13 March 2017. "Report on the human rights situation in Ukraine 16 November 2016 to 15 February 2017." Accessed 16 March 2017. http://www.ohchr.org/Documents/Countries/UA/UAReport17th_EN.pdf.

United Nations Human Rights Office of the High Commissioner (OHCHR). 15 March 2017. "Escalation of hostilities has exacerbated civilian suffering – UN report." *United Nations Human Rights Office Of The High Commisioner.* Accessed 5 April 2017. Http://www.ohchr.org/EN/NewsEvents/Pages/DisplayNews.aspx?NewsID=21383&LangID=E.

United Nations Human Rights Monitoring Mission in Ukraine meeting 19 and 20 April 2016.

United Nations Peacemaker. 2 December 2016. "Package for Implementation of the Minsk Agreements." Accessed 2 April 2017. http://peacemaker.un.org/ukraine-minsk-implementation15.

United Nations Security Council. 30 November 2012. "'Wherever there is Conflict, Women must be Part of the Solution,' Security Council Told in Day-Long Debate Urging their Inclusion in Restoring Fractured Societies." *United Nations Meetings Coverage and Press Releases.* Accessed 6 April 2017. https://www.un.org/press/en/2012/sc10840.doc.htm.

United Nations Security Council. 26 February 2014. "Letter Dated 26 February 2014 from the Permanent Representative of Ukraine to the United Nations Addressed to the President of the Security Council." *S/2014/132.* Accessed 1 April 2017. http://undocs.org/S/2014/132.

United Nations Security Council. 15 March 2014. "Albania, Australia, Austria, Belgium, Bulgaria, Canada, Croatia, Cyprus, Czech Republic, Denmark, Estonia, Finland, France, Georgia, Germany, Greece, Hungary, Iceland, Ireland, Italy, Japan, Latvia, Liechtenstein, Lithuania, Luxembourg, Malta, Montenegro, Netherlands, New Zealand, Norway, Poland, Portugal, Republic of Moldova, Romania, Slovakia, Slovenia, Spain, Sweden, Turkey, Ukraine, United Kingdom of Great Britain and Northern Ireland and United States of America: Draft Resolution." *S/2014/189.* Accessed 1 April 2017. http://undocs.org/S/2014/189.

United Nations Security Council.21 July 2014. "Resolution 2166 (2014)." *S/RES/2166(2014).* Accessed 1 April 2017. http://undocs.org/S/RES/2166(2014).

United Nations Security Council. 17 February 2015. "Resolution 2202 (2015)." *S/RES/2202(2015).* Accessed April 1, 2017. http://undocs.org/S/RES/2202(2015).

United Nations Ukraine. "Ukraine to develop a National Action Plan for Human Rights." Accessed 4 April 2017 http://www.un.org.ua/en/information-centre/news/1932-2014-11-28-01-45-27.

United States Department of State. 2008. "Ukraine." Accessed February 2017. https://www.state.gov/j/drl/rls/hrrpt/2007/100590.htm.

United States Department of State. "Trafficking in Persons 2016 Report: Ukraine." *State.gov*. Accessed 4 April 2017. https://www.state.gov/j/tip/rls/tiprpt/countries/2016/258885.htm

USC Shoah Foundation The Institute for Visual History and Education. 5 December 2016. "Institute News: USC Shoah Foundation Hosts Seminars on Teaching about Human Rights in Ukraine Conflict Areas." Retrieved on 2 April 2017. https://sfi.usc.edu/news/2016/12/12698-usc-shoah-foundation-hosts-seminars-teaching-about-human-rights-ukraine-conflict

Vannay, Gaetan. 2016. "Ukraine: Media in a Time of War." *Geneva Centre for Security Policy.* Strategic Security Analysis. March 2016, No.3.

Valiyeva, Kamala. December 2016. "The EU's Eastern Partnership: Normative Power or Geopolitical Power Projection?" *Eastern Journal of European Studies* Vol. 7

Vasilyeva, Nataliya. 22 September 2015. "Ukraine's Richest Man Plays both Sides of Frontline." *Associated Press.* Accessed 28 March 2017. https://www.usnews.com/news/business/articles/2015/09/22/ukraines-richest-man-plays-both-sides-of-wars-frontline.

Vosta, Milan; Svitlana Musiyenko, and Josef Abrham. 2016. "Ukraine-EU Deep and Comprehensive Free Trade Area as Part of Eastern Partnership Initiative." *Journal of International Studies* Vol. 9(3).

Way, Lucan A. 2004. "The Sources And Dynamics Of Competitive Authoritarianism In Ukraine." *Journal of Communist Studies and Transition Politics* 20 (1): 143-161. doi:10.1080/13523270410001687145.

Whitmore, Sarah. 2014. "Political Party Development in Ukraine." *GSDRC Helpdesk Research Report 1146.* Birmingham, UK: GSDRC, University of Birmingham. http://www.gsdrc.org/docs/open/hdq1146.pdf .

Williams, Brian Glyn. 2001. *The Crimean Tatars: The Diaspora Experience and the Forging of a Nation*. BRILL.

Williams, Brian Glyn. 2015. *The Crimean Tatars: from Soviet Genocide to Putin's Conquest.* London: Hurst & Company.

Wilson, Andrew. 2014. *Ukraine Crisis: What It Means for the West*. New Haven, CT: Yale University Press.

Women of Maidan. 2014. Documentary. Directed by Olha Onyshko.

Wood, Elizabeth A., William E. Pomeranz, E. Wayne Merry, and Maxim Trudolyubov. 2016. *Roots of Russia's War in Ukraine*. Washington, DC: Woodrow Wilson Center Press.

Yekelchyk, Serhy. 2015. *The Conflict in Ukraine: What Everyone Needs to Know*. 1st ed. New York: Oxford University Press.

Zartman, I. William and Maureen Berman. 1982. *The Practical Negotiator*. New Haven: Yale University Press.

I. William Zartman. 2008. "Ripeness Revisited: The Push and Pull of Conflict Management." In *Negotiation and Conflict Management: Essays on Theory and Practice*, edited by I. William Zartman, 232-244. London and New York: Routledge.

Zavoli, Ilaria. 3 August 2016. "Peacekeeping in Eastern Ukraine: The Legitimacy of a Request and The Competence of the United Nations General Assembly." *Journal of Conflict and Security Law* 22 (1): 147-173. doi:10.1093/jcsl/krw008.

Ziener, Markus. 20 April 20 2015. "Why are Germans so Sympathetic to Russia?" Blog Post, *German Marshall Fund of the United States*.